# CORE TEXTS
# IN
# CONVERSATION

Edited by

**Jane Kelley Rodeheffer**
**David Sokolowski**
**J. Scott Lee**

**Association for Core Texts and Courses**
**and**
**University Press of America, ® Inc.**
**Lanham • New York • Oxford**

**Copyright 2000 by**
**University Press of America, ® Inc.**
4720 Boston Way
Lanham, Maryland 20706

12 Hid's Copse Rd.
Cumnor Hill, Oxford OX2 9JJ

Copublished by arrangement with the
Association for Core Texts and Courses

**Library of Congress Cataloging-in-Publication Data**

ISBN 0-7618-1679-8 (pbk: alk. ppr.)

♾™ The paper used in this publication meets the minimum
requirements of American National Standard for Information
Sciences—Permanence of Paper for Printed Library Materials,
ANSI Z39.48—1984

# Contents

## II. Feminist and Modernist Issues in Core Texts

## III. Ancient and Medieval Gaps: Classical Core Texts from Eastern and Western Traditions

## IV. New Perspectives on Shakespeare as Core Text

# V. Core Texts and Writing

# *Preface*

As this volume attests, in 1998 the Association for Core Texts and Courses was (and still is) a growing, liberal arts, professional organization that seeks to fill an all-too-frequent gap in undergraduate education: namely, the integrated and common study of world classics and other texts of major cultural significance. The core text programs which use these texts are coherent, yet pluralistic, aimed at bachelor degree students as such, not at students of this or that major. These programs are the widest ranging interdisciplinary programs on the landscape of current higher education. And because of that interdisciplinarity, this volume is an illustration of how these texts—when used in structured, often required, general education curricula — address the issues which enliven higher education today.

Inside, the reader will find sections with arguments about texts and curricula which bridge the gaps between science and the arts, East and West, and the ancients, medievals, and moderns. Our last section shows how one great writer, Shakespeare, may be presented, thought about, and used in a core-text program. Teachers, scholars, and administrators who are serious about cohesive liberal education will find papers on feminist and postmodern writers linked to intellectual histories accessible to all undergraduates. In turn, those histories are used not only as invaluable appreciations of who "we" are, but as an inexhaustible resource for both liberal arts and professional colleges to expand the power of student thought through writing and critical analysis.

In short, a reader might think of this volume as an illustration of one possible core curriculum that could be made available to students.

True, this volume could not possibly recreate the particular curriculum which each of our 80 attending institutions offers to its respective students. Also, the many writers, herein, come from universities, colleges, and community colleges, and these institutions run the gamut from public to private, secular to religious, Canadian to U.S. American --all with different educational philosophies. So, one might say, even if the volume succeeded in presenting a "curriculum," it could never exist in practice. But such an objection would miss the point of this volume; for this volume represents faculty and adminstrators repeatedly facing the challenges of synthesizing and structuring core-text, liberal education. Usually, these educators' solutions display the successful construction of finely wrought curricula which, like a suspension bridge spanning an impassible divide, allow many to take an individual journey of exploration and discovery. If, then, this volume helps other administrators and faculty to build future curricula, it will have done its work well.

J. Scott Lee
Jane Kelley Rodeheffer
David Sokolowski

# Introduction

## Where the Wild Things Are: The Competencies We Teach

*Dr. Stephen Zelnick*

It is a wonderful thing to be here in Asheville, North Carolina. You can open a drawer and there sits a Bible and not only does it sit there but it is open prophetically to a page. This morning it was Job, and I glanced into the drawer and my eye hit a line that is right where I am. The line is not a particularly pleasant line—it is Job after all. But it anticipates the flavor of my talk today, which is not a pleasant talk. The line reads "Even today is my complaint bitter." The second half of the verse reads, "my stroke is heavier than my groaning." And about that, we shall see as my talk proceeds.

There are wonderful things about our organization, The Association for Core Texts and Courses (ACTC), and I want to talk first about our growth and our future direction. In his kind words of introduction, Scott Lee recalled the moment when I first broached the idea of establishing a national organization devoted to core text courses. And since that time it has been growing in a way that I really could only dream about ugh in 1995. In that year at our initial conference we had twenty-four institutions and thirty-three people. That seemed miraculous, and I was ready to fold my cards right there and call it a success. But we've kept going and this year we have eighty-eight institutions—four times the number—and a hundred and thirty-five people, from thirty-two states and Canadian provinces. And we are well on the way of becoming truly continental throughout all of North America and representing a wide variety of institutions—large state schools, small liberal arts schools, great universities and hard-working community colleges, secular schools and schools with religious affiliations. And throughout the organization I find excellent and committed people, who consider ACTC important and who are doing marvelous things. To me that is terrifically gratifying.

We've begun to develop networks of contact for ourselves. We have developed our own WebPage (thanks to the folks at St. Mary's in Minnesota). We have an ACTC listserv, where there's some interesting conversation going on and I hope there will be more. We have a nice little newsletter, thanks to the people at BU, and the published Proceedings should begin to appear at the end of the summer. The next thing we have to be happy about is the development of sponsorships. In the beginning it was all Temple—believe me we spent a lot of time and lot of effort on making ACTC function. People who have been around our office at Temple University the last three months know how much ACTC is at the very center of things and how much paper flies around the room and how many phone calls go out of our office to make this conference happen. And all that is gratifying, given the result, but even more gratifying is then being able to move on to UNC-Asheville and Peg Downes and her many hardworking people, and I really want to thank Peg and the people at UNC-Asheville. She and her assistants have done a terrific job. There's no ACTC without that close and caring attention to detail.

I'm happy to say some people have come forward about next year's conference, which we're going to take to the ugly old town of New Orleans if we are able. Two of our Louisiana affiliates have agreed to take on the burden of handling our conference next year, and I hope to see all of you here. Another very gratifying development is how many people I see here that I know from previous meetings and how warm the feeling is from them to one another and from me to them.

Our growth has been remarkable. Student enrollment of ACTC schools is close to two-thirds of a million students—687,000 go to schools that have ACTC affiliated programs. Our guess is that there is another two-thirds of a million students at schools with programs that will fit well under the ACTC aegis. We expect in the next year or two to reach to them.

It's at this point that some of the Jobean bitterness enters the story. I don't know how many of you know but Scott Lee will not be with Temple University next year. Because of the rule of the University, it is impossible for us to continue his employment. This is one of the battles I fought this year and lost, not against the administration but against a faculty heavily worried about tenure issues. At our school, as at many others, there is a limit to the number of years faculty not eligible for tenure can be kept on. We requested a review of our seven-year limit and lost. So, Scott is gone from Temple University and I've been unable to find other funding sources.

There are a few people out there who know this and who are making efforts right now to find Scott a position for next year. ACTC is in serious difficulty without Scott Lee. He said some find things about me, let me say one or two good things about him. Scott Lee is a man of extraordinary character. You know how hard he works and how personal he comes to know you and how when he calls you on the phone he knows who you are and what you are doing. He remembers the details, he has a personal touch and a deep concern, and he's worked twelve hours a day or more, day after day. He comes in on the weekends. He's there at 9:30 at night. And he's done all this knowing that very likely he's not employed for next year. That's the kind of courage and stamina of the spirit that I respect and I rarely see. When I see it, it just leaves me breathless. And that's been Scott Lee for me.

One thing that I know will have to happen for us to grow is that I need more participation, we need more participation from you out there. In the newsletter you may have notice the plan to ask you to become representatives of ACTC, and take on the responsibility perhaps of next year of calling ten or a dozen people who are new and explaining who we are and what we do and seeing if there's possibility of enlisting many of these other schools and programs that are out there. I'm going to ask you to think about that commitment to spend some time in the Fall, to make a dozen phone calls on behalf of ACTC. You can do it well because you represent programs that are in many cases are very powerful and long standing, programs that are full of new energies, and that can help the organization to expand in a way that we would like.

To continue on happy thoughts. Although Roger Shattuck is one of those who didn't return, he said some of the nicest things about us, and when I want to think about what ACTC is I look at his remark. Roger said that ACTC "stands for a much needed readjustment of our double commitment as professors to teaching and research. Most professional associations encourage specialized research far removed from the activity of teaching at the undergraduate level. Here in contrast every session I visited engaged in probing, high level discussion of core authors. Discussions were addressed to the application of advanced knowledge to the practicalities of curriculum course design in teaching in subjects vital to liberal education."

I ll march under that banner anywhere. There is no organization that is doing what we do, none that is fighting the battle for liberal education at the undergraduate level, fighting for the great books, for canon, for the real development of the young people we work with. I do, however, want to talk about some of my concerns. So I ll start off with the sunshine and then the sun will set and things will get stormy.

Reviewing last year's meeting, we identified five items that we all address. Our commitment to core texts has been a deep concern for us from the beginning. There are books that have been essential to our developing humanity, and we are the preservers of those texts for our culture for our society. And we have high criteria for great books. We believe that certain books are really special. They have depth and complexity. They address our humanity with a special kind of power and vividness. When we read them we are no longer the same. And in many cases when we read them we find they are reading us. They are interrogating who we are, what we believe, and where we've come from and what we dream and have visions about. We like to think that we do pretty well at being able to spot those books and knowing the difference between them and other quite good books that lack their weight and power. Much of our most interesting discussion at meetings like this has been about that very question. What are the qualities of these great books? And how do we come to know them and pass them along.

Another thing we have chosen to talk about at great length is interdisciplinary concerns. One of our great difficulties and the great tension in our schools is between the people around us who know a discipline, maybe know an author within that discipline, and maybe know a piece of that author's work in that discipline and not much else. The university and its development has fostered that kind of specialized knowledge, which is crippling I believe, not only to the people who are compelled to develop knowledge that way but certainly no happy news for students and particularly the undergraduate students. While many of us do have specialized training and knowledge, we have added to that first a reach into the general understanding of different disciplines and their relatedness and second a reach into the connection between what goes on in the academic project and the big world that goes on around us—and bringing all that to young people at a moment of their growth that is critical as they move from their childhood into the first stirring of their maturity. This is our special privilege as teachers and program designers. ACTC people teach and write poetry but are not afraid of science. And we even a few scientists who are not afraid of poetry. We have been brave that way—we've been interested and we've been vagrant and we've been wanderers. And we go from place to place to find the things we are not professionally compelled to know but that we just need to know and want to know, that becomes a part of our more general sense of who we are and what we pass along.

The challenge is to balance special knowledge and this general knowledge, to master some of the methods that belong to these disciplines without being trapped inside of them. And sometimes it is difficult to put aside something highly technical and highly refined and ask what does this mean to me as a human being in the moment of my life. What do I do with this? And these are the kinds of concerns that people who have showed up here have a powerful interest in. I just had a moment of that in my class before I left to come here. We were about to move on to Machiavelli, the Prince, and I asked my students what liberators we had studied along the way. They came up with Plato, the philosopher, coming from the cave and returning to lead others from the cave. And Moses reluctantly assuming the mantle of prophethood. It's a wonderful joke that goes on through all these traditions, God chooses the liberator, chooses the prophet and the prophet's response is:"can't you find somebody else?" Not me, I have a speech impediment!" They won't know me, I voted Republican." And nevertheless they take on this powerful mantle of history and wear it sometimes with great pain to accomplish what has to be accomplished. And Jesus, students recognize Jesus as another liberator, of course as a teacher and many other things. As a person possessing skills that made all the difference. And Sundiata, we study that West African epic, that marvelous thing, whose central character is the warrior and a nation builder of a different kind. And finally the Prince and they begin to see that through all these different kinds of texts and these different disciplines there's an ongoing concern, in the first of our courses, for how communities are put together. How they raise up people who are prostrate? How they make the law powerful? And how they build human dignity? And that's the project that we are involved in and the projects we want our students to be involved in too and it has no disciplinary label. It's much bigger than any field or methodology.

We have a lot of discussion on the third point, on teaching and pedagogy. I had a discussion before the conference started at the little gathering with someone from Saint John's of Santa Fe. It was a discussion I have all the time with people from ACTC. I asked her what sort of students went to Saint John's; I assumed they must be very strong in their scholarship and very committed students. And she said, "Well, actually, they're often people who have mid-line grades, and not particularly great SAT's. They are young people who stood away from rules and stupid demands of their schooling. They took risks and went in another direction and thought about things. And we prize this in our young people. We hope to cultivate that along with their scholarship. Because the scholarship itself is not so very important if there isn't a person behind it who has some courage and character who'll make good use of it."

And I thought that was a splendid way to think about what education is and it represents what ACTC people tend to do generally and that is to think about our project as a human project rather an abstract, schooling or merely intellectual project. And that's very important so our discussion of pedagogy tends to carry that forward. We take our young people very seriously. And part of what's involved there is to remember at that age, to remember that time our lives when we were just emerging into something important and something new and something that would mark us forever as who we were.

And that conversation was opportune for me because Asheville is a magical place for me. Thomas Wolfe captured me at fifteen and I always dreamed of Asheville but have never been here. Reading Wolfe changed me utterly. I don't know whether I could read those sentences again without howling. But at the time it was just right for the kind of fellow that I was and the kind of person I would grow to be. And part of what we do and we do well is to remember those silly moments at sixteen, seventeen, eighteen, nineteen—when we had our first elation's about reading and about books and learning. Have you ever had this experience? you go back to your books from your freshmen year and you look at the marginalia and it says things like: "Oh, yes!!" I went back to my Plato, "The Last Days of Socrates" those four dialogues, expecting find some insight into my students and I found "Oh, yes!" on pager after page, that was insight into my students.

That's right, that's what I hope they would be doing at eighteen, nineteen, looking into the "Apology" the first time and getting excited about it while not understanding all that well but writing in the margins in a quaking hand, "Oh, yes!". Well, remembering all that is part of pedagogy and part of the human process of passing on the wealth that we have carried a long the way. It is a challenge to us to remember, a challenge to us to be generous and to give back what was given to us and maybe more.

The fourth challenge area is cross- and multi-cultural perspectives bordering the outlooks within our own tradition. There was a very useful talk this morning on those issues. It is part of our project to try always to be looking at the edges and in the center of what we do, to think about what has come down to us and what it is we pass on. We have a responsibility to form the tradition that we work within, and reform it constantly. One of the points I did agree with in this morning's presentation is the effort on the part of students on many campuses who demand multicultural attention but who really mean only "my culture." That is so very confining. We in ACTC do represent a culture—it is the culture of great thinkers; in almost all cases, the culture of very rebellious people. Often students and others will say "Well, you represent a culture that affirms the mainstream." And that is pretty funny when you look at the fate of many of the writers that we teach. Socrates was so loved by the Athenians for supporting the mainstream, as was Jesus. They thought what everyone thought. And Moses was your typical mainstream Aaron-type person, who watched the polls and did just what the people wanted. We know better. These were trouble-makers, and of the worst sort. Machiavelli, now he wrote to get a job, though I don't know whether he ever got that job. He was, of course, instantly cheered for his cheering thoughts. And Galileo, as I recall, had his little difficulties with the power system of his time. None of the writers we teach were comfortable in any way. They challenged at every step what it was that people most fundamentally believed—and sometimes paid dearly for it. And I like to think that we belong to that tradition of trouble-makers, not to the mainstream male-Euro, whatever, but a tradition of people who compel other folks to look again at everything they thought they knew and learn something new.

So, we are part of that discussion as well. For me this semester it has been the Sufi Saint who carried around in one hand a bucket of water and in the other a bucket of fire, and who is ready to say she was prepared to pour water upon the fires of hell and to burn down the glory of heaven and then to see who loved God. Think about that, that's wonderful, that's really spectacular and has opened up a whole new discussion for my students about what the scriptures are about and how to think about the religious tradition. So, I keep finding, and I hope you do too, treasures outside the boundaries of what we know—treasures that refocus what we think we know in a powerful way.

And the fifth thing we in ACTC have been about is faculty. Building collegiality and building a sense of our common endeavor. Six of us from Temple rode down in a van, a twelve hour ride in a fifteen passenger van. And I had to think of what an odd crew we were and how much love and affection there is among us. The six characters in search of, I don't know what, included a rabbi, a minister, a communist, a Straussian or Neo-Straussian, or perhaps Neo-Leo-Straussian, a Foucaultian, and a Aristotelian. And we manage to actually speak to one another. It was really quite astonishing . We had a lot of fun. We had a lot of conversation about what this word meant in Moabite, and Aramaic, and Hebrew. We were sitting in one of those strange little restaurants the "Crackle Barrel," I don't know what that is, the "Kitch Hillbilly," or something like that, having this conversation about Moabite, Aramaic, Hebrew and there are people at the table next to us listening in. I can't imagine what they thought we were, having such a conversation.

But, what everybody agreed to, and we all talked about it, was how much fun it was and how much affection there was and how much in our program the idea of collegiality, includes a kind of friendship that I've only very rarely seen little bits of in a departmental setting. However, this collegial affection seems to be there in a setting where there a project to do something special. And all that is wonderful, I think that in the four years we have had people to come these conferences. I sense some of that same spirited openness and friendship among the people that come to ACTC.

And all that is wonderful and grand and yet I feel a great bitterness. And let me get on to the Job part, now so long delayed by sunshine.

One of the other principal aims of ACTC was to uplift the professional status of people who do this important work in the academy—to correct the imbalance where people who were generalists were always last in line or were forced to move from one adjunct job to another, or taught only part-time, or received the sabbatical and never the recognition. We saw the need to do what we could to see that this kind of teaching was professionalized and accorded some power within the institution. And at that I think we have surely failed. If anything the situation seems to have worsened. And I want to talk about some reasons why I believe it has gotten worse. And let me observe, too, what I hear in the sessions that I have attended. At the official conference table the comments are brave and forward looking and optimistic, and then in side discussions you start to hear some disturbing, some disturbing things.

At the table the first night I talked to someone who represented a very powerful program and who said next week we have to have a meeting because there's a challenge to the ongoing existence of a an old and venerated program. This person went on to observe that those who are forty-five and older understand what a commitment to general education is and what a commitment to undergraduate teaching is but that many of those who are younger grew up in a regime of such specialization that they see nothing in teaching core courses for themselves. They don't understand it, and furthermore they lack the competence to work within multidisciplinary, ACTC style programs. That's a problem. How do we reproduce ourselves? How do we pass on what we have done through our own work and onto a next generation?

This is happening with my own college, too. And I want to talk about some of the signs of this. And that's were my title came from: "Where the wild things are: the competencies we teach." I think were having great difficulty communicating what we do outside our own circles. And this problem comes at a time when the University itself is under assault, and being compelled to account for itself. Legislators want the university to account for itself in terms of dollars spent for their constituency, and I agree with that. I think it is right they should be doing that. If only the universities themselves would learn how to make that representation correctly. Because what happens in the places that I look at is that the representation in done in purely practical terms. "Growing the work force the next millennium," to use that kind of hideous language.

We seem to be living up to an hegemony of economic trauma, and the need to solve the work force problem has suddenly fallen upon ourselves. The legislators want that. Parents of our students want that very much. They want to know what the connection between all this money I am laying out for tuition, the studying my child will be doing, and the job that just has to be there the very minute the student steps out of the school door at the end of the four years and that will last a lifetime. That circuitry of "expectation, tuition, credit gathering, good job" is a real problem for us.

It dovetails all too well with another circuitry that has our students in its thrall, the circuitry of the goods that are dangled in front of their eyes. The car that they must have. The school they must go to get the job, to make the income, to get the car, to which is appended the notion of happiness and satisfaction. We don't fit into that model very well, if in any way at all, except that we deliver the credentialing that allows the circuit to function. And I see that many in educational leadership are willing to fold under that pressure and redesign the notion of education along the line of these narrow goals. I notice, too, that increasingly very few university presidents come from us. Instead, they are economists, they are lawyers, or they emerge from the business school.

Though some are open to our discussion, we don't talk to them enough; or if we do, they don't hear us. The days when university president's themselves spent an evening reading Plato or a Shakespeare play seem to be long gone. And that's a problem for us. How to represent ourselves to the people who have the power and shape the institutions in which he try to do our business. This is very serious.

I have noticed also that this style of leadership has crept down into the dean's level and even into the faculty itself. A recent retreat was organized in my college to identify the competencies that we were responsible for in teaching our students. The lists were stunningly off the mark. Each of the three divisions of the college composed its own list. When we compared the results, number one in all three divisions was to understand human and cultural diversity. Now that's a noble end, but I cannot imagine why that would appear as the principal goal of an undergraduate education. Why is understanding diversity the main priority? Except that faculty have learned that that's a thing we are supposed to recognize as critically important. Yet things she did not know. Quite extraordinary. She didn't see anything strange about that at all. But what seems clear to me is that we're operating within a realm that we haven't made clear to other people and perhaps to ourselves what it is that we really are about and what it is that the university does.

I see ourselves in the humanities and the more interesting kinds of the sciences and the social sciences being shoved into a corner and hemmed in by the new practicality of our time. And we live in a strange time. Although our society is enjoying unprecedented wealth, no one seems to be enjoying it. And we have something to offer to solve that quandary.

So for me there are many happy things about ACTC and there's a great unhappiness we face. ACTC is about something that is really important and that draws more people to us every year. We see the importance of it and we know what that is. And yet we fail at so far at our political agenda, and that includes protecting the practitioners of this fine art. We need to raise the profile of what we do and support the careers of people that teach the hardest. It's not an easy thing to do we have to have more talk about that. And, in a larger sense, to protect ourselves against the new idiocies that are transforming the university into a job service and reducing what we do to a terrible confusion. So I thank you for sitting through my tirade—it has been really only a small tirade. I allow myself this because I trust you since we are about the same thing. And I want to see ACTC move on as much as it can on to the issues that I think threaten what is most important to us, not only in the present moment but as we try to perpetuate ourselves and the legacy we bear.

# I. Core Texts and the History and Philosophy of Science

CHAPTER 1

# Core Text/Context:
# Reading Darwin Between the Lines

*Timothy Lenoir*

In the *Origin of Species* Charles Darwin sets himself the impossible task of persuading his readers of the evolution of species by natural selection. I say "impossible" because Darwin did not, of course, have indisputable facts to support his claim, such as would have been provided, for example, by a clear fossil trace of species transformation or by a controlled laboratory experiment demonstrating the gradual emergence of a new form. Moreover, the explanatory strategy in Darwin's account ran strongly counter to what most of his contemporaries expected. Where most readers assumed either explicitly or tacitly a notion of rational design at the basis of discussions of natural history, Darwin inserts chance as a key element in the appearance of novelty. To make matters even more complicated, Darwin embeds his entire discussion of how accumulated variation and novelty transform species in a framework of natural agents operating gradually, almost imperceptibly over an immeasurable period of time, according to law. And, of course, apart from this blatant break with the framework of creationist natural theology familiar to his audience, nowhere explicitly present but to be read between every line of Darwin's text is reference to human origins and human evolution.

In addition to these problems of being properly understood Darwin wrestled with the problem of not being misunderstood. Darwin's *Origin of Species* was not the first text that proposed the notion of a transformation or development of species; indeed transformationist doctrines were all too common, and, Darwin feared, associated with radical commoners. A major threat to social stability in Darwin's day were radical socialists, such as the Owenites, who drew upon Lamarckian theories of evolution in advocating the transformation of society. Darwin sought the middle ground. He did not want his views to be dismissed as another form of radicalism; and while Darwin's work raised the hackles of some among the most religious, the fact is the work was widely accepted. How did Darwin manage this? How did he avoid the wrath of creationists on the one hand and being misidentified as a radical on the other? George Henry Lewes, a contemporary of Darwin, formulated a response to this question that suggests the line I want to pursue this evening in understanding Darwin. Lewes wrote:

> No work of our time has been so general in its influence. This extent of influence is less due to the fact of its being a masterly work, enriching Science with a great discovery, than to the fact of its being a work which at once clashed against and chimed with the two great conceptions of the world that have ruled, and still rule the minds of Europe.[1]

The "two great conceptions" Lewes had in mind were the reductionist/materialist line of thought and the dualist approach that separated matter and final causes.

Lewes did not explore the reasons–as I intend to here–for Darwin's uncanny ability to write a text that could appeal both to materialists and creationists who would disagree with certain aspects of Darwin's theories while accepting others as completely compatible with their own position. However, Lewes was onto something important here about the rhetoric of scientific texts. This evening I want to explore the situation of Darwin's text and the manner in which he developed metaphors and analogies that enabled him to draw upon a common stock of narratives in his culture, including some drawn from the tradition of natural theology he was very much opposing, and how he turned these into supportive scaffolding for his own evolutionary theory.

From my perspective, the most appropriate approach to Darwin can be rendered in the slogan: "Text not Core." In other words, the reason Darwin's *Origin* deserves the status of Core Text depends only secondarily on the empirical evidence for the theory, which in any case, only came well after *the Origin* had been canonized; primarily its status depends on the manner in which it is actively woven into a web of texts. As core texts, scientific texts are no different from literary or philosophical texts, and in addressing the relevance of a scientific text to a core curriculum of canonical texts it is, in my view, crucial to judge them with much the same criteria that we apply to works of literature, philosophy, or theology. Darwin's *Origin* weaves itself into the textual web of our cultural imaginary not because it provides a true description of nature–though most biologists today would claim it basically does–but because it participates in the imagined world and the narrative structures shaped by other texts and by itself and serves as a rich source of metaphor crucial to the construction of other textual worlds. Darwin's text should be treated like Descartes' *Discourse on Method or Meditations,* even though the majority of contemporary philosophers and cognitive scientists are now abandoning Cartesian conceptions of a central-processing mind as the basis for experience of a coherent world and self in favor of notions of embodied mind run by parallel distributed networks, Descartes' views have been central to almost every philosophical position since the seventeenth century as well as to our literary traditions. Similarly, many would today dispute the scientific validity of Freud's theories, but no one can dispute the constitutive value of Freud's work for modern literature and film. So even if Freudian psychology is dismissed as "false," we would want to include *The Interpretation of Dreams* as a core text that has participated in the dialogue shaping other core texts. In short, the way I propose to look at Darwin's text may serve as a useful allegory for appreciating the role of scientific texts in a curriculum of core texts.

**Darwin's Metaphor: The Branching Model of Descent**

One of the reasons Darwin's texts are so interesting is that he chose to publish them in the genre of popular works intended for an educated but not necessarily scientifically-trained audience. In Darwin's day natural history was not the preserve of scientific specialists, and indeed, when Darwin set forth as the ship's naturalist on the *Beagle,* he was very much an amateur naturalist debating about returning to a country parsonage, where like other of squire's sons, he would pursue a life botanizing and collecting while tending to his flock of parishioners. Darwin's choice of genre for publishing his work could not have been more apt for persuading readers, scientists, and laymen alike of new ideas they were likely to find objectionable. Darwin was writing against the grain, attempting to fashion new concepts and new language in which to express them. For this purpose a popular medium in which analogy and metaphor were stock-in-trade was ideally suited. Darwin's text is written in a lively, engaging style in which metaphor and analogy are core strategies of presentation. It is devoid of footnotes, tables, and dense argument of the sort one would find in works of Cuvier or Richard Owen, for instance. In fact it reads much more like one of the Bridgewater Treatises aimed at popular audiences and intended to demonstrate the presence of God in nature.

Darwin's entire enterprise is based in metaphor. Rather like the forces of nature he hypothesizes, he modifies existing concepts through expansion and accommodation. In this process of semeiotic change and adaptation, he reshapes key terminologies through naturalization. In this enterprise Darwin instinctively implements a strategy of metaphoric thinking outlined by his contemporary William Whewell, who wrote that metaphors are useful in scientific reasoning as tools for extending the meaning of key terms while disguising change, accommodating it, and in the process establishing the new expanded sense of meaning.[2] Indeed, exactly this strategy applies to the main concept of Darwin's work, namely that of natural species. For his contemporaries, species are archetypes, Platonic essences with fixed boundaries having phenomenal instantiations as individuals. For Darwin, species are not essences. They are historical communities of individuals related by genealogy and descent. "We can dimly foresee," Darwin writes, "a revolution in natural history, "[in which] ... we will be freed from the vain search for the undiscovered and undiscoverable essence of the term species."[3] In this future the creationist perspective of fixed essences will give way to the view that every production of nature is one which has had a history. In the process of describing this revolution, Darwin enacts a small revolt which can be viewed as the advance guard of the new order:

> The terms used by naturalists of affinity, relationship, community of type, paternity, morphology, adaptive characters, rudimentary and aborted organs, etc., will cease to be metaphorical, and will have plain signification.... Our classifications will come to be, as far as they can be so made, genealogies; and will then truly give what may be called the plan of creation.[4]

A curious exchange has occurred. Here at the conclusion of the *Origin* Darwin erases the work of expanding existing notions, of metaphoric transition. Reversing the ground on the old distinctions, the new historically based significations will be grounded in nature, the old categories rendered metaphorical.

In such passages Darwin makes explicit use of metaphors and analogies, but as Gillian Beer, Edward Manier, and Mary Hesse have all pointed out, an equally important aspect of the use of metaphor is the polysemous qualities of metaphoric extension and the manner in which metaphors tap hidden, unconscious registers in their readers. Gillian Beer has elaborated upon the manner in which the history plays of Shakespeare, with their emphasis on lineage and continuity of descent, and the writings of Milton, particularly *Paradise Lost* with its emphasis on the superfecundity and the productivity of the earth, served Darwin as imaginative resources in his reading and writing practices. Darwin's audience, presumably trained in the same founding narratives of British culture, shared with him these common resources as topoi, storehouses of clustered thoughts, systematically organized formulas, ranging from stylistic to allegorical, that made up the "building blocks" of a common British upper class cultural tradition. Darwin could count on such topoi to provide prefabricated molds for experience, enabling his carefully crafted prose to take on familiar shape among his readers. Such topoi are diffuse. More explicit are those connected with natural theology. I will return to these.

### The Structure of Darwin's Argument in the *Origin of Species*

I want to turn now to examine some concrete textual strategies Darwin employs in establishing natural selection. One of the major contributions of recent Darwin studies has been extensive examination of the annotations Darwin made to his readings during the period when he was seeking a model of the transformation of species. Some excellent work by Schweber, Ospovat, Sloan, and others has shown that Darwin was heavily influenced by his reading of Herschel, Whewell, Comte, Brewster and a number of Scottish writers on morals and political economy. These authors led Darwin to believe that an argument convincing to the community of scientists he wanted to impress would have to be based on quantitative natural law as well as on some experimental model that could confirm the operation of the mechanism through which the law is enacted. A crucial feature of Darwin's reasoning was drawn from William Whewell's philosophy of the inductive sciences. Whewell argued that a principal means of confirming a general theory was through what he termed the "consilience of inductions." Darwin had no direct evidence of natural selection acting as a vera causa in nature, but he could argue natural selection's plausibility by showing that it is imminently suited to a unified account of the disparate facts of several areas, such as paleontology, embryology, classification, etc.

Crucial to Darwin's entire discussion in the *Origin of Species* is an analogy between the practices of artificial selection and natural selection. Introduced in the first chapter of the *Origin,* the model of artificial selection, which illustrates the mechanism behind natural selection, is invoked at every turning point of Darwin's argument. In arriving at his model of artificial selection,

Darwin spent a great deal of energy researching the practices of breeders in producing domesticated varieties and races. The breeder, according to Darwin, operates on the natural variability of individuals in domesticated populations. Among the examples Darwin uses to illustrate the practice of selection, the example of different races of pigeons is most memorable. Domestic pigeons, says Darwin, have noticeable variability in the length of their tail feathers. This is the kind of difference that could catch the eye of a breeder, who would select the pigeons with the longest tail feathers and allow them to breed only with one another in the next generation. Fantail pigeons do not emerge all at once through a single mutation event but gradually through the accumulation of inherited differences. If this trait– elongated tail feathers–turns out to be heritable, the offspring from the first mating will have elongated feathers. If this same procedure is repeated for each successive mating generation, eventually over many generations, so Darwin argues, a distinctive race of pigeons like the fantails will emerge. Darwin notes that characters do not vary singly. Any trait can vary, in fact will vary, since all individuals are different unless one of a pair of identical twins and individuals vary in multiple traits. Moreover, it is not just external, visible characters that vary, but internal characters as well, such as size, shape, and position of organs. Traits can vary at any stage of life and are perhaps most subject to variation in the embryo and in early development. A final crucial fact for Darwin is that behavioral characteristics are also "traits," can vary, and hence be the subject of artificial selection by a breeder. Some of our most impressive domestic breeds, such as the tumbler pigeon or the Portuguese Water Dog, have been developed by artificial selection of behavioral characteristics.

Darwin argues that what the breeder does in artificial selection is done by Nature in the wild. In fact while man can only scrutinize the most visible characters and those for the most part only singly, Nature by contrast can select for multiple traits, both internal and external, behavioral and structural, all at once. Nature is an all–scrutinizing selecting force–like a thousand wedges shaping an organism to an adaptive niche. And whereas man selects primarily for his own fancy or utility, Natural Selection adapts an organism to the complex web of its environment.

Can the principle of selection, which we have seen is so potent in the hands of man, apply in nature? I think we shall see that it can... Let it be borne in mind in what an endless number of strange peculiarities our domestic productions, and in a lesser degree, those under nature, vary; and how strong the hereditary tendency is. ... Let it be borne in mind how infinitely complex and close-fitting are the mutual relations of all organic beings to each another and to their physical conditions of life. Can it, then, be thought improbable, seeing that variations useful to man have undoubtedly occurred, that other variations useful in some way to each being in the great and complex battle of life, should sometimes occur in the course of thousands of generations? If such do occur, can we doubt (remembering that many more individuals are born than can possibly survive) that individuals having any advantage, however slight, over others, would have the best chance of surviving and of procreating their kind. On the other hand, we may feel sure that any variation in the least degree injurious would be rigidly destroyed. This preservation of favorable variations and the rejection of injurious variations, I call Natural Selection.

Clearly a crucial addition to the discussion of artificial selection is the notion of struggle for existence. In nature any lessening in checks on the ability of organisms to reproduce will lead to competition and struggle among members of the same species for survival and the ability to reproduce. Any advantage given to an organism as a result of some chance individual variation will aid it in the struggle for survival, and if that favorable variation is heritable, then it will be passed on to the organism's progeny.

The role of metaphor and analogy are patent in this comparison of artificial and natural selection. Darwin takes something known and well understood and translates it element-for-element to something new and different. But in the case of artificial selection we are clearly dealing with intention, design, and a rational agent making the selection. Darwin wants to convince us, however, that Natural Selection is a blind force fueled by chance and the struggle for survival among individuals differently endowed. Throughout the *Origin* Darwin's treatment of Natural Selection hovers on personification and anthropomorphization:

> As man can produce and certainly has produced a great result by his methodical and unconscious means of selection, what may not nature effect? Man can act only on external and visible characters: nature cares nothing for appearances except in so far as they may be useful to any being. She can act on every internal organ, on every shade of constitutional difference, on the whole machinery of life. Man selects only for his own good; Nature only for that of the being which she tends. Every selected character is fully exercised by her; and the being is place under well-suited conditions of life ... How fleeting are the wishes and efforts of man! How short his time! And consequently how poor will his products be, compared with those accumulated by nature during whole geological periods. Can we wonder, then, that nature's productions should be far "truer" in character than man's productions; that they should be

infinitely better adapted to the most complex conditions of life, and should plainly bear the stamp of far higher workmanship?[6]

In the wake of such passages, we can see the sometimes unpredictable, perhaps unintended results of an argument by analogy. It is not surprising that many read Darwin's argument as a piece of teleological reasoning permeated with arguments from design. Indeed, in moving toward the first sketch of his ideas in the "Sketch of 1842," and even more obviously in the work had been one of Darwin's favorite early texts in natural history, and it was one of the books he took with him on the Beagle voyage. In explaining how God's providence is effected through his divine governance in term of general laws, Paley had proposed a metaphor in which he imagined that the Creator supplied another "Being" with materials and rules from which it was given the task of bringing forth the creation. In Darwin's "Sketch of 1842" Paley's metaphor served as a means for drawing the analogy between artificial selection carried out by plant and animal breeders and natural selection. The "materials" in Paley's discussion became the variations upon which natural selection operates in bringing about adaptations.

In drawing the analogy between artificial and natural selection, Darwin now supposed "a Being with penetration sufficient to perceive differences in the outer and innermost organization quite imperceptible to man, and with forethought extending over future centuries to watch with unerring care and select for any object the offspring of an organism." As we have seen, the same metaphor appears in the *Origin of Species,* only here Darwin replaced the "Being" in the metaphor with "Nature." But having thus relied on teleological concepts drawn from natural theology in arriving at his mechanistic model, Darwin attempted to kick away the scaffolding. Darwin was ever worried about controlling this metaphor, and by the third edition of *the Origin* he disclaimed that natural selection is an active power or some form of expression of a Deity. He still thought it was important for heuristic reasons, however, to personify nature:

> Everyone knows what is meant and is implied by such metaphorical expressions; and they are almost necessary for brevity. So again it is difficult to avoid personifying Nature; but I mean by Nature, only the aggregate action and product of many natural laws, and by laws the sequence of events as ascertained by us. With a little familiarity such superficial objections will be forgotten.[7]

Darwin was no doubt sincere in his effort to replace Paley's active, designing God with impersonal laws of nature, but in this effort he was confuted by the solid company of the broad majority of his Christian brethren who were intent upon developing a newly vitalized natural theology which could embrace the findings of modern science. In the new natural theology God did not directly intervene in nature but rather carried out His plan for creation through natural laws. Indeed, a motto on the frontispiece of the *Origin* is from one of William Whewell's Bridgewater treatises, directly expressing the sentiments of the new natural theology:

> But with regard to the material world, we can at least go as far as this—we can perceive that events are brought about not by insulated interpositions of Divine power, exerted in each particular case, but by the establishment of general laws.[8]

Supporters of the new natural theology did not find Darwin's theory at all problematic. They could embrace most of it, particularly natural selection, which they now regarded as God's law for working out his plan for creation. Writing at the end of the century, James Iverach of the Princeton Theological Seminary, for instance, argued that natural selection was a useful tool in seeking to enlarge upon Paley's teleology. Iverach observed:

> No Bridgewater treatise is so teleological as almost any Darwinian book we may happen to open ... [Natural Selection] may be described as metaphorical, but as soon as we begin to work with it its metaphorical character disappears, and it becomes intensely real, and is quite capable of doing anything. It has the character constantly ascribed to it both of a directing agency and of a presiding intelligence; and it does seem as if both were needed if evolution is to be an intelligible process.[9]

Deeply immersed in the same textual tradition of natural theology that Darwin had used as scaffolding for his own ideas, men like Iverach would have immediately recognized and appreciated Darwin's efforts to rework Paley as compatible with their own views and in fact, a valuable transition to a new theistic evolution. Unlike Darwin, however, they were not interested in kicking away the ladder after reaching the roof.

Whether Darwin intended it or not, the ambiguity of his metaphorical language served him as an effective rhetorical device for assimilating potential opponents of his theory. On certain occasions, Darwin even actively promoted this accommodation of his theory to natural theology. The case of Asa Gray, an American exponent of Darwin's views, is revealing. Gray (1810-1888) was professor of natural history at Harvard University from 1842-1873 and thereafter the director of the University Herbarium. A pioneer in the field of plant geography, he did fundamental work on the botany of North America. Gray's comparative studies of the flora of Japan and eastern North America provided important evidence for Darwin's evolutionary theory. Gray entered into correspondence with Darwin in 1855, supplying Darwin important information relevant to his theory. Darwin sent Gray a summary of his theory in 1857, which later served to establish Darwin's priority over Wallace as the first to develop the theory of evolution by natural selection. Gray was thus intimately familiar with Darwin's theory. In fact, Darwin once described Gray as understanding the *Origin* as well as Darwin did himself. Gray was not only orthodox in his science. He was also orthodox in his religion, and it was in this capacity that he stepped forward as the leading interpreter of natural selection to American intellectuals. Gray nonetheless held that organic evolution, even on Darwin's principles, "leaves the argument for design, and therefore for a designer, as valid as it ever was."[10]

Darwin's third edition of the *Origin* contained an advertisement for Gray's articles as a favorable review. As James Moore has demonstrated, Darwin intended to bring out this American edition of his book as a joint publication with Gray with Gray's glowing review at the head, but this project was never realized. Moore has shown that Darwin nonetheless had Gray's articles reprinted at his own expense and distributed to more than one hundred naturalists and divines, periodicals, and libraries. The title of the pamphlet Darwin supported was entitled *Natural Selection Not Inconsistent with Natural Theology.*[11]

Darwin's intertextual strategies for securing assent to natural selection were not limited to treatises in the natural theology tradition. Another important influence on Darwin's model of natural selection was Adam Smith's *Wealth of Nations.* Crucial to the operation of natural selection is the production of divergence of character. In our earlier example of artificial selection applied to the rock pigeon, for instance, fantails might be presumed to have some peculiar advantage over the standard rock pigeon enabling them to exploit a particular environmental niche in which their survival is enhanced. By selecting for the character that enables them to exploit their niche the group and its descendents diverge from the parent group. In general for organisms competing with one another in nature, Darwin argues that natural selection will favor divergence of character, since specialization around a character that confers advantage will reduce the pressure of competition among members of a group. As this divergence of character progresses eventually the character gap between members of related groups of a species is so great that they are prevented from interbreeding and leaving fertile progeny. In this way one can see the branching character of Darwin's model of distinct groups of organisms separated from one another by a character gap but related by descent from a common ancestor.

Scholarship by Sam Schweber and Ed Manier[12] has demonstrated Darwin's deep immersion in the tradition of Scottish moral philosophy and political economy. In Adam Smith Darwin found exactly what he needed to break the old typological model of traditional natural history and focus instead on groups of individuals. Smith, you'll recall, argued that the most efficient way to advance the collective good of society, to generate the greatest wealth for the greatest number, was to remove artificial barriers to the pursuit of individual talent. Free market competition among individuals should be favored instead of an economy regulated from above. Smith argued that individuals know best what their own particular advantage might be in competition with others and that unfettered competition would lead to increased specialization and diversification of the economy. Smith argued, furthermore, that competition would not lead to the dissolution of society in a war of all against all, but rather that market forces would guide the economy in a harmonious, progressive fashion. To express this guidance, Smith used the of the Invisible Hand of the market place. Darwin adapted to the model of natural selection not only Smith's emphasis on individual competition leading to diversification and specialization but also his notion of the Invisible Hand.

## Conclusion

These are just some among many examples I could choose to illustrate the manner in which Darwin's theory of evolution is actually constructed from metaphors and narrative fragments–topoi–common to the progressive liberal segment of British intellectual culture. Rather than having been cast in the field or lab through discoveries of transitional forms to modern day animals and put into the specialist language of biology, the account of evolutionary theory I've depicted here actually goes the other way: Darwin shapes his biological theory from the ground up in terms of models, analogies, and metaphors drawn from and compatible with fields seemingly extraneous to biology such as political economy, natural theology, and Gillian Beer would argue, even literature. If anything, the intellectual and political contexts–the set of texts that this "core text" resonates with–are core to this text. I want to urge that we can find a similar situation in most of the scientific texts we might include in a curriculum of core texts. For example, Descartes' and Freud's texts, like Darwin's, achieve such power because they tap deeply into the *topoi* of their age.

## Notes

1. GeorgeHenry Lewes, "Mr. Darwin's Hypotheses." *Fortnightly Review* 16 (1868), 353. Cited by Gillian Beer, in *Darwin's Plots: Evolutionary Narrative in Darwin, George Eliot and Nineteenth-Century Fiction* (London: Routledge & Kegan Paul, 1983), 22.

2. William Whewell, "Of the Transformation of Hypotheses in the History of Science," *Transactions of the Cambridge Philosophical Society*, 1851; reprinted in *William Whewell: Selected Writings on the History of Science*, ed. Yehuda Elkana (Chicago: Chicago University Press, 1984), 385-392, especially 385. Whewell's influence on Darwin's thought has been analyzed by Michael Rouse, "Darwin's Debt to Philosophy: An Examination of the Influence of the Philosophical Ideas of John F.W. Herschel and William Whewell on the Development of Charles Darwin's Theory of Evolution," *Studies in the History and Philosophy of Science*, 6 (1975), 154-181. A crucial work for understanding the influence of various philosophical works on Darwin is Silvan Schweber, "The Origin of *the Origin Revisited*," *Journal of the History of Biology*, 13 (1981), 195-289.

3. Charles Darwin, On the Origin of the Species, facsimile of the first edition [1859], (Cambridge, MA; Harvard University Press, 1964), 485.

4. Ibid., 486.

5. Ibid., 80-81.

6. Ibid., 84.

7. Darwin, *Origin of Species*, 3rd edition, 1875, 6-7.

8. Whewell from the frontispiece to Darwin, *Origin*, 1st edition, 1859.

9. James Iverach, *Christianity and Evolution.* (London: 1894), 114-115, 121.

10. Asa Gray, *Darwiniana: Essays and Reviews Pertaining to Darwinism.* ed. A. Hunter Dupree (Cambridge, MA; Belknap Press, 1963), reprint of the 1876 edition, 144.

11. See James Moore, "Deconstructing Darwinism: The Politics of Evolution in the 1860s," *Journal of the History of Biology,* vol. 24, no 3 (Fall 1991), 353-408, especially 368-369.

12. Edward Manier, *The Young Darwin and his Cultural Circle: A Study of influences Shaped the Language and Logic of the First Drafts of the Theory of Natural Selection.* (Dordrecht: D. Reidel, 1978).

CHAPTER 2

# Gould's "Nonoverlapping Magisteria": The Real Issue Between Theism and Darwinism

*James Woelfel*

My remarks are directed to the handling of the theological issues raised by evolutionary theory in core text courses that include readings on Darwinism. (In the Western Civilization course at the University of Kansas that covers the modern period, our current readings are Darwin's and Wallace's *Linnaean Society Papers* of 1858 and T. H. Huxley's 1893 essay "Evolution and Ethics.") Despite the fact that creationism is intellectually untenable, for two good reasons some of our students (and, if the polls are to be believed, a substantial percentage of Americans generally) consider it a genuine alternative to evolutionary theory. The first reason is student and public ignorance of the fact that there has been a long and lively tradition of theistic evolutionism represented by "mainstream" Catholic and Protestant theologians and scientists. The second is student and public awareness, however inarticulate, that the writings of some of the leading scientific popularizers of Darwinism and biology textbook authors identify evolutionism with a naturalistic worldview. I want to suggest that presenting theistic and naturalistic evolutionism as the two sides of the real theological issue when we discuss Darwinism in the classroom is likely both to enlighten and to relieve all but the hard-core fundamentalists among our students, and as a by-product expose creationism for the nonissue it is.

The focus of my remarks is Stephen Jay Gould's essay "Nonoverlapping Magisteria" in the March 1997 issue of *Natural History*.[1] The essay is a lively discussion of the document issued by Pope John Paul II, entitled "Truth Cannot Contradict Truth," to the Pontifical Academy of Sciences on October 22, 1996, in which he defended the evidence for the theory of evolution and affirmed its consistency with Catholic doctrine. A good bit of Gould's essay is a close comparative study of the texts of John Paul's statement and Pope Pius XII's 1950 encyclical *Humani Generis*, which also dealt with evolutionary theory positively but much more tentatively.

But what makes Gould's essay fascinating and, I think, significant is that he provides a context for his exegesis of the papal documents by sharing his own views on science and religion and presenting a theory of the relationship between the two. Gould is always infectiously engaging and characteristically very broadly informed, but in this essay he additionally shares his lively personal interest in and respect for religion as a "Jewish agnostic. " The theory of the relationship between science and religion that he uses to discuss the papal pronouncements is what he calls "nonoverlapping magisteria" or NOMA, borrowing the term *magisterium*, teaching authority, from the Catholic Church. Gould describes the "NOMA principle" as follows: "The net of science covers the empirical universe: what is it made of (fact) and why does it work this way (theory). The net of religion extends over questions of moral meaning and value. These two magisteria do not overlap, nor do they encompass all inquiry (consider, for example, the magisterium of art and the meaning of beauty)."[2]

What interests me about the *Natural History* essay is that it shows Gould as a leading evolutionary scientist and a foremost popularizer of science who considers himself–in sharp contrast to, say, Richard Dawkins–a genial skeptic and good friend of religious faith. In the essay Gould relegates creationism to the status of a peculiarly American and parochial movement and fully recognizes that the Catholic Church and most major Protestant and Jewish bodies have for decades officially accepted critical-historical interpretation of the Bible and affirmed evolution as compatible with theistic faith. At the same time, a close look at Gould's friendly "NOMA principle" on the relationship between science and religion precisely reveals something of the secular evolutionist outlook that can make theists, including some of our students, uneasy.

**Theological Evolutionism**

When I lecture on Darwin (and also on Galileo) I always give the students what I call my "little homily" on the so-called "conflict between science and religion." I point out that historically the great paradigm shifts in science have split both the scientific community and the religious community, so that the conflict is much more accurately described as science vs. science and religion vs. religion. I add that most of the great scientists of the sixteenth through the eighteenth century were themselves believers, some of them devoutly so. The publication of Darwin's *Origin of Species* in 1859 divided the scientific community: for example, America's distinguished biologist Louis Agassiz (religiously a liberal Unitarian) rejected it and Asa Gray (religiously an orthodox Presbyterian) became Darwin's main champion in the U.S. On the religious side, while some church leaders, famously Bishop Samuel Wilberforce, attacked Darwinism, some prominent theologians and religious writers quickly accepted it and set about incorporating it into Christian thought: in Britain alone, Anglican priest and novelist Charles Kingsley and influential Anglican theologians Aubrey Moore, J. R. Illingworth, and Bishop Charles Gore among many others. Although the theory of natural selection made Darwin himself a reluctant agnostic, Alfred Russel Wallace eventually became a convert to Catholicism, not rejecting evolutionism but taking what would become the official Catholic position that humankind's uniqueness could not be accounted for simply as a product of evolution.

Late-nineteenth-century theologians, like just about everyone else at the time, found irresistible the identification of evolution with progressive development in both the natural and the human spheres, which conveniently cohered with the progressivist interpretations of the divine purpose that dominated the age. A good example is the American theologian Lyman Abbott's book *The Evolution of Christianity*.[3] But the twentieth century has been the age of theistic evolutionism *par excellence*, and it has been represented by theologians and theologically–informed scientists who have been fully aware that scientifically evolution does not mean progressive development culminating in *homo sapiens*. Time constraints permit me only to mention some of the major figures: among them scientist–theologians such as Pierre Teilhard de Chardin, C. A. Coulson, Arthur Peacocke, John Polkinghorne, and Ian Barbour, and theistic philosophers from A. E. Taylor and F. R. Tennant to Charles Hartshorne and Richard Swinburne. To these thinkers who have worked specifically on the issues raised by evolution we may add virtually all the "famous names" of twentieth–century theology–Barth, Tillich, Bultmann, Moltmann, Rahner, Lonergan, Küng, and many others–who have accepted evolutionary theory within the context of a variety of understandings of the relationship between science and faith. My point here is simply that our students badly need to be informed that there is a long and highly respected tradition of theistic evolutionism that has in fact come to define "mainstream" Catholic and Protestant thinking on the issue; that there is a wealth of serious literature by experts which thoroughly explores the implications of Darwinism for faith and finds the two compatible.

## Naturalistic Evolutionism

The real issue, then, is the fact that evolution may be interpreted within either a theistic or a naturalistic metaphysical framework. Underlying his many criticisms of aspects of evolutionary theory, what I think really agitates Phillip Johnson, the author of *Darwinism on Trial*,[4] is the uncritical identification of scientific evolutionism with a reductionistic philosophical naturalism by many of its leading proponents. A case in point is Douglas Futuyama, author of the most widely used college textbook in evolutionary biology. In the book, *Evolutionary Biology*, Futuyama writes: "By coupling undirected, purposeless variation to the blind, uncaring process of natural selection, Darwin made theological or spiritual explanations of the life processes superfluous."[5] This is Futuyama's own view, and, of course, one notes the unscientifically "loaded" language and the philosophical assumptions in the quotation.

Stephen Jay Gould is a much more interesting case, for the reasons I've mentioned. He genuinely has "enormous respect for religion" and believes "with all his heart" in "a respectful and even loving concordat" between religion and science. Ian Barbour, in his book *Religion and Science: Historical and Contemporary Issues*, presents a typology of approaches to the relationship between science and religion: conflict, independence, dialogue, and integration.[6] Gould's approach, the "NOMA principle," clearly sees science and religion as *independent* of each other, each legitimate in its own sphere and coming into conflict only when one claims to pronounce authoritatively on something that is properly within the other's sphere. For obvious reasons this has been an attractive solution to some theologians as well, particularly those whose theology has been shaped by existentialism or analytic philosophy.

But when we look closely at Gould's fleshing out of the NOMA principle, we see something interesting. He seems generally to interpret religion as "the search for proper ethical values and the spiritual meaning of our lives,"[7] as dealing with "questions of moral meaning and value."[8] There is an old tradition of interpreting religious claims functionally as moral claims, from Spinoza to Kant to R. B. Braithwaite, which conveniently leaves science and indeed naturalism the undisputed claimant to the epistemological and ontological realms. Gould, reminiscent of Einstein, happily defers to religion as the proper source of moral values and also, somewhat vaguely, as answering people's need for meaning to their lives.

Somewhat inconsistently with the above, however, Gould also recognizes that religion makes certain distinctive epistemological and ontological claims, and he specifically mentions the existence of the soul. But even here, he says, "My world [science] cannot prove or disprove such a notion, and the concept of souls cannot threaten or impact my domain." He then offers his own humanistic interpretation of language about souls: "I surely honor the metaphorical value of such a concept both for grounding moral discussion and for expressing what we most value about human potentiality: our decency, care, and all the ethical and intellectual struggles that the evolution of consciousness imposed upon us."[2] What Gould apparently will not allow for is the possibility that concepts such as the soul might point to a competing epistemological and ontological framework for which scientific descriptions of the universe have the status of essential but selective abstractions from a richer and deeper range of knowledge and reality. Anyone who has read his books or heard any of his popular lectures knows that Gould attacks the traditional belief in purposiveness in nature with a zest and attentiveness which clearly imply that a philosophical naturalism is the proper context of interpretation and rule out non-naturalist alternatives.

It may be that naturalism is true, but it needs considerably more than simple assertion and assumption presented as science. On the issue of metaphysical assumptions the theistic evolutionists, for perhaps obvious good reasons, seem more critically aware of the necessary distinctions. But the whole point of my discussion is not to enter into that philosophical debate, but rather to urge that our students need to know that for well over a hundred years evolutionism has been interpreted theistically as well as naturalistically, and that the impression created by prominent secular evolutionists that evolutionism is equivalent to a reductionistic naturalism results from a failure to distinguish critically between science and philosophy. This is the genuine, intellectually and spiritually significant issue, in the light of which creationism can clearly be viewed as the spurious alternative it is.

Notes

1. Stephen Jay Gould, "Nonoverlapping Magisteria," Natural History 106:2, March 1997, 16-22, 60-62.

2. Ibid., 19-20.

3. Lyman Abbott, *The Evolution of Christianity.* (Boston and New York: Houghton Mifflin, 1892).

4. Phillip E. Johnson, *Darwinism on Trial*, 2d ed. (Downers Grove, IL: InterVarsity Press, 1993). He is generally concerned about what he sees as the subtle and pervasive influence of naturalistic assumptions in science and other areas, as is clear from his recent book Reason in the Balance: The Case Against Naturalism in Science, Law and Education. (Downers Grove, IL: InterVarsity Press, 1995).

5. Quoted but not referenced by Phillip E. Johnson in his article "What (If Anything) Hath God Wrought? Academic Freedom and the Religious Professor," *Academe* (Sept.-Oct. 1995): 19.

6. Ian G. Barbour, Religion and Science: Historical and Contemporary Issues. (San Francisco: HarperCollins, 1997), 77-105.

7. "Nonoverlapping Magisteria," 18.

8. Ibid., 19.

9. Ibid., 62.

# CHAPTER 3

# Galileo's Faith

*Darrel D. Colson*

I often try to assign my students some readings in Galileo, for I think that by reading the words of a man who had so much to do with the birth of modern science, we can best understand what I, somewhat perversely, like to call the "scientific faith."

Galileo expresses his "faith" in his *Letter to the Grand Duchess Christina*, in which he purports to draw a sharp distinction between Scriptural faith and what he is up to–namely science. He insists that where Scripture *seems* to conflict with "reason and the evidence of our senses" (Galileo 179), the apparent meaning of Scripture must give way. Committed to a version of heliocentrism, Galileo insisted that when physical matters are "demonstrated beyond doubt or known by sense-experience" (199), we ought to read the Bible so as to conform to these so-called *demonstrations*.

The problem with his argument, however, is that Galileo, like most thinkers of his day, accepted the causal theory of perception, "representative realism." That is, he believed that in human consciousness are mental representations mirroring or corresponding to material substances out in the world. These material substances, the theory goes, cause images of themselves to appear in our minds. The problem posed by the theory is pretty clear, and at least since Berkeley, has been an essential lesson in almost every introductory philosophy course: if we are only aware of mental images, how can we be sure of what causes them? Moreover, how can we be sure that our mental images are accurate portrayals of their causes?

Galileo's answers to these questions are the answers, the "Lockean" answers, which we would expect a scientist to give. First of all, in *The Assayer*, Galileo separated "real qualities"–shape, size, location, motion, number–from those that are no more than "mere names" residing "only in the consciousness"–color, taste, sound, odor (274). Then he declared that the "real" qualities accurately portray their causes, for he "cannot separate" them from "material or corporeal substance" by "any stretch of [his] imagination" (274). The others, though, he "does not feel compelled to bring in as necessary accompaniments" to material substance (274).

If I had time, I would rehearse Berkeley's arguments against this artificial distinction. Suffice to say, we can no more imagine an object without, for instance, color, than we can imagine one without shape. The two go hand in hand. I recognize the shape of something because it has a different color than its background.

What then, accounts for Galileo's distinction between the two sorts of qualities? Well, there is no real mystery. The so-called "real" qualities are all quantifiable; and, we have all heard that oft-quoted comment of Galileo's:

> Philosophy is written in this grand book of the universe, which stands con-tinually open to our gaze. But the book cannot be understood unless one first learns to comprehend the language and read the letters in which it is com-posed. It is written in the language of mathematics. . . . (237-8)

Let us think for a moment about Galileo's key assumption that the mea-surable qualities of our perceptions "really exist." In a superficial, uncriti-cal way, I understand what he means. My perception that this book is 7 inches long is more reliable than my perception that it is white, yellow, and blue because I can stretch out a ruler and measure it. But if Galileo is right to raise questions about my sensation of the book's color, then would not his questions apply equally well to my sensation of the ruler? I can measure the ruler with another ruler, of course, but that merely pushes the question farther back and starts me on a treadmill.

In short, once Galileo decides that some of our perceptions are merely "names" in our "consciousness," he cannot maintain that others of our per-ceptions actually represent reality, for the only possible evidence he can cite must come from additional perceptions. This is the Achilles' heel of repre-sentative realism: the only way really to discriminate between sensations of what is "real" and sensations that are mere "names" would be to escape the human condition, to slip out of one's skin and stand apart, holding up human perceptions on one side and comparing them to the physical objects that supposedly compose them. (Even if one could do this, however, we would have to question the accuracy of his new perceptions of these physical objects, and then we would be on the same treadmill once again.)

Although Galileo confidently separates "real" perceptions from illusory ones, his confidence does not strike me as scientific. Why? One cannot possibly construct an experiment to test his claims. What we get from Galileo in *The Assayer* is a creedal profession of faith grounded less in science than in philosophical systems such as Pythagoreanism, or Platonism, or Neoplatonism: This "grand book the Universe ...is written in the language of mathematics. . ." (237-8).

What I am suggesting, and what I think that we can learn from reading Galileo, is that even a splendid scientist can betray science. As Aristotle understood, and as the most sophisticated among the 17th-Century Churchmen understood, science is the attempt to explain observational data, to systematize the "phenomena," a word derived from the Greek verb for "to appear." Cardinal Bellarmine, a major player in the Church's dispute with Galileo, did not close his mind to the promises of modern science. He acknowledged that *if* scientists proved–really *proved*–heliocentrism, then the Church would have to go along. But he simply did not believe that Galileo or any of the other Copernicans had come up with such a proof. Galileo, of course, insisted that his discoveries of Venus's phases, the sun's spots, and Jupiter's moons all proved the theory true; but Bellarmine thinks that Galileo's inferences go too far.

Responding to Galileo's *Letter to Christina*, Bellarmine warns him to stick to science and to avoid metaphysical speculation:

> I say that if there were a true demonstration that the sun was in the center of the universe and the earth in the third sphere, and that the sun did not go around the earth but the earth went around the sun, then it would be necessary to use careful consideration in explaining the Scriptures that seemed contrary. . . . But I do not think that there is any such demonstration. . . . To demonstrate that the appearances are saved by assuming the sun at the center and the earth in the heavens is not the same thing as to demonstrate that in fact the sun is in the center and the earth in the heavens. I believe that the first demonstration may exist, but I have very grave doubts about the second. . . . (164)

You see, the Cardinal is willing to adapt Scripture to a proven conclusion, but he wants Galileo to provide the proof. And this, obviously, Galileo cannot do. Why? Because Galileo's theory of perception entails skepticism about any scientific claims. Urban VIII, the pope under whom Galileo was eventually condemned, held a position that I find plausible. He believed that strict proof of any system of the universe was impossible for humans to achieve, for human capacities are limited. As Galileo was so quick to point out on other occasions, humans perceive the world by untrustworthy sensations. Thus, even if all the perceptual evidence seems to prefer one system over another, it cannot finally prove either system true with absolute certainty. For, as Urban VIII puts it, "God, who is all powerful, could have established the machinery of the universe in such a way that no man could ever penetrate its mysteries" (Langford 114).

Although Galileo's own theory of perception implies this sort of skeptical outlook on human capacities, he still insisted on making claims about the reality that lies behind the phenomena, the reality that is irremediably veiled by appearances. These claims are metaphysical claims, and yet, he cloaks them in the language of science. That language, which is often our language, disguises the fact that Galileo's commitments, like many of our so-called "scientific" commitments, are really expressions of faith–faith, say, that nature is written in the language of mathematics.

## Works Cited

Galileo. 1957. *Discoveries and Opinions of Galileo*. Trans. Stillman Drake. Garden City, NY: Doubleday.

Koestler, Arthur. 1959. *The Sleepwalkers: A History of Man's Changing Vision of the Universe*. New York: Viking.

Kuhn, Thomas S. 1957. *The Copernican Revolution: Planetary Astronomy in the Development of Western Thought*. Cambridge: Harvard University Press.

Langford, Jerome J. 1971. *Galileo, Science, and the Church*. Ann Arbor: University of Michigan Press.

# CHAPTER 4

# Following the Passionate Atoms: Epicurus and Lucretius

*Stephen Duguid*

In Anatole France's 19th century novel The Gods Will Have Blood, an elderly former aristocrat named Brotteaux wanders through Paris in the midst of the chaos of the Reign of Terror, seemingly oblivious to the dangers he faces. In his pocket is a leather-bound copy of Lucretius, his "faithful solace, companion and comforter."[1] After three years of witnessing the Revolution, Brotteaux had concluded that the universe was mad, that the "sole destiny of all living beings [was] only to become the fodder of other living beings fated also to the same end."[2] Hence since there was clearly no God to give objective sanction to subjective values, a life dedicated to the pursuit of pleasure was all that both reason and the senses could justify. But this 'pleasure' for Brotteaux was neither Sadean license nor a monkish retreat, but rather it reposed in a life dedicated to the Epicurean values of physical contentment, inner peace, social reconciliation, individual friendships and rational self-awareness.

Brotteaux's Paris in 1792, the Greece of Epicurus in the 3rd century B.C. and the Rome of Lucretius in 100 B.C. were all cultures in crisis, crises that were manifested first in the public sphere: the realm of community, politics, citizenship and concerns by the individual for the well-being of the body. If the polis is in crisis, if one can no longer presume citizenship as a primary identity, if the health of the body-self is in constant jeopardy, reason and philosophy often lead us toward the private sphere, the realm of family, the household, the self, and concerns for the well-being of the soul. This path to the private traced by Epicurus and his Roman disciple Lucretius has ever since proved an attractive alternative to the more 'public' traditions established by Socrates, Plato, and Aristotle. In her recent writings on Epicureanism, Martha Nussbaum has placed this tradition in the context of 'therapy', a kind of ancient therapeutic counseling which targets not the ills of society or state or citizen, but rather the ills of the self when faced with chaos, collapse, or corruption in the public sphere.

The Epicurean intervention, strongly therapeutic in Nussbaum's construction, consists of a set of simple philosophic premises resting on some very complex science. The key to happiness or contentment – in fact, simply the absence of anxiety – is seen as freedom from disturbance and anxiety in the soul and freedom from pain in the body. To achieve these freedoms involves acceptance of the following basic premises:

1.  There are no divine beings who threaten us
2.  There is no next life
3.  What we actually need is easy to get
4.  What makes us suffer is easy to put up with[3]

What we actually need is limited to three things: the necessities of life, bodily health and peace of mind and the latter, the central concern of Epicurean philosophy, requires:

a)  Avoiding unpleasantness from fellow humans
b)  Escaping the pangs of conscience
c)  Avoiding worry about the future (including death)

In the early practice of this philosophy the focus on the inner peace of the self meant avoidance of the public sphere in favor of immersion in a small community of friends. Since in this setting the choice of needs is the responsibility of the individual, self-fulfillment can be guaranteed by setting ourselves as few needs or desires as possible, indeed only those that we can realize completely on our own, without being helped or influenced by others. It is necessary, then, to restrict the truly valuable to things which are readily attainable and to condemn what is unattainable as valueless and indifferent.[4]

In the context of our times, this might be seen as a rejection of the welfare state, whether capitalist or socialist, with its intent on bringing the good things of this world to each and every human being, in favor of what in modern ecological thinking might be called 'sustainable communities' which focus on fundamental changes in belief and desire designed to make the individual less dependent on external forces or objects. As Nussbaum says, in Epicurus's Garden they "do not so much show ways of removing injustice as teach the pupil to be indifferent to the injustice she suffers."[5]

Arriving at such indifference is, however, a complicated process. There is the issue of the 'meaning' of life, the yearning for a greater purpose, even immortality. There is the persistent feeling which easily becomes a conviction grounded in reasoned argument that for humans there must be more to 'being' than just material existence – an undeniably powerful anthropocentrism that has come to dominate many human cultures. Even more fundamental is the issue of pain and death and the fear of both. How might one become indifferent to such obvious calamities? How do we get from the Epicurean here – meaninglessness, pain, chaos – to there – contentment? Lucretius, following the lead of Epicurus his mentor, insists that we postpone such difficult questions and start at the foundation, insisting that, "Garments of piecework came before garments of woven cloth." (5: 1350). The piecework of the Epicurean system, in essence its physics, starts from the materialist base of the atom. The Epicureans deduced a 'smallest particle" of being, the atom, from which all observed objects were composed. In this ancient atomic theory:

- Atoms fall downward with the same velocity in empty space (void) owing to their weight;
- Interactions between atoms which result in the formation of bodies take place as a result of swerves which occur by chance and lead to collisions;
- While there are a limited number of shapes of atoms there are an infinite number of atoms within each shape;
- On collision, atoms become interlocked by little branches or antlers, with only the atoms of the soul being spherical. The infinite number of atoms produce an infinite number of universes in infinite space.[6]

Thus, as Carolyn Merchant summarizes an Epicurean universe, it "postulated the existence of an infinite number of unchanging atoms of different shapes and sizes moving ceaselessly through infinite void space, falling, swerving, combining, and separating to form the objects of the changing sensible world."[7] The earth like all objects, then, is a result of accident. The universe is a material system governed by the laws of matter and filled with structures, some stable and others unstable. "The stable ones will persist and give the appearance of being designed to be stable, like our world, and living structures will sometimes develop out of the elements of these worlds."[8]

One of the most salient aspects of post-Newtonian understandings of the natural world is the idea that the occurrence of random fluctuations within natural systems have the potential to make them unpredictable. Thus the future need not, indeed does not derive deterministically from the past because within any natural system apparently random choices and catastrophic bifurcations can spread quickly and thereby radically alter the existing system.[9] These unforeseeable directions, of course, result in a new kind of order – hence from chaos comes order – from the swerving atoms of Epicurus comes Creation, the Universe, ourselves. Lucretius referred to this as "chance," the chance swervings of the atoms being the primal case in point. In Darwinian theory the same process can be seen in the work of Stephen Jay Gould and his theory of "punctuated equilibrium" through which evolution moves in fits and starts rather than smooth progression. Weather is the most often given example, but cancer may fit the pattern as indeed might humans per se. As well, there is renewed interest in science in holistic conceptions as opposed to dualisms or separations. Thus in modern physics matter and energy (motion) are increasingly seen to be inseparably connected and neurophysiologists are drawing links between mind/brain/consciousness/spirit.

Epicurean science was based on creating a middle position between the helplessness or resignation implied in a world run by gods and the determinism of a world governed by immutable Laws or Necessity by allowing for spontaneity and chance in the natural world and thereby a form of free will in the human world. The spontaneity that Epicurus envisaged in the atom was inside the atom, not given to it by an outside force (God).[10] Thus Chance is the form under which the spontaneity inherent in the atom reveals itself to us. It was this provision for free will that persuaded the Jena University graduate student Karl Marx to write his dissertation on "The Difference between the Democritean and Epicurean Philosophies of Nature", rejecting the determinism inherent in Democritus' insistence that the atoms fall in straight lines and favoring the Epicurean position of the 'swerve' because it implied the freedom of man's consciousness to change his surroundings. Thus Marx argued that for Epicurus the atom was "not only the material basis of the world of phenomena, but also the symbol of the isolated individual, the formal principle of abstract individual self-consciousness."[11] The world, the realm of reality, was in a perpetual process of dissolution and rebirth which opened up all kinds of possibilities – whatever is could be otherwise. Above all, for Marx the power of Epicurus' theory lay in its rejection of religion and its creation/ discovery of an "energizing principle." Like Epicurus, Marx saw philosophy and religion as being in "radical opposition." Hence the 'materialist' nature of Epicurean thought: everything is material, even the soul or spirit of man is composed of atoms. Indeed, even the gods are atomic.

But this was an activist version of epicureanism which Marx could not sustain and for most the philosophy seemed to point more toward quietism, a retreat into the self or at least into a restricted private sphere. The options may be more contextual than intrinsic. The essential lesson derived from Epicurean science was the more fundamental one that in a world of chance and chaos there remained an element of will and choice, albeit much more limited than the grandiose wills of secular reformers or spiritual transcenders. One could in the shelter of a private world of self, family, and friends overcome the rule of chance and chaos and attain both bodily and inner peace.

For Epicurus and Lucretius, human beings are troubled and driven creatures – their bodies are vulnerable to numerous pains and diseases, and we can do little to control this. However, bodily pain is not the central source of general unhappiness – far worse is the disturbance of the soul, the causes of which can easily be removed. These causes are false beliefs about the world and about value – about the empty desires that are generated by these false beliefs. Epicurus sees people rushing about after all sorts of objects of desire – wealth, luxury, power, love, the immortal life of the soul – all objects the seeking of which can only cause pain and anxiety. This issue of false beliefs, or 'false consciousness' to use a more modern term, leads Epicurus necessarily to the unconscious layers of motivation which result in emotions, desires, needs which in turn can only be controlled or eliminated by discovering their source in belief, in thought, in the mind. These unconscious layers are socially constructed, the result of living in a human culture obsessed (even in the 4th century B.C..!) with wealth and status and the desire for immortality.[12]

The central false belief is the fear of death which has over the millennia persuaded humans to create gods and construct an 'afterlife', with the result that life becomes one long struggle to attain access to an imaginary afterlife. All this, Lucretius argues, is based on a fear of death that is at its base irrational. Given Epicurean science, death is actually a form of birth. Entropy, the inevitable loss of energy, is a condition of being and leads always to creation. Given this, any notion of mastery of the 'problem' of life and death is futile. "We and the world we live in are shifting aggregations of imperceptibly minute atoms falling endlessly through empty space, hence for each of us death is the end, as our component atoms move on to form new alliances."[13]

To make this case convincing for the mortal who must face death, Lucretius poses what for him is clearly a logical case for death being meaningless. The argument is as follows:

1. An event can be good or bad for someone only if, at the time when the event is present, that person exists as a subject of at least possible experience, so that it is at least possible that the person experiences the event.
2. The time after a person dies is a time at which that person does not exist as a subject of possible experience.
3. Hence the condition of being dead is not bad for that person.
4. It is irrational to fear a future event unless that event, when it comes, will be bad for one.
5. It is irrational to fear death.

The problem of the pain that often accompanies death proves more difficult, applied logic often meeting its match in combat with a mere toothache. Both Epicurus and Lucretius insist, however, that a proper mental attitude, an understanding of the atomic processes that are occurring, and a mental concentration on fond memories of home and friends can overcome the misery of the pain.

While some modern psychiatrists interpret Lucretius's apparent welcoming attitude toward death as symptoms of a "suicidal personality,"[14] the issue is in fact central to his case. If the secular dreams of the public sphere with their statues and arches are to be abandoned along with the spiritual promise of immortality, then the ultimate fate of the private self must be celebrated along with the daily pleasures of life in the restricted realm of the Epicurean garden. The argument made by Lucretius must center, then, on the limitation of desire as the central factor in attaining individual contentment while living and with the attainment of resignation and repose while dying. There is no design, only atoms and void, infinity and chance. All 'being' is merely a temporary coming together of compounds of atoms and all such compounds will eventually disintegrate and then reform in new shapes and qualities. There is, then, no intrinsic superiority of one form of being over another and no eternal beings, compounds or qualities, only eternal atoms. Hence there is no sense to any notion of 'progress' or 'development', no need or ability to 'conquer' the natural, and no ability to affect the future. There is, in the language of the modern Enlightenment, no individual authenticity to be achieved or realized in struggling for liberty, selfhood, or justice. What there is 'being' and the conscious drive for pleasure within that state. There is, then, no need to have the public sphere make sense, be progressive, prosperous, or victorious. There is only the need to maximize the opportunities for pleasure, and because our particular atomic formation has resulted in consciousness, that pleasure must be both sensual and cognitive since "mental pleasures depend on a right attitude to bodily feelings," including in this case both death and annihilation.[15]

## Notes

1. Anatole France. *The Gods Will Have Blood* (Penguin, 1979), 82.

2. France, 73.

3. Epicurus died painfully after a two-week bout of kidney failure and kidney stones, but he apparently died cheerfully because he "...kept in mind the memory of his friends and the agreeable experiences and conversations they had together." D.S. Hutchinson, "Introduction" *The Epicurus Reader* (Indianapolis: Hackett Publishing, 1994), viii.

4. M. Hossenfelder. "Epicurus - hedonist malgre lui," in *The Norms of Nature: Studies in Hellenistic Ethics,* eds. M. Schofield and G. Striker (Cambridge University Press, 1986), 247.

5. Martha Nussbaum. *The Therapy of Desire* (Princeton University Press, 1994), 10.

6. A.C. Crombie. *Medieval and Early Modern Science*, vol 2. (New York: Doubleday, 1959), 38.

7. Carolyn Merchant. *Death of Nature: Women, Ecology, and the Scientific Revolution* (New York: Harper, 1980), 200.

8. Hutchinson, x.

9. Eric Charles White. "Negentropy, noise and emancipatory thought," in *Chaos and Order: Complex Dynamics in Literature and Science,* ed. N. Hayles, (University of Chicago Press), 263.

10. John Masson. *Lucretius: Epicurean and Poet* (London: John Murray, 1909), 68.

11. Franz Mehring. *Karl Marx* (Ann Arbor: University of Michigan Press, 1959), 29.

12. Martha Nussbaum. "Therapeutic arguments: Epicuris and Aristotle," in Schofield and Striker, 32.

13. David West. *The Imagery and Poetry of Lucretius* (Bristol Classical Press, 1969), vii.

14. Charles Segal. *Lucretius on Death and Anxiety* (Princeton University Press, 1990), 9.

15. J.M. Rist. *Epicurus: An Introduction* (Cambridge University Press, 1972), 105.

# CHAPTER 5

# Symbol, the Infinite, and Paradox: Euclidean Essentials

*Don Thompson*

Werner Heisenberg observed, "It is probably true quite generally that in the history of human thinking the most fruitful developments frequently take place at those points where two different lines of thought meet" (Heisenberg 1958). In the spirit of such convergence, this paper will investigate the intersection of two lines of thought lying at the nexus between mathematics and natural philosophy.

Euclid's *Elements* is a foundational mathematical treatise providing first-level description and axiomatic practice in the essentials of symbol, the infinite, and paradox. Furthermore, these essentials transcend their mathematical framework and find life as echo-structures resonating in other great writings within natural philosophy. In particular, this paper will discuss ways in which the writings of Plato, Aquinas, and Kierkegaard, when viewed in juxtaposition to Euclid, provide fruitful developments.

Our contact with symbols, the infinite, and paradox occurs as we encounter even the most basic Euclidean elements. Euclid begins his work with a mere twenty-three definitions, five common notions, and five postulates, following which he constructs some four-hundred sixty-five propositions. Thus, he builds a massive intellectual edifice from a mere mustard seed, creating life virtually *in vacuo*. He begins by examining the most fundamental geometric entity: the point. Euclid's first definition is both intriguing and problematic: "A point is that which has no part" (Euclid 1956). It is an object containing no thing, an empty entity. Thus Euclid's geometric system must rely, at the atomic level, on objects having no interior, no inside, no substance. This means that at the base level, we are dealing with symbolic entities or representatives that point back to our world of approximations. These symbols are the hidden skeletons within the images we sketch on paper or draw on chalkboards. Moreover, Euclid constructs trees and forests from these sinewy, skeletal forms, thereby capturing the essence of symbol without being drawn into the imperfect copies. Though we may take issue with his "point" definition, how can he avoid the symbolic when attempting to capture mathematical precision or perfection itself? Furthermore, hasn't Euclid given us the perfect definition of symbol? It does not of itself exist (i.e. it has no substance) but only points back to our imperfect models. Finally, his definition of point contains a "that" which says: "I am pointing at it (the point) with my words and it is over there." Thus, his very language is symbolic. His own words are pointers, self-contained poetry.

By comparison, Plato's language of symbols is his language of forms. A casual reading of Plato reveals this connection, as in his discussion of the nature of unity: "The soul would be compelled to summon up thought and inquire into the true nature of unity. Hence the study of unity will be among those studies that guide and turn the soul to the contemplation of reality. We should persuade those who are to perform high functions in the city to undertake calculation, but not as amateurs. They should persist in their studies until they reach the level of pure thought, where they will be able to contemplate the very nature of number" (Plato 1985). Thus, Plato engages us in pure thought about unity (the nature of "one") through contemplation of this number's essence, the part which has no part. We are to contemplate the center of one, the symbol itself. Euclid and Plato are on the same wavelength – or at least pointing to the same sinusoid. The fruitful development that results from reading these authors is then a deepening of our understanding of both the nature of symbol and its broader universal applicability. Symbols, as essential as they may be, have no part but force us to find their essence in the things they symbolize.

In addition to exposing and engaging the reader in the symbolic, Euclid also gives us a look at the infinite: "It is possible to bisect a given finite straight line" (Euclid 1956). This seems innocuous enough. A closer look reveals, however, that we can continue bisecting any finite straight line indefinitely. Thus, there are infinitely many points on any finite straight line. Furthermore, Euclid proves this possibility by a "compass—straightedge—stylus" construction. He does not rely solely on words but on their completed action. In so doing, Euclid demonstrates that the incremental, elemental, essential parts of the infinite consist of symbols in action. In other words, one does not contemplate the infinite without activity. Infinity takes a stand, then moves beyond all barriers, unwilling to be limited or static. Glimmering and twinkling for a moment, infinity allows us a glimpse we draw briefly into our lungs, then it moves on to its next level. Infinity is the shark imperative – to understand, we must keep moving.

Thomas Aquinas uses infinity to formulate several proofs of the existence of God. By infinite chaining he proves that God exists, relying on "argument from motion," "efficient cause," "possibility ... necessity," "gradation," and "order in the universe" (Aquinas 1988). At root, all of his arguments rely on the possibility of the infinite, the consistency of infinity, and on infinite processes. Infinity does not break down or careen out of control. It is manageable, performing and moving with predictability: "Everything that moves must be moved by something else" (Aquinas 1988). Without movement, we most certainly metastasize, freeze, and die. Indeed, death is the ultimate sensate absence of God, being infinite inactivity. Ironically, God built into the system the possibility and guarantee of the infinite. His very existence contains the possibility of our describing and discovering his very nature, as if He left the proverbial key under the front door mat. God, the perpetual motion machine, reveals his workings, while both Euclid and Aquinas have caught him in the act. Again, the fruit of juxtaposing mathematics and theology occurs in a deepening of our understanding of the use and universal applicability of the infinite.

We now move to a combination of symbol and the infinite, as manifested in the notion of mathematical paradox. As point and line intersect, Euclid presents us with a thorny paradox: "The extremities of a line are points," and "[a] line is breadthless length" (Euclid 1956). Apparently a line is made up of points and nothing else. It consists of things having no part. We are led to the paradox of existence within nonexistence, infinite and infinitesimal, being and nothingness. Zeno, the Eleatic philosopher, took matters even further: "If a straight line segment is infinitely divisible, then motion is impossible, for in order to traverse the line segment it is necessary first reach the midpoint, and to do this one must first reach the one-quarter point, and to do this one must first reach the one-eighth point, and so on, ad infinitum. It follows that the motion can never even begin" (Eves 1969). Therefore, we are intellectually transfixed, unable to move; a far cry from Aquinas' infinite chain of movers!

What is the problem with paradox? Why does it confuse, frustrate, and even intimidate us? Perhaps it is because local logic fails to confine it. We must step up to a higher system level in order to contemplate, let alone understand it. We must mentally jump to a higher dimension in order to catch it in the act: to not be drawn into its vortex and hopelessly dragged down by its force, but rather to take a detached view of its scope. Admittedly, few of us are disturbed by something like Zeno's paradox or the notion of lines being made up of infinitely many nothings. We do, after all, manage to move, despite the logical paradox in Zeno's words. But, the next notion of paradox is a bit more challenging.

Abraham's dilemma with God occurs when, by faith, he is asked to sacrifice his own son, Isaac. Kierkegaard asks us to confront this life and death paradox with boldness: "I shall rely on the strength of the absurd, on the strength of the fact that for God all things are possible" and "it takes a paradoxical and humble courage then to grasp the whole on the strength of the absurd, and that courage is the courage of faith" (Kierkegaard 1985). Rather than retreat from or remain transfixed by paradox, Kierkegaard encourages us to embrace it, holding onto the tension of its absurd conflict. Indeed, one can't jump out of the system to look at this paradox because the author of the paradox IS the system! So, we must allow its mysterious nature to grasp us and we, in turn, must attempt to hold it within our grasp. Kierkegaard is teaching us to dive in, to let go, and have faith in the paradox itself. Thus, paradox leaves us with two choices: jump up a level or jump in.

We have briefly examined three mathematical essentials that produce fruitful developments when combined with other realities. Symbols are common currency in both mathematics and philosophy. The infinite finds a natural home in the world of points and lines as well as in our attempt to discuss the author of the infinite. Finally, paradox is unavoidable in the tangle of mathematical thought as well as in those attempts to reconcile theology with matters of faith. By considering these three essentials from apparently disconnected viewpoints, we capture extended glimpses at meaning and a greater understanding of their transcendent qualities.

## Works Cited

Aquinas, Thomas. *On Politics and Ethics*, trans. and ed. Paul E. Sigmund. (New York: W.W. Norton, 1988).

Euclid. *The Elements*. trans. Sir Thomas L. Heath. 3 vols. (New York: Dover, 1956).

Eves, Howard. *An Introduction to the History of Mathematics* (New York:

Holt, Rinehart and Winston).

Heisenberg, Werner. *Physics and Philosophy: The Revolution in Modern Science.* (New York: Harper Collins, 1958).

Kierkegaard, Soren. *Fear and Trembling,* trans. Alastair Hannay. (London: Penguin, 1985).

Plato. *The Republic*, trans. Richard W. Sterling and William C. Scott. (New York: W.W. Norton, 1985).

CHAPTER 6

# A Crack in the Surface, 1601:
# *Hamlet* Reads Lucretian Atomism

*Theodora S. Carlile*

What is it that we are hoping for when we ask our students to read "core texts" or when we ourselves read and reread these works? One of the advantages of using texts of such depth and richness as Shakespeare's *Hamlet* or Lucretius' *The Nature of Things* in our courses is that they themselves often yield significant responses to our educational and pedagogical questions. Thus, rather than attempting to broach such questions head-on, I would like to look to *Hamlet* in the approach it takes to "reading" Lucretius–or at least Lucretian philosophy. In the following remarks I will suggest that the drama contains an exploration of Lucretius that provides a model of the best way to read.

Shakespeare's Hamlet stands on what has often been taken to be the watershed between the old worldview and the modem age. First performed in year one of the seventeenth century, it seems to both inaugurate and embody the spirit of the age to follow. But even as *Hamlet* prefigures the future, the drama reflects the great turbulence of doctrine, discoveries, and conflicts of its own times. Among the "problems" of the play is the question of material causality. In Shakespeare's time a focus upon material causality was

viewed both in popular literature and from the pulpit as a dangerous challenge
to religious faith and social stability. Despite such views, however, thinkers
of the sixteenth century continued to pursue such questions avidly, advancing
in particular three explanations of the cosmos. The first was based on the
theory of the four elements of earth, air, fire, and water–ultimately derived
from the Aristotelian doctrine of four primal qualities; the second was based
on the Alchemic theory of the *tria prima* of matter– salt, sulfur, and mercury.
A third view, the atomistic account, inherited, via Roman antiquity and
Lucretius, from Democritus and Epicurus, was also current. Though this third
view was the least prevalent in the practice and theory of its own time, it was,
as we know, to exert a far greater influence on the future. Among the philosophers of the late sixteenth century who evinced a willingness to wrestle with
conflicting issues of the old versus the new was the Italian philosopher
Giordano Bruno. Bruno, a follower of Lucretius, exerted wide influence
among Shakespeare's contemporaries. In *Hamlet* in particular the sorts of
questions pursued by Bruno and the influence of such thought are apparent.
Thus, while Shakespeare's direct familiarity with Lucretius, though probable,
remains uncertain, the basic tenets of the philosophy were generally available to the age.

In exploring the Lucretian atomism manifest in *Hamlet,* I turn in particular to Gertrude's narrative descriptions of Ophelia's death by drowning:

> ... on pendent boughs her crownet weeds
> Clam'ring to hang, an envious sliver broke,
> When down her weedy trophies and herself
> Fell in the weeping brook. Her clothes spread wide,
> And merinaid-like awhile they bore her up,
> ... [b]ut long it could not be
> Till that her garments, heavy with their drink
> Pull'd the poor wretch from her melodious lay
> To muddy death. (4.7.167-184)

Ophelia s death is depicted here as a gradual melting. Her being is native
and indued to the watery element (1 1.1.80-181), and she merges passively into it. Later Ophelia s corpse makes its entrance, reinforcing the suggestion of her body s imminent disintegration. Because of her suicide
Ophelia s burial is maimed (5.1.242), and one consequence, according to
the stage directions of the quarto text of the play, is that her body be denied
the stone or leaden casket of burial customarily accorded to the nobly born.
Instead her unprotected remains, her cloth-wrapped body , would have

been carried on stage to be lowered into the grave. The contrast between the ornately carved stone or leaden casket of customary noble burial and the soft swaddled remains of Ophelia, handed into the earthen grave, accentuates the vulnerability of her flesh. Laertes words underscore this stage image:

> Lay her i'th' earth:
> And from her fair and unpolluted flesh
> May violets spring. (5.1.231-233)

Thus her parts will disperse into the earth and ultimately transform into violets. In death Ophelia melts into her inner parts, her core of matter.

Ophelia's life matches well her death–the disintegration and ultimate demise of her personality begun well before her physical drowning. She has both appeared on stage and been described in a state "distract," murmuring strange bits of verse, "spum[ing] enviously at straws," speaking "things in doubt" (4.5.4-7). The disintegration of Ophelia's social persona and her wits (as "mortal" as Laertes laments, "as an old man's life" [4.5.160]) prefigures her body's sinking into "muddy death." Thus Ophelia's passage from life to death suggests a model of mortality which is characterized by a breaking apart and a return of both the spirit and the flesh to the world of physical nature.

In the Lucretian cosmology there is at base only the void and the atoms. The void is empty, undifferentiated space through which the atoms move in a continuous unending downward flow. The atoms are of many types and forms, each one eternally itself, infinitely durable, and impenetrable. All difference and identity in the universe is the consequence of random combinations of varieties of atoms brought on initially by chance "swerves" in the atomic flow. There is no eternal nature apart from material. The soul exists but is merely a conglomerate of the subtlest atoms which, with the body, disperse at death. All is finally in matter itself. In death, then, what ceases to be is the accident, the happenstance arrangement into which the atoms have shaped themselves, the form. What persists is the smallest unchanging part, the atom. Just such a notion of death is suggested by the account of Ophelia's drowning and her prefiguring madness. Her death is a melting–a dispersion of the combined elements back into material nature. Her being sinks into the mud of elemental matter. What remains of Ophelia are the atoms of her body which will persist after her death and regroup into new beings, vegetal matter in the world of nature. Her soul, a collection of the subtlest and most diffuse atoms will not persist after death, but will likewise disperse, its parts as well reverting to the material nature from which it came.

Interestingly, the form taken by Ophelia's madness suggests even more pointedly this Lucretian view. For Lucretius, madness, a palpable symptom of psychic mutability, is strong evidence of the material composition of the soul. More particularly Lucretius based a model of the cosmos on an analogy to the letters, words, and sentences of literature. In his analogy the individual atoms are letters which, when combined with one another according to their particular properties, form an infinite variety of elemental things, the "words" of nature. The whole of the universe is a "poem" written and ever combined anew by *nature,* the prolific goddess who is herself her own ever-changing composition. While Ophelia's death by drowning is an image of the atomist's notion of physical death, her madness is literally Lucretian. The integrity of her verbal thought breaks apart into nearly meaningless pieces of this and that, the flotsam and jetsam of speech. If our world is merely a chance combinations of atoms, then Ophelia, in her madness, becomes a sort of new *nature,* creating other possible worlds in her fecund language.

I return now to the question with which I began: What do we hope for our students when we ask them to read core texts? I propose that there are two sorts of valuable ways of reading towards which we may direct our students. There is a way of reading which holds the text almost as an artifact– at its best treating the text systematically, examining its lineage, analyzing its "message," and bringing critical thinking to its ideas and their implications. This is the sort of reading towards which scholars and professional critics aspire and certainly some portion of this is what we ask of students. In contrast to this way of reading, however, there exists another model, one perhaps more appropriate for students, especially in their first encounter with a text. Such a reading is exemplified by the reading of Lucretius' *The Nature of Things* in Shakespeare's *Hamlet.* In comparison to the model of reading described above this is a way of reading that is both more and less respectful of the original text. It is not a fully critical reading in that it does not attempt to remove itself from the text, nor to accomplish an overview. Yet it is a reading which is deeply imbued with the language, imagery, and tone of the original. Such a reading imbibes and digests the original, as *Hamlet* does Lucretius. Interestingly, moving for inspiration from *Hamlet's* reading of Lucretius to Lucretius' work itself, this way of reading reflects a kind of Lucretian transformation of ideas, at their most elemental level, from one mind to another– Lucretius' work, for example, digested and transformed into Shakespeare. Beyond this, however, even as Lucretius is transformed into Shakespeare, Shakespeare has been as thoroughly transformed into Lucretius. It is just such a transformative process that, I believe, we must envision for our students and, indeed, for ourselves. In looking to such a model, we would, I admit, be aspiring to nothing less than alchemy.

## Works Cited

Lucretius, *On the Nature of Things,* trans and ed. Anthony M. Esslen (Baltimore: Johns Hopkins University Press, 1995).

William Shakespeare, *Hamlet*, ed. Anthony B. Dawson (New York: Manchester University Press, 1995).

# CHAPTER 7

# Why Read Ptolemy?

*Peter Kalkavage*

Everybody knows that Ptolemy was wrong: the earth is not the immovable center of a finite, spherical cosmos. The earth is a planet, and the sun rather than the earth is the center of the planetary system. Everybody also knows that Ptolemy's Aristotelian assumptions were wrong: the heavenly bodies are not divine. The physical universe – so most scientists seem to believe–is simply matter moving in empty space according to fixed laws of nature. Matter is the same everywhere, and there is no fundamental distinction between the "down here" and the "up there," between my throwing a rock at the wall and the revolution of Mars. Whereas Aristotle's physics is aristocratic, modern physics is egalitarian – and modern physics has prevailed. Indeed, its technological achievements are staggering. We know, as I have said, that Ptolemy was wrong. What, then, can we teachers and our students possibly learn from him? Why read Ptolemy?

At St. John's College, every student spends considerable time with Ptolemy's great work, the *Almagest*. Freshmen take up the motion of the sun right after their long journey through Euclid's *Elements*. Sophomores continue the study of the *Almagest* with Ptolemy's complex account of Venus. This account of Venus in turn paves the way for the study of Copernicus as students move from the beautifully clear skies of the Mediterranean to the cloudy skies of eastern Europe.

The sequence of the St. John's curriculum suggests my first answer to the question "Why read Ptolemy?" The answer is very simple: One cannot hope to understand the so-called Copernican Revolution (and therefore the astronomical origin of modernity) without a close study of Ptolemy. We tend to have very fuzzy notions about why the Polish astronomer did what he did. We tend to believe, mistakenly, that somehow or other Copernicus *observed* something that Ptolemy didn't. But if observation wasn't the issue, then what was? Why was a revolution deemed necessary? I shall return to this question at a later point.

*Sozein ta phainomena*, "to save the appearances." Thus did Simplicius, commenting on Aristotle's *De Caelo*, famously define the goal of the mathematical astronomer. This saving of the appearances is deeply connected with the mathematical character of Ptolemy's book. Ptolemy begins with the grand assumption of a beautifully ordered whole, in Greek, a *kosmos*. Fundamental to this view is the distinction between the human and the divine, the deathbound and the deathless. Is there experiential evidence for this view? Yes. As we look around us with an eye unprejudiced by theory, we observe all sorts of things undergoing all sorts of motions. Flowers emerge from the ground, blossom, and then die. Leaves change their colors, fall from the trees, and then reappear. Various animals creep, fly, or swim. This variety of motions reaches its peak with man who not only moves physically but also changes his mind and is constantly beset by those inner motions known as the passions. As we turn our gaze to the sky, although we still observe motion or change, whether the daily arc of the sun or the whirl of the stars in the course of a night, we behold – that is, we pre-scientific observers behold – a realm very different from our own. To all appearances the brilliant Beings in the Sky neither change nor die: they simply move in place. And what's more, they appear to do this one thing they do the same way all the time. In the realm of pre-scientific experience, nothing on earth, certainly not man, approaches this marvelous regularity of being and behavior. To the scientifically disposed human being, the inquisitive human being, this prescientific experience is the surest sign that the world is not only visible but also thinkable, that if we look for order we will find it.

But order and regularity are not perfectly preserved in the heavenly appearances. There is overall order, but there are observable irregularities within that order. The sun always rises in the same place and sets in another. Its whole daily cycle takes the same amount of time every day. But the sun's arc, its height above the horizon, changes as the year rolls on. Then there is the fact that if we measured the durations of the four seasons, we would find that these durations are unequal – that the sun in its yearly course around the ecliptic seems to speed up and slow down. The irregularities become much more disturbing when we conduct careful and prolonged observations of the so-called planets or "wanderers," which not only seem to move at an inconstant rate but also are observed to "stop" in their course through the fixed stars and then move backwards! To save the appearances the astronomer must rescue them from this apparent irregularity and disorder. The Ptolemaic astronomer is thus the advocate and defender of the visible gods to human beings: he defends these gods, these starry symbols of our better selves, from the hasty though not ill-founded charge of disorderly conduct. He does so by means of mathematical hypotheses. Armed with these devices, the astronomer seeks to demonstrate that apparent irregularity is really the product of a complex and not altogether apparent regularity. Why rescue these motions and not the manifestly irregular jumps, starts, and vicissitudes of plants and animals? Why limit the mathematical rescue of the appearances to the Beings in the Sky? Because they alone for Ptolemy deserve to be rescued, because they alone of all the things in the familiar observable world manifest themselves as deathless and admirably dependable in their motions.

The heart of Ptolemy's science is the mathematical hypothesis of regular circular motion. Such motion has the following theoretical advantages: first, it is eminently intelligible because accountable in terms of Euclid's geometry and theory of ratio; second, regular circular motion accords with the divine nature of the Beings in the Sky; and third, that's the way celestial motion by and large *looks*. In Book III, Chapter 3 of the *Almagest*, Ptolemy lays out his two basic forms of this hypothesis: the eccentric circle and the epicycle with its so-called deferent, that is, the circle around which the epicycle's own center moves. So what does the Ptolemaic astronomer do with these hypotheses? Well, he starts by looking at the world and taking measurements of time and position for a given star or planet. On the basis of these measurements he constructs tables. The tables serve as a means by which the astronomer can "plot the course" of a star or planet. The next step is to wed the specifics of the table, the "facts," to an appropriately adjusted mathematical hypothesis of regular circular motion. The astronomer must demonstrate that how the Beings in the Sky actually look, especially in their apparent irregularity, can be regarded as the result of some nonapparent, hypothesized regularity. It would be like taking the various events in the life of a human being and constructing the single story or plot to which these events belong – or can be imagined to belong. Needless to say, the hypothesis must have predictive power: it must not only accord with chronicles of the past but also serve as the basis for tables of future times and positions.

Now you cannot really understand Ptolemy by just extracting the doctrine from his book, by reading his general assumptions and conclusions. You must spend time actually working through his artful and sometimes confusing demonstrations. Generally speaking, a proper understanding of science can be gotten only from actually attempting to do the work of science. This is precisely what students do when they take up Ptolemy in the mathematics tutorial at St. John's College. By immersing themselves in Ptolemy's activity, our students counteract the defects of both the "history of ideas" approach to great works of science and the professional study of astronomy: they are compelled to take Ptolemy on his own terms.

It is an eye-opener for teachers and students alike to realize what Ptolemy is *not* setting out to do in the *Almagest*. He is not setting out to "explain the world" in the sense of getting at the true causes of motion and paths of the heavenly bodies. For all the circles we see in his book, not one of them is an actual orbit. We can, of course, generate the orbits that Ptolemy's mathematical hypotheses would produce. But only in the case of the sun do we actually get a circle. The rest are elaborate floral patterns with petallike loops. Nor is there a single, coherent picture of the cosmos. The absence of such a picture goes hand in hand with the absence of a single, mathematical *account* of the heavenly bodies taken as a whole. In other words, the *Almagest* is a sequence of separate "savings" of separately taken appearances. And yet Ptolemy never doubts that there is a single and coherent whole of things, a *kosmos*. We can only conclude that such a whole does not for Ptolemy emerge in the purely mathematical study of the heavens but belongs in the province of another science.

The absence of a single mathematical account of the whole in the *Almagest* horrified Copernicus. But what really horrified him was something called the "equant." At one point in his account of Venus, Ptolemy realizes that even combining the eccentric hypothesis with the epicyclic can't account for the apparent irregularity of the motions of Venus. So what does he do? He lets the motion of Venus' epicycle around its deferent be irregular and then postulates *another* center around which this irregularity is made regular. This "equalizing" or regulating center is the equant. The *ad hoc* hypothesis of the equant, which surely seems to compromise Ptolemy's own veneration of regular circular motion, is eliminated at one stroke by the heliocentric hypothesis of Copernicus. Furthermore, under the heliocentric hypothesis all the celestial appearances are mathematically accountable together as belonging to a single coherent system. The Copernican hypothesis does all this – but at a price: the world no longer looks like what it is. *Terra firma* seems to be at rest but in fact is not; the sun and stars seem to move, but in fact they don't. From the Aristotelian perspective that Ptolemy holds dear, the ordering principle of the world, the natural "placedness" of things within a hierarchy, is gone. With the triumph of Copernicus, humanity has gained a system but lost a *kosmos*.

These remarks should make clear that a careful study of Ptolemy is absolutely essential to an understanding of Copernicus and his world-shaking hypothesis. It should make clear that the great revolution in astronomy was generated, as it were, from conflicts within Ptolemaic science. What seems to be at stake in the revolution is not the facts of the science but the form of science itself, the scientificness of science. This issue – the form of science – is of central importance to the development of modern thought, from Descartes up through Kant's Copernican Revolution in philosophy, and beyond to non-Euclidean geometry, relativity, and quantum physics.

But we don't need the moderns to get at the problematic nature of Ptolemaic astronomy. Ptolemy himself stresses the perplexing character of his science. He thus encourages us to persist in exploring the question, What is astronomy? Ptolemy at one point warns us that we must be careful not to confuse the mechanisms of our mathematical models with the actual motions of the Beings in the Sky. Echoing Plato's character Timaeus, Ptolemy refers to his mathematical accounts as *likenesses* or *images*. He reminds us that the Beings in the Sky move the way they do, not because they are subject to laws of nature and experience either inertial or accelerative force but because, as Ptolemy says, they are *free*, free of the chance and impulsiveness that characterize the realm below the sky.[1]

By way of conclusion, I propose the following list of answers to the question "Why read Ptolemy?" First, without a study of the *Almagest*, as I have said, we cannot hope to understand the Copernican Revolution and the origins of modernity: not to study Ptolemy is therefore a failure to know ourselves. Second, Ptolemy represents a magnificent example of how the visible world seems indeed to be mathematically ordered. Third, Ptolemy's theory, the truth of the Copernican hypothesis notwithstanding, actually succeeds in accounting for all the motions that are detectable with the naked eye. Fourth, Ptolemy presents his science within a comprehensive philosophic view of the whole, so that by studying Ptolemy we are led to the deepest questions about being and knowing, truth and appearance, the human and the divine. Fifth, in working through the details of Ptolemy's argument, we get firsthand experience of mathematical model-building in physical science. Sixth – and forgive me if this sounds frivolous – Ptolemaic astronomy is *fun*. The very limits and difficulties of the science are intimately connected with the imaginative play of telling "likely stories" about the visible world.

My seventh and last answer derives from the Preface to the *Almagest*. Here Ptolemy, again echoing Plato's *Timaeus*, tells us that mathematical astronomy is *good for our souls*. He speaks of the *eros*, the passionate love, "of the discipline of things that are always what they are." In studying the motions of the Beings in the Sky, we become more like them – regular, orderly and good. We thus acquire and cultivate the right perspective on the human in its relation to the divine. To study Ptolemy is to realize that knowledge of the visible world need not be a stranger to nobility. Yes, Ptolemy seems to have been wrong about the facts. But his theory does save one appearance, one important fact, that modernity seems bent on repressing: that when we mortals observe the Beings in the Sky, we are compelled to look *up*.

**Note**

1. See *Almagest* XIII, vol. 2, "Great Books of the Western World," (Chicago: Encyclopedia Britannica, 1975), 429.

# II. Feminist and Modernist Issues in Core Texts

CHAPTER 8

# Under the Gaze of the Ancients: Dante, Foucault and the Discipline of Being Seen by the Curriculum

*Stewart W. Herman*

The Principia course at Concordia includes both Dante and Job, which virtually mandates a unit on the meaning of suffering in both its deserved and undeserved modalities. After the students have stumbled over the question of justice in God's speech in Job, they are ready for an equally troubling question regarding Dante's *Inferno*: Who controls this place of eternal torment? This query has proven a fruitful line of inquiry into the text, for it encourages the students to dig for evidence rather than simply witness the long parade of unusual characters and bizarre punishments. It also is fruitful in that the result tends to rattle their inherited convictions about hell. As they proceed through canto after canto, they are astonished to discover that no one really appears to be in charge. Minos, Cerberus, and the other monsters from Greco-Roman mythology? To be sure, these colorful figures ply their trade of torment in many of the circles, yet they are not overtly subject to divine or even satanic control. God's intentions become visible at only a few points and even then indirectly—as when approving Dante's tour in the first place or when sending a messenger to usher Virgil and Dante through the gates of Dis.[1] Satan, for his part, appears only at the very bottom of hell, mute, locked in ice, and seemingly completely preoccupied with the three traitors he chews eternally upon. In short, Dante's hell is unorganized. Indeed, it presents what Dante likely would have seen as the epitome of bad government for his high middle ages: a kingdom nominally presided over by one sovereign but actually rent into feuding fiefdoms, each of which is presided over by thugs jealous of their turf.

Given this state of anarchy, why don't the sinners simply leave? There are no meaningful physical barriers to escape or rebellion. Dante's hell falls far short of twentieth-century inventiveness in law-enforcement techniques of mass control: there are no bars and no barbed wire; no radios or telephones to link the various circles into a gulag of bureaucratically systematized torment. Dante may have been aware of the problem. He carefully points out that the lost souls have chosen to be in hell by their habituation to vice. As his schedule of sins and punishments shows, their earthly lives groove them into the particular sin, which becomes their torment for eternity. Their alienation from God becomes complete when, shortly after death, Charon approaches to ferry them across the Acheron when "their dread turns wish; they yearn for what they fear."[2] While this explanation captures the Christian logic of sin and punishment in a simple and profound way, it still seems incomplete. Perhaps I am too modern, but I can't help but wonder how the damned can suffer so horribly and not seek some relief, whether through escape, rebellion, or concealment from God.

This puzzle sent me back to Michel Foucault's interpretation of how the punitive practices and disciplinary institutions during the past two or three centuries asserted their control over the minds and bodies of the condemned. In an odd and interesting way, Foucault's argument illuminates the issue of why the damned stay in a hell so loosely organized, and I suggest what for me is a new way of framing a central problematic in devising a curriculum which focuses upon classic Western texts. The key idea I want to look at here is "surveillance"—the evocative term Foucault uses to explain the emergence of such practices and institutions, particularly the prison.[3] Surveillance is to be observed, and especially to become consciously aware of being observed, of being subjected to the focused, evaluative gaze of a guard, a teacher, or even a text.

Foucault distinguishes an earlier, monarchical theory of punishment from two theories which emerged seriatim in the eighteenth and nineteenth centuries. He opens with the gruesome dismemberment of a would-be regicide named Damien. The "ritual marks of vengeance" were applied to the body of the condemned, in the name of the sovereign, presumably to terrorize the observing public (130). Surely the punishments in Dante's *Inferno* partake liberally of this primitive theory of punishment and intimidation. Far underneath God's righteous throne, the souls of the damned are afflicted with ever-renewed extremities of pain, with or without the thuggish assistance of demons. Yet however much such torments might terrorize us, much as a young Joyce listening to the dark artistry of Irish priests, we do not witness them this side of the grave. For Foucault, this primitive theory was abandoned as eighteenth-century reformers argued persuasively that prisoners—and the entire populace—could be deterred from criminal activity if they were conditioned to experience such pain vicariously when faced with a representation of the punishments they might suffer.[4] Prisoners and law-abiding citizens alike should see the "legible lesson" of chain gangs, scaffolds, and the other "theaters of punishment"; they should learn to shudder and reorder their desires within the confines of the law. Now, this theory also helps explain how punishment functions in Dante's *Inferno*. Ciacco the gluttonish hog of Florence must wallow in garbage while Paolo and Francesca whirl forever in an unconsummated windstorm of desire; the damned are forced to reexperience eternally their sins as represented in their punishments.[5] But there is no intent to reform these souls, and no reason why these representations of punishment should serve to keep the prisoners in hell. This theater of punishment is aimed at saving Dante and his audience from damnation. They are to be energized for the arduous climb through Purgatory and Paradise by observing and participating vicariously in such vivid representations of damnable sin.

To explain why the damned remain in a hell so loosely organized, Foucault's third theory of punishment is of most help. In nineteenth-century America and Europe, he argues, the public spectacle of representation, the theater of punishment, was replaced by the prison. Punishment was withdrawn from public view into a discipline of correction applied behind opaque prison walls.[6] He describes, with a fascination born of horror, Jeremy Bentham's invention of the panopticon, a central tower which permitted prison authorities to keep not only prisoners but wardens under constant yet invisible surveillance.[7] The watched could not know when they were seen; they only knew that they might be observed at any moment of day or night. As Foucault puts it, "Disciplinary power . . . is exercised through its invisibility; at the same time it imposes upon those whom it subjects a principle of compulsory visibility. In discipline, it is the subjects who have to be seen. Their visibility assures the hold of the power that is exercised over them."[8] The prison, like the military, the factory, the school, the reformatory, and the hospital, became a technology for manipulating its populations— through constant observation and the coerced inculcation of appropriate habits, rather than through representations of what they must avoid.

Of course, Dante's sinners are beyond habituation to virtue, and so they are beyond the reach of discipline. But they remain subject, eternally and at every moment, to the baleful gaze of God. Again, Foucault: "It is the fact of being constantly seen, of being able always to be seen, that maintains the disciplined individual in his subjection."[9] In their lives the sinners stopped up their ears and would not hear God's Word admonishing them to change their lives. In hell they still refuse to hear, but they cannot refuse to be seen. God sees immediately and without hindrance into all nooks and crannies of the universe. Seen by God but unable to see back into the heavenly panopticon, the damned cannot escape that gaze. This surveillance renders them vulnerable at any moment to God's thundering intervention, as when Christ harrowed the gates of hell following his Crucifixion, or when the heavenly messenger strides down and blows open the gates of Dis only moments after the Furies have refused entry to Dante and Virgil.[10] In short, the damned do not escape because there is no escape, in the sense that they cannot hide from the panoptic glare of God and the ineluctable power implied by that universal vision.

Many of my students harbor a residual, or more than residual, anxiety about being damned. For them, that baleful glare of God is real and Dante's vision inspires shivers of anticipatory dread. For students with such piety, *The Inferno* can be a powerful instance of what we might term the panoptic gaze of the classics. The texts are there, however we may interpret or misinterpret them. Lying in a meaningful sense beyond our manipulations, they look at us with disturbing questions which will not go away. By such surveillance I mean not paranoid delusion, but the uncanny experience of being looked at by a statue, when its blind sightedness cuts through our privacy and invisibility and challenges who we are. When we are seen in this way, the questions can be uncomfortable. The Socrates of the *Apology* asks whether we are any better than the Athenians, whether we really do care for "wisdom, truth, or the best possible states of our souls."[11] Augustine in his *Confessions* asks whether we have not been worshipping tokens of success and pleasure rather than God; Francis Bacon and Rene Descartes ask whether we have been sufficiently skeptical about the knowledge we receive; Charles Dickens asks whether we have not become timid slaves to our own bourgeois righteousness; Martin Luther King, Jr., asks whether we really believe in the love and justice preached by the prophets and Jesus.[12]

If we ask how the students experience themselves as being observed by the texts they study, we might make headway against the solipsistic narcissism and relativism which shrinks their moral universes. Many if not most of my students want to be seen, even the guys with the seed caps pulled down low. They want their essays to be read, they want their opinions to be heard, at least sometimes, and they want to be recognized as being worthy of being heard.[13] Some recent sociological research at Concordia suggests that participation in class discussion is strongly dampened by the anxiety students feel about appearing unintelligent to their peers—no matter how much they are affirmed by their teachers.[14] What is needed here is for students to see themselves as being pulled beyond such group dynamics onto a wider plane of view. The experience of being seen by the texts might transcend their experience of being seen by each other.

The challenge, therefore, is to make real for students the experience of being seen in a vivid and constructive way by the ancient texts with which they are wrestling. Since Concordia is a self-consciously Christian (Lutheran) college, and the theme of its first-year required class is "The Examined Life," some of the more significant texts we read are tilted prophetically towards introspection in the Judeo-Christian tradition. Obviously here lies a danger. There is a potential for the book of Job, Dante's *Inferno*, or Augustine's *Confessions* to reinforce rather than moderate student anxiety about being judged. While I have not heard such anxiety voiced, this risk nevertheless suggests that we employ what I term a panoptic criterion for selecting texts and constructing a curriculum. We first can ask of any candidate text, does it possess the mystic power to convince students that they are being seen and known in some sense? That mystic power alone might serve to help us distinguish enduring texts from texts of passing importance.

Second, we can ask, what kind of gaze will students experience? Three alternatives immediately suggest themselves. Students may experience a baleful, judgmental gaze which reinforces the absolute worst that they have suspected of themselves. They may experience a naturalistic, unsentimental gaze expressive of what is rather than what should be. Or they may experience a yet more benign gaze which draws them out of themselves, and gives them heart, and informs their passions. Needless to say, I vote primarily for the latter but would want to include texts upon undeserved suffering, eternal punishment, and the like, so that students might grow into a conversation with that nagging question of divine judgment. That crude but inexpugnably personal question provides a first growing edge for a particular kind of moral growth: the growth that occurs when one sees oneself as seen even when one is not seen.

As Dante illustrates in *Purgatorio* and *Paradiso*, some souls thrive under the inescapable eye of God. But even without an ascent to heaven, the state of being observed invisibly need not be an oppressive apparatus of external, bureaucratized control, as Foucault argues. Rather, the conviction that one is seen can provide a powerful comfort. For if one is seen, one is understood, and one has a place in a larger, even if invisible, community of affirmative souls. It is such a conviction that drives, for example, the distinctively American philosophy of Josiah Royce, or the theology of H. Richard Niebuhr.[15] In short, experiencing oneself as seen by classic texts can provide a powerful bulwark against moral meaninglessness.

## Notes

1. Dante, II, where God is evident only as having endorsed Beatrice's mission of mercy, and IX, 76-99, where the "Messenger from God's Throne" scornfully reminds the rebel souls at the gate of Dis that they periodically have their punishments intensified for "butt[ing] against Fate's ordinance." Dante, *The Inferno*, trans. John Ciardi (New York: Penguin USA, 1954).

2. Dante, III, 123.

3. The significance of this term for Foucault is obscured by the fact that it was omitted in the translation of the title: *Surveiller et Punir* became *Discipline and Punish*, trans. Alan Sheridan (New York: Pantheon, 1977).

4. Foucault, 104-114.

5. Dante, III, 73-140, IV, 37-90.

6. Foucault, 114-131, 135-169.

7. Ibid, 170-177.

8. Ibid, 187.

9. Ibid, 187.

10. For references to Christ's cataclysmic passage through hell, see Dante, IV, 53-63, XII, 34, XXI, 112ff; regarding the heavenly messenger, see IX, 61-102

11. The Apology, 29e in Plato, *Five Dialogues*, trans. G. M. A. Grube (Indianapolis: Hackett, 1981).

12. Bacon, "The Four Idols"; Descartes, *Discourse on Method*; Dickens, *David Copperfield, Oliver Twist, Bleak House*, etc.; King, "Letter from Birmingham Jail."

13. Some twenty years ago Christopher Lasch argued that a general collapse of parental authority has distorted the development of superegos in children, in particular, leaving their fragile egos open to harsh, dictatorial and punitive elements from the id, *The Culture of Narcissism* (New York: Warner, 1979), 11-12, 176-80. If such Freudian conceptions retain any cogency, I wonder whether the panoptic gaze students can experience from classic texts might not bring some wiser voices into the construction of their superegos, particularly where parental influences have been weak. Enlarging and rounding out other influences through conversation with the ancients might strengthen student superegos against the harsh perfectionist attacks by the id. Students might learn from Dante or Dickens what they never experienced from their fathers or mothers.

14. Polly Fassinger, "Classes Are Groups: Thinking Sociologically About Teaching." *College Teaching,* 45:1 (Winter 1997): 22-25.

15. See, for example, the American theologian H. Richard Niebuhr's account of *The Responsible Self* (New York: Harper & Row, 1963), with elements borrowed from the social psychology of George Herbert Meade and Josiah Royce's theory of loyalty. To become a self, according to Niebuhr, involves understanding oneself to be in a network of action which encompasses the "universal community" (chapter 2): "The responsible self is driven as it were by the movement of the social process to respond and be accountable in nothing less than a universal community (88)."

## CHAPTER 9

# Marguerite De Navarre, Louise Labé, Rabelais, and Montaigne: Feminist Issues in the Sixteenth Century

*A.G. Arthur*

Instructors in Core Text or Great Books Programs often have to confront the fact that their students' interests or beliefs, on the one hand, and new methodological or cultural concerns, on the other, require them to rethink the ways in which they analyse and employ the great texts which define or serve as the basis for their pedagogy. For an historian of the early modern period like me, who also teaches in a Great Books Program, thinking about how to use primary sources and which ones to use in order most effectively to engage students and foster productive, intellectually stimulating discussion is a doubly problematic obligation. Fields like gender studies, environmental studies and child studies, and approaches like structuralism, feminism, and discourse analysis all have altered students' ideas about how to approach texts and what they expect to learn from them.

Historical study of fifteenth- and sixteenth-century Europe has been dramatically widened by the analysis of historians like Caroline Walker Bynum,

Christiane Klapisch-Zuber, Natalie Zemon Davis, and Lyndal Roper.[1] History courses on the period must reflect and draw students' attention to feminist scholarship and the issues it raises. The ways in which we employ primary sources in teaching and the very sources we choose to read are altered both by new approaches and by changed student expectations and interests.

Similarly, in more broadly-focused courses based on a series of major texts or 'great works' written over the centuries, there has been an increasing reluctance automatically to defend the reading only of works by dead white males; the addition to the canon of Hildegard of Bingen, Mary Shelley, and George Sand, to name just three, has brought increased depth and new perspectives to student learning and professorial understanding. Other additions, like Hroswitha von Gandersheim, Christine de Pisan, and Aemilia Lanyer are more disputable.

I wish here to examine a number of the choices available to instructors proposing to use primary sources from the sixteenth century, particularly in the context of a decision to address gender issues, male-female relationships, and feminist analysis of the text and /or the society for which it was produced. The sixteenth century was clearly an age in which gender issues were fraught; any convincing explanation of the growth of witch persecutions, for example, must address the changing nature of patriarchal power structures and new ideas about the shape and function of the nuclear family. It is clear that the century saw a substantial diminution in the importance of ascending lineage in defining one's moral responsibilities and obligations to ancestors and distant kin. Any reading of the *Tiers livre* of Rabelais makes the question of male-female relationships and gender tensions rapidly apparent, and they are usually a central issue for discussion. Even before this, a reading of Rabelais' first book (in order of publication), *Pantagruel*, confronts one with amazingly discomfiting evidence of a war between the sexes which seems on first reading to make modern misogyny seem gentle, and one is tempted to sympathize with the desire of some to find a more discreet or tasteful means of access to sixteenth-century culture.

To suggest, however, that the best way to approach gender and feminist issues in any era is to begin with the works of women seems to me to misconstrue the relationship between texts and the culture they embody. To see Marguerite de Navarre's *Heptaméron* as an alternative to Rabelais and as a way to feminize the canon seems to me to elevate a clearly derivative and etiolated recapitulation of the *Decameron* and *The Canterbury Tales* beyond its essential worth and to ignore a masterpiece which transcends and reconfigures much of the oral tradition of the later Middle Ages. One needs merely to compare story eleven[2] of the *Heptaméron* with Chapter XIII of *Gargantua*[3] to distinguish between a cautious discussion of defecation as unpleasant and malodorous, which leaves the reader merely uncomfortable with the author's efforts to maintain a respectable tone, and Rabelais' rollicking excremental celebration of what Bakhtin characterized in modern Rabelaisian academic language as "the material bodily lower stratum."[4]

This is not to say that the *Heptaméron* is unworthy of study or an unprofitable subject for academic examination. I do not believe, however, that it is merely male bias that underlies my assertion that it is a far less impelling work and provokes much less productive student discussion and understanding. In a course where court culture and noble values are a major concern, much can be drawn from it and the evidence of an ongoing *évangélique* tradition, well into the 1540's can be used to underline the orthodox religious antecedents of a Calvinist Huguenot movement, but the complexity of the presentation of religious, scholarly, and social concerns in Rabelais makes his work a far more obvious choice, despite his masculinity and what many see as his apparent misogyny.

Most students are horrified and disgusted by the story of the trick Panurge played on the great Parisian lady who rejected his propositions and advances. Making sense of it and asking how it is that Rabelais could seem to approve, or at least not to abhor, his character's behavior requires a considerable effort and an ability to read through the text to some of the social realities it implies. The story is profoundly ambiguous, as Panurge seems truly to believe that he

> never any wrong to [her] had done
> In word or deed, in slander or in slight,[5]

despite the fact that in his initial approach to the lady he asserted that it would be most beneficial to the whole state, delightful for you, and an honor to your progeny, as it is a necessity to me, that you should be covered and breed from me. [6] After her immediate and shocked rejection of his advances, however, he changed his tune considerably and moved into a rhetorical mode more consonant with what one might expect from a sixteenth-century gentleman:

> Your beauty is so transcendent, ...so singular, and so celestial that I believe
> Nature has made you for her paragon, so that we can understand how much
> she can do if she chooses to employ her full powers and her entire wisdom.
> There is nothing in you that is not honey, that is not sugar, that is not heavenly manna. It is to you that Paris should have awarded the golden apple, not

to Venus, oh dear no; nor to Juno, nor to Minerva.[7]

Of course, this did not last and the speech rapidly declined into a request that she let him "rub his bacon with her,"[8] suggesting either a profound cynicism on his part or the possibility that Rabelais is contrasting the formal speech of polite discourse with the animal passions (the kindest way to describe them) that he believes underlie our social behavior. Such an interpretation can be reinforced by a reading of the pseudonymous stories of Bonnivet's efforts to seduce Marguerite in the *Heptaméron*,[9] but these are both less straightforward and less psychologically convincing than the fictional tale of Rabelais. They may be useful to someone wishing to understand sexuality and male-female relationships among sixteenth-century aristocrats, but their factual base tends to make them less true and less impelling.

Whatever his motives, Rabelais' words are profoundly alarming to most modern readers and the apparent expectation that his readers would find the lady's "punishment" hilarious is appalling; tying the implicit sensibility underlying the whole episode to the vision of the Abbaye de Théleme requires a real effort of cultural reconstruction and forces students to reframe their initial responses. The humanist vision that shapes the rules of the abbey and the apparent equality between the sexes, coupled with the assertion that "people who are free, wellborn, well-bred, and easy in honest company have a natural spur and instinct which drives them to virtuous deeds and deflects them from vice"[10] suggest strongly that Rabelais' vision of appropriate social behavior is not that assumed by Panurge and his companions. One needs to consider that satire, or social criticism, or an alternative sixteenth-century distancing of author from story is an essential part of the Rabelaisian vision. Here, writ much larger, is the problem faced by many who see Marguerite, the author of the *Miroir de l'âme pechereuse*, as an early proponent of a more serious, personalised faith but must make sense of the bawdiness of many of the tales in her compendium. Careful consideration of the form and the butt of Rabelais' humor, however, produces repeated evidence of a sophisticated and internally coherent vision of the limitations and self-delusion of many of the educated elite of sixteenth-century France, whether courtiers, lawyers, judges, monks, mendicants, theologians, or humanist scholars. His humor deepens the more one knows about the complex and often arcane cultures he attacks. The objects of Marguerite's humor, on the other hand, are much less difficult to limn — unfaithful husbands, horny suitors, and greedy and/or lascivious friars, Franciscans for the most part — and the male-female tensions her stories embody are much less complicated and thoroughly conven-

tionalized. For the most part, her pictures are merely an extension of the traditional medieval vision of men and women based in Chrétien de Troyes and worked out in Bocaccio, the *Roman de la Rose*, and Chaucer's *Canterbury Tales*. One can learn from it and it can provoke meaningful discussion, but to replace Rabelais with it would be to confuse gentility with truth and to diminish a student's experience of the sixteenth century.

Asserting Montaigne's importance as one of the foremost writers of the sixteenth century is rather less likely to arouse substantial opposition from the politically correct, but his maleness and his implicit sense of the superiority of the male does make for a problem, even when one notes that he entrusted a woman with his literary inheritance. One can easily cite passages like his assertion that "women are in truth not normally capable of responding to such familiarity and mutual confidence as sustain [the] holy bond of friendship."[11] In part, his suspicion of unaided human reason and of all opinion masquerading as fact or truth implicitly undercuts his cultural biases and makes them less assertive than they might otherwise seem. I have always found that his essays, whichever I choose — and I must admit that I have never chosen the "Apology for Raymond Sebond" — stimulate a wide-ranging discussion in a Great Books / Liberal Studies setting and provide helpful *entrées* into the cultural world of the sixteenth century for history students. His openness and the seeming lack of focus or clear purpose of some of his essays on first reading provide a helpful beginning for a discussion of the ways in which one can connect disparate themes and ideas at other than a narrative or sequential level. For history students his essay "De l'amitié" leads to an understanding of the constraints of arranged marriage and the ways in which men and women were defined by their marital and familial roles rather than individual personality. Montaigne saw marriage, "apart from being a bargain where only the entrance is free (its duration being fettered and constrained, depending on things outside our will) ...is a bargain struck for other purposes" than friendship — and even companionship, though that might result — and involving "hundreds of extraneous tangled ends."[12] Reading him provides a picture clearer than any modern commentator can draw.

Nonetheless, an approach to the sixteenth century based on the works of Erasmus, Sir Thomas More, Machiavelli, Ariosto, Rabelais, Montaigne, Shakespeare, and Luther and Calvin has to be admitted to be gender-biased, however much gender issues are raised. Marguerite's *Heptaméron* is not the answer to this problem; her book is too long and can't readily be excerpted, as the most useful parts are the discussions among the storytellers which separate the stories and these depend on the stories as their context (in any

case even these sections are less interesting in sum than they might be).[13]
A possible answer, if it does not seem like mere tokenism, can be found in
the poetry of "La belle cordonnière," Louise Labé, one of the Lyonnais poets
relatively quickly passed over in most survey histories of French literature
as their authors move from Villon to the *Pléiade*, avoiding the *rhétoriqueurs*
and making only brief bows in the direction of Clément Marot, perhaps
Maurice Scève, and Louise. The daughter and wife of a ropemaker, she is
more clearly bourgeois in background and life circumstance than any of the
authors on my list of great *littérateurs* and thus offers a number of unique
perspectives on the world of her time. History students can learn about the
urban culture of the most dynamic economic center of France as well as
about the ways in which a woman thought about and presented the female
situation and male-female relationships. Her picture is a useful balance to
Montaigne's for she assumes that women have different capacities for social relationships than he does. On the other hand, it is difficult to characterize her vision as especially or particularly female; what is most noticeable
is the extent to which her writing parallels and resembles that of her male
contemporaries. One rapidly discovers how sophisticated, latinate, and even
multilingual learned urban culture was — Louise wrote in French, but also
in Italian, Latin and Greek (the latter, in particular, more as a self-displaying
exercise than a real poetic achievement) — and that some women, at least,
participated in it, if not as equals, then at least as respectable colleagues who
were able to take full advantage of an education which was available to those
of less than substantial wealth and power. The breadth as well as the depth
of humanist culture and learning in the decades before the spread of the
French Reformation is made clearly apparent. Here, however, while I have
no doubt about what history students in an upper-year course on sixteenth-
century France might learn from a reading of her work, I find myself won-
dering if in its very specificity Louise's work makes her a less than necessary
part of a broader effort to engage students in a dialog with the great works
of the past. The themes she develops and the ways in which she works with
them are not particularly challenging and do not make us rethink what it is
that we believe. She, like Marguerite, pales beside Rabelais and Montaigne
and forces me to the conclusion that to present the culture and ideas of the
sixteenth century, except at a relatively specialized level to undergraduates,
one must rely almost exclusively on male voices. This obliges me to make
even greater efforts to ask provocative questions of them and to attempt to
make sense of a culture in which substantial literary achievement by women
was exceedingly unlikely, if not impossible.

## Notes

1. C.W. Bynum, *Holy Feast and Holy Fast; The Religious Significance of Food to Medieval Women* (Berkeley, 1987); C. Klapisch-Zuber, *Women, Family and Ritual in Renaissance Italy*, trans. L.G. Cochrane (Chicago, 1985); N.Z. Davis, "Women in the crafts in sixteenth-century Lyon", in *Women and Work in Pre-Industrial Europe*, ed. B. Hanawalt (Bloomington, 1986), 167-97; *Fiction in the Archives; Pardon Tales and Their Tellers in Sixteenth-Century France* (Stanford, 1987); *Women on the Margins; Three Seventeenth-Century Lives* (Cambridge, Mass: 1995); L. Roper, *Oedipus and The Devil; Witchcraft, Sexuality, and Religion in Early Modern Europe* (New York, 1994).

2. Marguerite de Navarre, *The Heptameron*, trans. P.A. Chilton (New York: Penguin, 1984), 156-7. "Madame de Roncex visits the [privy of a] Franciscan convent, is taken short and is discovered in an embarrassing condition by her male companions."

3. "Comment Grandgousier congneut l'esperit merveilleux de Gargantua à l'invention d'un torchecul."

4. M. Bakhtin, *Rabelais and His World*, trans. H. Iswolsky (Cambridge, Mass: 1968), 368*ff*.

5. "Veu que à vous ne feis austere tour / En dict ny faict, en soubson ny libelle," Rabelais, *Pantagruel, roy des dipsodes, restitué a son naturel, avec ses faictz et prouesses espoventables*, Ch. XXII in *Gargantua and Pantagruel*, trans. J.M. Cohen (Harmondsworth: Penguin, 1955), 243.

6. "Ce seroit bien fort utile à tout la republicque, delectable à vous, honneste à vostre lignée et à moy necessaire, que feussiez couverte de ma race," *ibid.*, Ch. XXI, trans. Cohen, 239.

7. "vostre [beauté] est tant excellente, tant singuliere, tant celeste, que je crois que nature l'a mise en vous comme un parragon pour nos donne entendre combien elle peut faire quand elle veult employer toute sa puissance et tout son sçavoir. Ce n'est que miel, ce n'est que sucre, ce n'est que manne celeste, de tout qu'est en vous. C'estoit à vous à qui Pâris debvoit adjuger la pomme d'or, non à Venus, non, ny à Juno, ny a Minerve," *ibid.* trans. Cohen, 240.

8. "frotter son lart avecques elle," *ibid.*

9. Marguerite de Navarre, *Heptaméron*, stories IV and X.

10. "gens liberes, bien nez, bien instruictz, conversans en compaignies honnestes, ont par nature un instinct et aguillon qui tousjours les poulse à faictz vertueux et retire de vice...," *La vie très horrificque du grand Gargantua*, Ch. LVII, trans. Cohen, 159.

11. I:28 trans. M. Screech, *The Complete Essays* (New York: Allen Lane, 1991), 210.

12. *Ibid.* trans. Screech, 209.

13. The classic work of Lucien Febvre, *Amour Sacré; Amour Profane; Autour de l'Heptaméron* (Paris, 1944) gives a clear indication of the ways in which historians can tease a great deal of information from a work like Marguerite's.

# CHAPTER 10

# Milton's Satan: Victim of Sibling Rivalry?

*Joan Faust*

The theme of this year's ACTC Conference—"Core Text Education: Knowledge, Action, Creation?"—To me, is not a question but epitomizes the task with which we, as instructors of core text courses, are charged: not only must we impart knowledge of the literary works in question, but we must actively create a connection between the modern reader and the core text. The rationale of calling a text a "core text" is that it somehow touches the very core of our humanity—that no matter how many years or even millennia have intervened between the original composition and our reading, the actions and values remain significant and inspirational in our own lives. The job of a core text instructor, then, is to reveal that significance, that relevance, to our often skeptical young students who perhaps have not yet ascertained just what is significant to their own lives. I have found a very fruitful approach is demonstrating relationships between the text and other diverse fields of study and experience, in a type of metaphysical conceit, "yolk[ing] by violence together" aspects of the text and life perhaps not realized by our students. I have compared epic hero Aeneas to an American politician; I have shown dissimilating tactics recommended by Castiglione in *The Courtier* are the sources of our modern business behavior; and I have interpreted Dante's use of light in the *Paradiso* by analyzing medieval theories of sight.

When it came to teaching *Paradise Lost*, however, the obvious phenomenon that needed explanation was why readers were able to relate much more closely to Satan than to God or even Adam. I looked for modern sociological or psychological studies that might explain human fascination with evil but so far have been unsuccessful. Critics who have tackled Milton's enigmatic character generally fall into two opposing groups: Satanists who, like William Blake and Percy Shelley, justify Milton's charismatic character in Books I and II as representing human desire and creative energy; and Anti-Satanists who focus especially on the final books of *Paradise Lost* and on the substance (or lack thereof) of Satan's complaints. One of the leading anti-Satanists, C.S. Lewis, sees Satan as an absurd egoist whose rantings and posturings eventually become comic.[1]

So, I challenge my students, which do you believe—is Satan hero or clown? Then I offer them a third alternative, one that not only acknowledges Satan's virtues as well as his vices, his human qualities as well as his divine, his status as creator and created; but also explains our sympathy for the character: Satan is a victim of sibling rivalry.

Freudian psychologist Bruno Bettelheim has shown that competition among siblings presents a profound and largely unconscious problem to children and even adults. He has analyzed popular fairy tales like *Cinderella* to show that fairy tales speak to a child's unconscious, giving him or her tools to help resolve these inner conflicts. When children see Cinderella, a good and beautiful young woman who is unfairly debased and mistreated by her stepsisters, finally overcoming adversity to take her rightful place with the prince, they feel somehow justified and hopeful that they, too, will surpass their threatening brothers and sisters.[2] I suggest to my students that Satan's story, at least in his own mind, is *Cinderella* without the happy ending.

Bettelheim explains that despite the term "sibling rivalry," the feelings of resentment toward one's brothers and sisters have little to do with the sibling but have their real source in the child's feelings about his parents. When another child is given special attention, the child fears that his relationship with his parents is threatened: "Fearing that in comparison to them he cannot win his parents' love and esteem is what inflames sibling rivalry."[3] Of course, the child is usually not consciously aware of his anxiety about his parents' love but only feels animosity toward his siblings who seem to usurp his share of that love. And though the story of Satan's revolt is not definitively set down in canonical scripture, accounts of sibling rivalry are.

From Cain's first fratricide to Joseph's brothers selling him into slavery to Jacob's stealing Esau's birthright, the Bible abounds in stories of good, unsuspecting children being tormented, cheated, and even killed by jealous siblings. But, says Bettelheim, these extreme accounts attract us because they speak to the unconscious child in us all who feels himself unfairly used by siblings, even when those feelings have little basis in fact.

These feelings of being slighted by a parent are very evident in Milton's Satan. In Book V, Raphael admits that Satan did merit greatness. He was "of the first, / if not the first Archangel, great in power, / in favour, and preeminence. . . " (V.559-61).[4] His existence was a happy one until God, somewhat arbitrarily, declared and anointed one of his creation "My only Son" (V.604) and commanded all other creatures to "bow / All knees in Heaven and . . . confess him Lord" under pain of utter exile (V.607-08). Critics have commented that this exaltation does appear arbitrary, since Christ to this point had not done anything to show his worth.[5]

In Satan's own mind, God's exaltation of what the fallen angel considers just another son, another creature, threatens his own high place in heaven. Like any selfish, insecure child who loves his father, Satan feels God's love is a finite commodity which decreases as it is shared. Bettelheim explains that the term "sibling rivalry" refers to "a most complex constellation of feelings and their causes":

> With extremely rare exceptions, the emotions aroused in the person subject to sibling rivalry are far out of proportion to what his real situation with his sisters and brothers would justify, seen objectively. While all children at times suffer greatly from sibling rivalry, parents seldom sacrifice one of their children to the others, nor do they condone the other children's persecuting them.[6]

And as abused sibling, Satan does seem to exaggerate his sufferings in heaven and to focus on his situation with rather childish egoism. At first, he reveals to Beelzebub that his revolt was from sense of injured merit (I.98) but gives no specific slight. Most of his speeches to the diabolic troops emphasize his own worthiness and selfishness, as he names himself possessor of hell (I.252), yet he claims he was unfairly tricked by God, who, concealing much of his power, tempted [his] attempt and wrought [his] fall (I.642).

Satan continues his distorted and immature interpretation of all things as a personal insult throughout his quest to destroy mankind. He views the glorious sun not as a source of warmth and light but as a tyrant, whose brightness effaces that of the lesser stars, and he sees in the overshadowing of those stars his own plight, drowned out by the greater light of God's Son: ". . . I hate thy beams, / That bring to my remembrance from what state / I fell..." (IV.37-39). He resents the new creation, Man, whom he comes to believe God created to take the place of those angels who fell. We see Satan's burning jealousy increasingly distort his interpretation of this new sibling group, first naming mankind "A generation, whom [God's] choice regard / Should favour equal to the sons of heaven" (I.653-4); then claiming that Man is to be "favored more / Of him who rules above" (II.350-1); and finally accusing mankind of totally supplanting his own position, calling this new creation "A race of upstart creatures, to supply / Perhaps our vacant room" (II.834-5). Satan evidences here the resentment of an older child who fears a younger sibling might supplant his place in his parents' affection. His childish inability to see objectively is the "hell within" of sibling rivalry that distorts all experiences and all creation.

Blinded by his own sense of "injured merit," then, Satan fails to see in his plan of revenge the ultimate *contrapasso* of his freely chosen fate: he must serve as a diabolical parody of Christ's own act of redemption. In an absurd imitation of Christ's incarnation, Satan thinks to raise himself to victor by slyly lowering himself to various animals—a cormorant, a toad, and finally a serpent. His ultimate punishment of being transformed into a serpent in hell along with his comrades, though, is not only fitting punishment but also links him to the sibling rivalry that prompts his every action. According to Bettelheim, "having to live among the ashes" was a symbol of being debased in comparison to one's siblings:

> Martin Luther in his *Table Talks* speaks about Cain as the God-forsaken evildoer who is powerful, while pious Abel is forced to be his ash-brother. . . a mere nothing, subject to Cain; in one of Luther's sermons he says that Esau was forced into the role of Jacob's ash-brother. [7]

This symbol of ashes explains the sibling rivalry link to Cinderella and her German counterpart, Ashputtle, who are forced to live among the ashes by their jealous siblings. Likewise, Satan and his compeers suffer a *contrapasso* worthy of Dante himself as they, writhing as snakes in Hell, forever reenacting man s fall, desire and eat the fruit before them, which turns to bitter ashes. . . soot and cinders (X.565-570). Forever they will be reminded that they are the ash-brothers of Christ.

Samuel Butler, in his *Note-Books* published posthumously in 1912, said we never heard the Devil's side of the case because God has written all the books. [8] As I advise my students, like any great character in literature, Satan must ultimately be interpreted by his audience, and each of us should come to terms with this enigma by carefully comparing what he says, what he does, what is said about him and what is done to him. Whether we see him as epic hero, Promethean rebel, absurd buffoon, or misused sibling, Satan touches a part of us, perhaps a part of which we're not proud, but at least a part of us all. So when we read his convoluted arguments and justifications for his revenge and hatred, we might try to read a bit between the lines: is he really that evil, that awesome, that terrifying, or is he really just lamenting, "Dad liked him best"?

## Notes

1. Harold Bloom, ed., *Modern Critical Views: John Milton*, "Introduction," (New York: Chelsea House Publishers, 1986), 3.

2. Bruno Bettelheim, *The Uses of Enchantment*, (New York: Alfred A. Knopf, 1977), 237-38.

3. Ibid., 238.

4. All quotes from *Paradise Lost* will be from the Lecompte edition listed in the bibliography.

5. William Flesch, "The Majesty of Darkness" in Bloom, 295.

6. Bettelheim, 237-38.

7. Ibid., 237.

8. Maximilian Rudwin. *The Devil in Legend and Literature* (Illinois: The Open Court Publishing Company, 1931, repr. 1959), 14.

## Works Cited

Bettelheim, Bruno. 1977. *The Uses of Enchantment*. New York: Alfred A. Knopf.

Bloom, Harold, ed. 1986. *Modern Critical Views: John Milton*. "Introduction" New York: Chelsea House Publishers, 1-7.

Flesch, William. 1986. "The Majesty of Darkness," in *Modern Critical Views: John Milton*, ed. Harold Bloom, 293-31. New York: Chelsea House Publishers.

Edward LeCompte, ed. 1981. *Paradise Lost and Other Poems*, 33-343. Penguin Books.

Rudwin, Maximilian. 1931; repr. 1959. *The Devil in Legend and Literature*, Illinois: The Open Court Publishing Company.

CHAPTER 11

# Confronting the Fragments:
# Eliot's *Four Quartets*

*Christopher L. Constas*

Boston College's Honors Program takes a historical approach to core texts. The first two years of the Honors Program sequence (called The Western Cultural Tradition) serve as an alternative to the university core in philosophy, theology, social sciences and literature. Each section is interdisciplinary: thus, the same instructor will be teaching Plato, Homer, and the Bible. Freshman year (12 credits) covers the Ancient world, the Bible, and ends in the high middle ages (Dante); sophomore year moves from the renaissance and early modernity up to the 20th century. As compared with the first year, there is decidedly less agreement among faculty of the second year as to where one should end up, or how much of the 20th century one should cover: some end with *The Brothers Karamazov*, others end with Nietzsche or Freud.

Over the past three years the Honors Program has developed a third year requirement on the 20th century. This yearlong, six-credit course— the 20th Century and the Tradition I & II— is divided roughly between modernism in the fall and postmodernism in the spring.

As one who has taught this third year course, I have sensed a problem, though I hasten to add that it is not a problem that is lacking a solution. The problem is that by ending a three-year encounter with Western Culture with the postmodern critique of the tradition, one runs the risk of instilling in students a series of ideas that one may not want them to go away with: that the core texts we teach are primarily instruments of domination; that the choice of texts that we have made as teachers are essentially arbitrary; that the culture made a wrong turn 4,000 years ago and is only now beginning to recover; that there is no truth, and that, consequently, the only possible epistemic postures on the eve of the millennium are skeptical relativism and dogmatic tribalism.

It is, of course, possible to guard against the formation of various extreme ideas about the function and value of a core text education. One strategy would be to ignore the postmodern critique, at least until we see how it plays out (it may, after all, turn out to be nothing more than a fad, a blip on the screen). I am not particularly sympathetic to this idea, primarily because there is much in postmodern theory that I find both plausible and valuable. Another strategy is to confront the postmodern critique of culture head-on and accept its fundamental insights (in particular, its anti-Cartesian critique of subjectivity and its anti-realist critique of representation) but still manage to avoid skepticism and dogmatism. I believe that this last strategy is feasible and that T.S. Eliot's *Four Quartets* can be of assistance in accomplishing this task. [1]

Why Eliot's *Four Quartets* ? First, because they are four didactic poems, each of which, in its own way, ruminates on the contemporary problems of fragmentation, subjectivity, and contingency. Each poem reflects an understanding of consciousness that is consistent with the understanding of postmodern theory. Second, each poem exemplifies the way in which art can help us to confront and be reconciled to our historicity. Each poem ends with a synthesis that resolves, however provisionally and humbly, the problem with which the poem is concerned (in all four poems, some variation on the problem of historicity). Finally, the *Quartets* represent just the kind of humility they ultimately counsel. They impose a pattern, for "Only by the form, the pattern, /Can words or music reach/The stillness, as a Chinese jar still/ Moves perpetually in its stillness" (BN, 140-3). But the pattern is the complex yet humble pattern of the quartet, not the lofty pattern of the symphony.

The *Four Quartets* are didactic. They endeavor to teach us many things. One thing they hope to teach is that consciousness is historical and contingent. We are historical beings— that is, finite beings in space and time. Reality is disclosed to us locally in time. Because of our historicity, however, the disclosure of reality is always radically incomplete. There will always be past disclosures that we missed, future disclosures that we will fail to anticipate, and present disclosures that we are not in a position to experience. A full disclosure of reality, a full grasp of what Eliot in "Burnt Norton" calls "our first world" (BN, 22), can only happen out of place and out of time, and a human being is a being in a particular place at a particular time.

But though humans are unavoidably historical in this sense, they are neither always nor wholly so. For though to be human is to be in time, there are moments when the timeless intersects with time and places which are the world's end. There are experiences in which we sense, however vaguely, the oneness of reality. Eliot prefaces *Four Quartets* with two quotes from Heraclitus. It is the first of these that is relevant here: "Although logos is common to all, most people live as if they possessed a wisdom of their own." There is, in other words, despite the fragmentary— because temporal— nature of our experience, a primordial synthesis that we apprehend, however dimly, in what Eliot refers to as "unattended moments."

Each of the *Quartets* begins with just such an unattended moment, "sudden in a shaft of sunlight" (BN, 169; cf. DS, 208). "Burnt Norton" describes a moment in a rose garden; "East Coker" revolves around a moment when light falls across an open field; "The Dry Salvages," a moment by the sea in Massachusetts; and "Little Gidding," a moment in a church in a small English village. Each moment is fleeting— "Quick now, here, now, always" (BN, 173; LG 252)— but each is an unmistakable apprehension of "The point of intersection of the timeless/With time" (DS, 201-02; cf. LG, 52).

What Eliot is describing are those moments in life when, in a flash of insight, it all makes sense to us— reality is coherent and unified. We sense the oneness of reality, we feel the synthesis. We are in "our first world." Eliot locates this experience in unattended moments. Joyce, to cite another Modernist, called such experiences epiphanies.[2]

It is, of course, only natural that we should want to fix this experience and represent it, to make this felt synthesis explicit, to secure for ourselves a world that is coherent and stable. Reality is disclosed to us in fragments, and our job is to impose some order on these fragments, to synthesize them into a coherent whole. We have to do this; we have no choice in the matter. We must impose an order on our experience. We are, as it were, condemned to the perpetual creation— not the discovery, but the creation— of meaning. The question, then, is the status of these meanings we construct and their connection to this primordial meaning that we sense in unattended moments. In other words, what should our attitude be towards those cultural artifacts that endeavor to represent our first world, to express its meaning?

Two possible responses have already been mentioned: dogmatism and skepticism. The dogmatic response is that my representations, or the

representations of my tribe, are the True representations. The skeptical response is that no representation is the true representation, and that one tribe's
representation of our first world is as good as any other tribe's.

But both responses are inadequate. The dogmatic response assumes that
our representations are not created but discovered, are not *re* -presentations
but presentations. The skeptical response assumes that representations are
constructed *de novo* and *ex nihilo*. Both responses lack an appropriate
measure of humility, because both fail to understand that we always speak
what Eliot calls "the dialect of the tribe."

> ...our concern was speech, and speech impelled us
> To purify the dialect of the tribe
> And urge the mind to aftersight and foresight... (LG, 126-28).

The dogmatist fails to see that the representations of the tribe are always
constructed in the *dialect* of the tribe. As dialects are local, historical, contingent and provisional, so, also, representations are local, historical, contingent and provisional. Even if we take the tribe to be the whole of the
human species, the fact remains that what we speak is a dialect, and not the
language, of the tribe. There will always be something that is left unsaid,
something that remains undisclosed, something that I cannot say because
I do not have the words ("...one has only learnt to get the better of words /
For the thing one no longer has to say, or the way in which / O n e is no
longer disposed to say it," EC, 176-78).

But a dialect is still derivative of a more primordial and original language,
and it is this that the skeptic fails to see. Though local, historical, contingent
and provisional, the dialect of the tribe— and thus the representations of the
tribe— emerge as a response to what the later Heidegger would call a disclosure or unconcealment of being. [3] Eliot, in a line that could easily be found
in the later Heidegger, notes that "Words, after speech, reach/Into the silence"
(BN, 139-40). We use words because we have been spoken to (by God? By
Being? By the logos?), and we are called to respond. Language, itself, origi-
nates in the need to respond.

We respond to our fleeting apprehension of the pattern of reality by trying
to represent the pattern. But because the pattern is intersecting with time in
time, our apprehension of the pattern is the apprehension that is appropriate at this place at this time ("Now and in England," LG, 38). We can only
apprehend it with the resources of the tribe. It is because of the limitations
imposed by the dialect of the tribe that it seems to Eliot that there is

> At best, only a limited value
> In the knowledge derived from experience.
> The knowledge imposes a pattern, and falsifies,
> For the pattern is new in every moment
> And every moment is a new and shocking
> Valuation of all we have been. We are only undeceived
> Of that which, deceiving, could no longer harm (EC, 81-88).

But though knowledge imposes a pattern and falsifies,[4] we should not refrain from imposing a pattern. For if we allow the inevitability of falsification to prevent us from imposing a pattern, we have misunderstood the purpose of imposing a pattern. As Eliot notes in his essay "Poetry and Drama": "It is ultimately the function of art, in imposing a credible order upon reality, and thereby eliciting some perception of an order *in* reality, to bring us to a condition of serenity, stillness and reconciliation; and then leave us, as Virgil left Dante, to proceed toward a region where that guide can avail us no farther."[5]

Our response, after speech, is always a response in and through words, in and through language (including the language of music). The pattern we impose is always a mediated representation of the pattern we have apprehended in an unattended moment. Language, however, is not fully adequate to the task. The fifth movement of "East Coker" begins by lamenting this fact:

> So here I am, in the middle way, having had twenty years—
> Twenty years largely wasted, the years of l'entre deux guerres
> Trying to learn to use words, and every attempt
> Is a wholly new start, and a different kind of failure
> Because one has only learnt to get the better of words
> For the thing one no longer has to say, or the way in which
> One is no longer disposed to say it. And so each venture
> Is a new beginning, a raid on the inarticulate
> With shabby equipment always deteriorating
> In the general mess of imprecision of feeling,
> Undisciplined squads of emotion (EC, 172-182).

Language is part and parcel of our shabby equipment always deteriorating (EC, 179). A similar observation is made in the fifth movement of Burnt Norton :

> Words strain,
> Crack and sometimes break, under the burden,
> Under the tension, slip, slide, perish,

Decay with imprecision, will not stay in place,
Will not stay still (BN, 149-53).

Observations about the instability of meaning and the ultimate inadequacy of our linguistic representations are central to postmodern theory and
deconstructive practice. But the instability of meaning is not language's vice
but its virtue. Because words do not have fixed meanings, what is left unsaid is not doomed to perpetual silence.

It is in this respect that one can see postmodern and deconstructive theory
as pushing us towards poetry. For poetry is that use of language, that response to being, that most exploits the instability of meaning. Through
poetry, perhaps more than any other art, we can represent unattended moments with the least violence. A poem fixes the moment, but fixes it in such
a way that the moment "Moves perpetually in its stillness" (BN, 143),
namely, the stillness of the poetic representation. If, as Heidegger suggests,
every unconcealment of Being is also a concealment, if every disclosure of
a dimension of reality unavoidably closes off some other dimension of reality, then we should endeavor to engage in those modes of disclosure that
conceal as little as possible. Poetry, because it embraces the instability of
meaning, is such a mode of disclosure.

The poet has no illusions of ever fully purifying the dialect of the tribe. He
has no expectation that he or anyone will ever find a form of expression that
is fully adequate, an artistic representation that fully discloses reality, a poetic synthesis that conveys the speech of the Absolute synthesis of the logos.
We can never fully overcome our historicity, we can only conquer it historically, that is, in a particular place at a particular time, "Now and in England."

Core texts are part of the dialect of the tribe. As such, they always leave
something unsaid. There are always fragments that have escaped the synthesis
that each represents. There will *always* be fragments that will escape the
synthesis (thus, the dogmatist is misguided). But some syntheses are more
coherent and comprehensive than others and, thus, better than others (so, also,
the skeptic is misguided). Our students should read the syntheses of others
and, from these fragments, accomplish new syntheses, secure in the knowledge that their synthesis will leave much unsaid, but confident that they have,
in good faith, said as much as the dialect of the tribe would allow.

I end with a passage from "Little Gidding," the fourth and final of the
*Four Quartets* :

The end is where we start from. And every phrase
And sentence that is right (where every word is at home,

Taking its place to support the others,
The word neither diffident nor ostentatious,
An easy commerce of the old and the new,
The common word exact without vulgarity,
The formal word precise but not pedantic,
The complete consort dancing together)
Every phrase and every sentence is an end and a beginning,
Every poem an epitaph. And any action
Is a step to the block, to the fire, down the sea's throat
Or to an illegible stone: and that is where we start (Eliot, "Little Gidding,"
214-27).

## Notes

1. T.S. Eliot, *Four Quartets* (New York: Harcourt Brace & Company, 1943). References to this volume will appear in the text of the paper. References will be to individual poem and line. Poems will be cited in the text by the following abbreviations: BN = "Burnt Norton"; EC = "East Coker"; DS = "The Dry Salvages"; LG = "Little Gidding."

The inspiration for using Eliot's *Four Quartets* as a way to confront the postmodern condition is owed to David Tracy of the University of Chicago, specifically to a paper he delivered at Boston College on December 4, 1997, entitled "Poetry as Theology: The Example of T.S. Eliot." The paper was derived from Tracy's work on his current book, *Naming God*. My own approach differs from Tracy's in that I focus less on the mystical—Buddhist and Christian— dimensions of *Four Quartets* and more on what the poem says about being, language and historicity. Instead of poetry as theology, I examine the possibility of poetry as ontology.

2. Cf. James Joyce, *A Portrait of the Artist as a Young Man.* The Viking Critical Edition of *Portrait* (New York: Viking Penguin, Inc., 1968) reprints a passage from *Stephen Hero* where an epiphany is described as "a sudden spiritual manifestation, whether in the vulgarity of speech or of gesture or in a memorable phase of the mind itself. He believed that it was for the man of letters to record these epiphanies with extreme care, seeing that they themselves are the most delicate and evanescent of moments" (*ibid.,* 288).

3. See, for example, Martin Heidegger, "On the Essence of Truth," in *Basic Writings,* ed., David Farrell Krell (New York: Harper & Row, 1977), 127ff.

CHAPTER 12

# When Learning Goes Awry: Meditations on the *Malleus Malificarum*

*Anne Leavitt*

Few people these days have heard of the *Malleus Malificarum* or *Witch's Hammer* although it is beginning to receive long overdue attention in a number of academic circles.[1] In its own day, however, it was a book that was not only well known in virtually all sectors of the academic, ecclesiastical and legal worlds, it was a book that had enormous impact on the day to day lives of ordinary citizens of all classes in virtually every country in Europe. Written in 1486 by two highly-placed and well-respected Dominican clerics, Heinrich Kramer and James Sprenger, it is divided into three parts. The first treats of the "necessary concomitants of witchcraft"; the second of "the methods by which the works of witchcraft are wrought and directed, and how they may be successfully annulled and dissolved"; and the third of "the judicial proceedings in both the ecclesiastical and civil courts against all witches and indeed all heretics." When it appeared, it quickly became an international best-seller (thanks, in part, to the printing press) and the handbook of every ecclesiastical and civil judge charged with trying accused witches, appearing in 35 editions in four different languages between 1486 and 1669. And, its direct impact on European culture and history was enormous. It was the *Malleus Malificarum* which sparked and justified the fires that led to the deaths of hundreds of thousands of women over the next three hundred years in a period now referred to as "the burning times."

When I was an undergraduate back in the seventies, the *Malleus* was not the kind of book that, even if my professors had known about, I would have been encouraged to read. My formative years as a young adult were spent in the Philosophy Department at McMaster University – a Department which was always very good to me and to which I returned, after many years of absence, to complete my Ph.D. Then, as now, young philosophy students grappled with serious questions of epistemology, metaphysics, logic and the rest over endless streams of beer and chips in one of the many campus pubs. It all seemed very important to us then and it troubled us not a wit if our friends in other disciplines or our parents hardly understood a word we had to say. We were intent upon examining the beliefs with which we had grown up in an attempt to discover what we knew and did not know, and we understood that our language and obsessions were bound to be different from most people's. Witches and witchcraft were things we did not think about much and, as I recall, they never came up in any of our many classes save for a couple of days after we had all seen Monty Python's *Holy Grail*. We had little time to spend arguing over superstitions which troubled "the medieval mind", the lasting legacy of which was only a Halloween costume that some of us had worn when we were kids. I guess that, if some one had actually asked us why we didn't trouble ourselves with witches, we would have been amused, confident in our knowledge that, thanks to the achievements of our philosophical forebears in the Enlightenment, all the interesting legal, political and philosophical issues surrounding witchcraft had been laid, forever, to rest.

In philosophical circles and others these days, that "rationalist" project (successfully marketed by thinkers as Rene Descartes and Thomas Hobbes) has come under serious attack. And I do not intend here (or anywhere) to offer a sustained defense of all that these thinkers were up to. After spending some time with the *Malleus Malificarum*, however, I have a much greater appreciation for what prompted them to embark on the rationalist course they chose and a much greater appreciation for why philosophical debates about the differences between knowledge and belief, about the meaning of human inquiry, and about the intellectual search for certainty are of perennial and political importance. I also have begun to lament the increasing technicality and obscurity of the language of many of these academic debates, and the diminishing place of courses which focus on primary works in the history of the Western tradition in most institutions of higher learning. I lament these things because I have come to wonder whether they might not be the very things which prevent intelligent and effective responses to modern versions of the *Malleus* of which I have seen, I think, a few, the most notable being the Nazi justifications and institutional measures for carrying out the Holocaust. But, before I outline some of my reasons for thinking these things, let me first say a bit more about the *Malleus* and how it came to be written.

Both authors of the *Malleus* were Inquisitors, given the authority by Pope Innocent VIII in a Bull of 1484 to investigate and punish people of every class for crimes of witchcraft and heresy in a large area of Northern Germany. It, also, called upon the Bishop of Strasburg to lend all possible support. The Bull, however, made it clear that the Pope was particularly concerned with the practices of witches in the area which included such things as: sexually abandoning themselves to incubus and succubus devils, slaying infants in their mothers' wombs, blasting the produce of the earth, hindering men and women and animals from the sexual act, preventing women from conceiving, and renouncing the faith that was theirs by Baptism. The Pope also expresses a grave concern over the fact that "not a few clerics and lay folk" in the area "are not ashamed to contend with the most unblushing effrontery that these enormities are not practiced in those provinces".[2]

Kremer and Sprenger clearly felt that the experiences and insights they gained as Inquisitors needed a wide audience. Convinced that the abominable and devastating practices of witchcraft were on the rise among all classes of the population,[3] they set out to all educated skepticism about the nature and dangers of such matters in a comprehensive work which also drew upon their own experiences. Their main object, as they tell us, was to lay out the methods of "trying, judging and sentencing" cases of witchcraft for provincial judges as the crime (given its temporal effects) fell within civil jurisdiction and the Inquisitors themselves were suffering under the "arduousness" of trying witches themselves.[4] That there was a great deal of skepticism is clear not only from Pope Innocent's expression of frustration at lay and clerical denials that witchcraft was being practiced in Northern Germany but also from the structure of the work itself. In scholastic fairness, the two Inquisitors lay out and rebut objection after objection to the notion that there is such a thing as witchcraft, that witchcraft is anything more than a psychological phenomenon, and that those who disbelieve in witches and their Satanic powers are themselves heretics.

Not unexpectedly, the *Malleus* covers a great deal of ground addressing, as it must, the nature of evil and its place in the divine scheme of things, resting its arguments on everything from scripture to the doctors of the Church to canon and Roman law. But the *Malleus* would not be the *Malleus*, and it would not have had the effect it had on the history of the West if it had not offered an equally comprehensive treatment of the morally corrupt nature of women and their susceptibility to the sexual seductions of "those Devils known as incubi." While the authors make it clear that witchcraft, in principle, knows no gender, in practice, they insist that the vast majority of witches are women. Why? Because, "All witchcraft comes from carnal lust, which in women is insatiable."[5] According to the *Malleus,* women are, by nature, intellectually inferior to men and this inferiority is rooted in their carnality. "The natural reason [for the intellectual inferiority of woman] is that she is more carnal than a man, as is clear from her many carnal abominations. . . [T]here was a defect in the formation of the first woman, since she was formed from a bent rib . . . which is bent as it were in a contrary direction to a man. And since through this defect she is an imperfect animal, she always deceives."[6] The intellectual inferiority of women, rooted in carnal lust, is what inclines them more readily than men to "abjure the faith," to enter into sexual relations with devils and to worship the Lord of Darkness.[7]

The effects imputed to witchcraft, laid out in the Papal Bull and explored in detail by Kremer and Sprenger, were truly horrendous, including as they did the habitual sacrifice of little babies and the habitual weakening and stealing of male sexual organs. The means employed by witches are said to include not only charms and curses but also sidelong glances and mere touches. In fact, given the notorious secrecy of witches, threatening words, odd looks, strange touches, and hidden birthmarks alone were, for Kremer and Sprenger, sufficient to justify a "grave suspicion" of witchcraft (if a confession could not be got through torture)[8] and a "grave suspicion" of witchcraft, according to the authors, merited capital punishment even for those who recanted.[9] Not simply because of their spiritual degradation but rather because of their "temporal effects," the authors urge that witches "deserve the heaviest punishment of all the criminals in the world."[10]

And punished they were. For the next three hundred years, hundreds of thousands of women of all classes and ages were sent to the stake in village and town squares all over both Catholic and Protestant Europe by judges whose handbook was the *Malleus Malificarum.*[11]

It is, of course, now easy for me to see why, even if my professors at McMaster had known about the *Malleus*, they would not have suggested that I read it. It really is a dreadful book by any standard and not the kind of text one wants students to read if one is interested in providing for them models of cogent, clear, critical and persuasive philosophical thinking and writing. But, if one is interested in not only providing models of such thinking and writing but demonstrating why such thinking and writing is important, one could do a lot worse than point to the *Malleus*. Even its outspoken misogyny can be instructive although not a few academics these days would be appalled at the idea that it ever be allowed on an undergraduate reading list.

Consider the travails of Arizona State University Theatre Professor, Jared Sakren, who came close to being fired for teaching the works of Shakespeare on the grounds that they are "sexist". It was suggested to him by his department that, if he insisted on teaching such plays as *The Taming of the Shrew*, he could, provided he change the ending so it "wouldn't offend women".[12] Arguments attempting to establish the misogyny of Shakespeare and any other number of writers of classic texts in the Western tradition have been around now for awhile. But to confront the *Malleus* is to confront the utterly unapologetic, genuine article. There it is as plain as day – not quietly beneath the surface requiring careful reading to be exposed and not described as an inferred object of theoretical reflection. Kremer and Sprenger believe what they write even as they argue against those who do not. All I had to do was to ask myself how I might raise my daughter in a world where this text was a judicial handbook and I got, in a way I had never got before, the origins of a great deal of women's habits and customs with which I am even now familiar. I also got why it might be that early liberal feminists like Mary Wollstencraft were so insistent upon downplaying the differences between men and women and so passionate in their defense and promotion of women's rational capacities. For me, confronting the *Malleus* was, in many ways, a personal act of exorcism. As one of my students who had just finished the text said to me recently, "Serious misogyny used to scare me. After reading the *Malleus*, I now find it hilarious. I mean, to think that men could be so afraid of women just because we can have multiple orgasms!"

To confront the origin of a sinister strand of thought in one's society, a text which led to the most horrible end for thousands of women can be profoundly disturbing. But it also has the capacity to provoke in one an understanding of the need for deep and serious reflection about serious things – something that Kremer and Sprenger and the judges who used their work ignored. The *Malleus* has led me to question seriously the assumption that students, female students in particular, should be spared the discomfort of reading any work which smacks of misogyny. To defeat one's enemy, one has to know him. The members of the Arizona State University Theatre Department might do well to remember that, while there were periodic attempts by members of the ecclesiastical and scholarly communities to refute the arguments offered in the *Malleus Malificarum*, the reason there were not more was because, according to the same text, disbelief in witches was heresy and merited serious legal consequences if not the accusation that one who engaged in such disbelief was a witch oneself.[13]

Students confronted with the modern rationalist approach to matters of reason and knowledge (whether in learning the methods of the sciences and social sciences or through studying the works and history of the Enlightenment) are often offended by the rejection that the rational approach requires of the fantastic and magical as based in anything other than illusion. But this is the approach that eventually brought to an end the admissibility of idle threats, sidelong glances, odd touches and birthmarks as legal evidence of a "grave suspicion" of witchcraft. If the founders of modern rationalism (e.g. Thomas Hobbes and Rene Descartes) seem, at times, overly harsh in their rejection of Scholastic reasoning, in their rejection of "occult causes", and in their rejection of "superstition", it is worth remembering what, for them, the alternative had produced.

I am no booster of modern rationalism in all of its many guises but reading the *Malleus* has encouraged me to rethink many of the reasons I have had for being hostile to it. And the one thing I have appreciated is that a great deal of my own education and the Program in which I now teach has given me a high level of exposure to the original arguments for many of the things with which are now familiar in the modern world. It is one thing to grow up in a world dominated by scientific learning where academic and professional success are premised upon one's ability to reason in fairly linear ways. When those things come under attack, it is another thing to be able to appreciate the reasons why the Western world embraced them. Those reasons are most powerfully offered by the people who first put them, who could not simply assume the worth of their own arguments but had to convince a world which had not yet heard them. The *Malleus* has led me to lament the fact that we do not often ask students to confront those arguments as they were originally developed but rather, far too often, treat the modern rational tradition as if, from the moment it emerged, it was as thoughtlessly self-evident to itself as it has, in fact, become in many circles today. The *Malleus* and its dark history have taught me that simply to assume as self-evident the "truths" of modern rationalism or simply to assume that modern rationalism has always been an unreflective prejudice of Western culture is to court a potentially dangerous intellectual passivity.

The *Malleus* has invited me to think about the ways in which learning can go awry and the horrifying things that can happen when it does. By any standard, it is a badly argued book and it is a deeply misogynist book, but it is also a highly learned book. Kremer and Sprenger offer a prodigious compendium of scriptural, philosophical, ecclesiastical, legal, historical and anecdotal evidence and argument both for and against their various positions. The number of sources cited is simply staggering. And it is all this learning, all this scholarship, all this technical virtuosity, that gives the book its weighty and authoritative tone. It is precisely the *amount* of scholarship which puts flesh on what otherwise would be a thin skeleton of plainly sophistical arguments and which also veils the extent to which the authors have been highly selective in the choice of the passages they cite, ignoring the context of many of those passages altogether when it is in their interest to do so. The text is not so much a Scholastic work as an unwitting and dark parody of Scholastic reasoning. At moments, like my student, I find it hilarious until I remember what happened when people took it seriously. And, when that happens, I am not convinced that such a thing could never happen again.

Like the Holocaust, the *Malleus* invites us to reflect upon how it is that learning is not necessarily an inoculation against evil but can actually serve it. As John Ralston Saul notes, ". . . the Holocaust was the product of decades of written, intellectual justification, which the rest of society failed to destroy as an expressible option by passively allowing the arguments to stand."[14] The reasons we ponder the Holocaust are not to simply beat our breasts and cry with shame over the mistakes of the past. Rather, we ponder the Holocaust in order to try to get our heads around human capacities for evil and some of the deep ambiguities present in our culture that need to be recognized, understood and confronted.[15] The *Malleus* certainly does not provide a model for the kind of philosophical reflection one might need in order to do this. But precisely because it does not and precisely because of what it triggered, like the Holocaust, it provides a reason for why such reflection is important. Like the Holocaust, it also sits as a warning against scholarship and learning which parade as reflection and which, for that reason, are easily co-opted by the powers of darkness ever present in any time and place.

## Notes

1. Heinrich Kramer and James Sprenger, *The Malleus Malificarum*, trans. Montague Summers (New York: Dover Publications, 1971).

2. "The Bull of Innocent VIII", *The Malleus Malificarum*, xliii – xlv.

3. *Malleus,* 20 – 21.

4. *Ibid.,* 196.

5. *Ibid.,* 47.

6. *Ibid.,* 44.

7. *Ibid.,* 45.

8. *Ibid.*, 248.

9. *Ibid.*, 77.

10. *Ibid.*

11. With the exception of Russia, where the numbers of men and women found guilty of witchcraft was approximately equal, throughout Europe, 85% of those found guilty of witchcraft were women.

12. *Arizona Daily Wildcat*, February 2, 1998.

13. *Malleus*, 8 – 10, 238.

14. John Ralston Saul, *The Doubter's Companion* (Toronto: Penguin Books, 1995), 3.

15. One way to have students confront the Holocaust which leads to the kind of reflection to which I have been pointing is to have them read and discuss Hannah Arendt's *Eichmann in Jerusalem* after having viewed and discussed Leni Riefenstahl's *Triumph of the Will*.

# III. Ancient and Medieval Gaps: Classical Core Texts from Eastern and Western Traditions

CHAPTER 13

# A Social Science Core Text from the Medieval Islamic World: Ibn Khaldun's *Muqaddimah* and its Models of Social Change.

*Thomas Barfield*

I would like to talk about two things today. The first concerns some of the issues that we face in the social sciences when creating a core texts program that has some general applicability. The second is to argue that in expanding our corpus of core texts into other world traditions, we should give priority to the contributions these works make to knowledge and not simply seek diversity for diversity's sake. To make this case I would like to introduce the work of one of my favorite authors, Ibn Khaldun, the 14th century North African social theorist whose models and observations still have great relevance today.

Teaching core texts in the social sciences immediately lays open disputes about what the social sciences are and where their value lies. Those taking the science aspect seriously argue that there are observable underlying characteristics in human activity and belief that can be identified and that these findings should be confirmed or replicated by the use of the scientific method. In this view model building or hypothesis testing are what distinguish the social sciences from the humanities. In designing our social science core text program at Boston University, however, we discovered two problems with this vision of the social sciences: one with the people who accepted it and the other with the people who did not.

The first group of people, who see the social sciences as being a variety of natural sciences, rejected the whole idea of core texts, arguing that they represented a history of the social sciences, not social science itself. As far as they were concerned these texts were like the python's skin, a product that was continually shed as the disciplines grew larger and larger by swallowing more and more material. Why should we give students mere snakeskins, when we should be introducing them to the snake? But in discussions we soon discovered that their idea of presenting the snake was to focus on each discipline individually, with a stress on methodology, so that the students could admire the beast scale by scale. In essence, over the course of a year, each discipline currently recognized by the university would get a week to present itself and its methodology in the best light, and then students would have sixteen weeks of "to be arranged" topics on the latest research findings of these same disciplines. Our students would then be well educated in the social sciences without the need of any musty old texts, many written by people who would never have obtained tenure in their departments anyway because they never got any grants.

Core texts did not fare much better among the opposing group of people who saw the social sciences as a variety of humanistic studies, not subject to model building, comparisons, or replication. For these scholars everything was unique and must be studied as such in its own terms, a form of relativism that has strong partisans in my own field of anthropology. In particular they wanted to stress the uniqueness of each individual, culture, or political system and were inherently suspicious of comparison because they believed comparison was essentially invidious. They, too, were impatient with the idea of core texts, particularly those texts produced by authors who were members of dominant suspect groups (by race, gender, class, ideology, etc.) Even attempting to create such a list of core texts, let alone teach them, was to engage in a hegemonic discourse of hubristic proportion. Their solution was not core texts but rather core theories, often referred to as "critical theories" (presumably so you could separate them quickly from the uncritical ones espoused by their opponents). Here the emphasis would be on exposing students to diversity with a moveable feast of readings with precedence given to what was most current and hot in academic circles. Again, there was no need for any musty old texts written by people who were woefully ignorant of current critiques of their work because they were dead. Besides many of them had written in a style that was far too clear to be real social science.

Chastened but unbowed by these responses, we proceeded to pull together a curriculum anyway because we argued that both sets of critics had missed the point of using core texts in an educational context. To those natural science types we pointed out that most of the issues facing human beings were fundamentally the same through time, and, when the world did change, the nature of human beings did not. Such questions as the relationship between individual and society, the essence of human nature, materialist versus idealistic explanations, the legitimacy and purpose of political order, or stability versus change could all be investigated but not necessarily resolved once and for all by any theory. By looking at these texts as they emerged historically, we were also looking at what problems social scientists first sought to engage and why. Equally important, we addressed the consequences of social theories when they were actually applied, for good or ill. It was also important to stress that we were drawing up a curriculum for education, not a proposal for research. There was methodology aplenty to be learned in any discipline's introductory course; our job was to educate students about why people asked such questions, how to judge the quality of their answers, and what was the connection between them.

To our humanist critics we argued that what we sought was a diversity of ideas, not necessarily a diversity of authors. Selecting core texts was no imposition of a rigid canon, but rather a task similar to that each professor faces every term: which readings should I assign for my courses from the much larger corpus of available works? The world is full of choices. As professors we are paid to make them and cannot shirk this responsibility on the grounds that no selection is perfect. More often than not we are far more uncomfortably aware of what is missing than our students, but tide and limited class time waits for no man. In regard to reaching out to a broader range of traditions as an anthropologist, I could not agree more. But I find it surprising that this call for more cultural diversity usually boils down to including only the limited historical traditions of ethnic groups in the United States and is not truly worldwide in scope. Similarly, there is a tendency to forget that because each culture is ethnocentric in its own way, studying more of them does not immediately solve the question of bias. It is all too easy to assume that if you have adopted a new set of arbitrary beliefs or prejudices from a culture different than the one you were born in, you have become more broad-minded. However, this is not broad-mindedness but "secondary ethnocentrism," a vice most common among scholars of foreign cultures (ancient and modern) and recent converts to religious or political movements.

There is a valid point to be made against restricting the core texts we assign only to "the usual suspects" of the western canon for readings. I do not see this flaw as a product of deliberate design but one of familiarity. It is hard enough to master the significant works in any single tradition, let alone to be a master of all of what the world offers. Here I think we need to be open to suggestions from the outside about seeking out what was valuable in each tradition as a contribution to knowledge or a way of seeing the world. We will always be limited about what it is possible to teach, but there are exciting and significant works that we might want to consider adding to our repertoire, works deserving of respect and study because of the quality of the ideas they present. I would argue that the *Muqaddimah* of Ibn Khaldun is one such work. One could go so far as to say that he should have been considered the father of social science, except that he was not rediscovered until long after it was reinvented in the West.

Ibn Khaldun was born in Tunisia in 1332 and died in 1406 in Egypt.[1] He received a classical Islamic education that allowed him to serve as an itinerant administrator for a number of different rulers in North Africa and Spain, moving from one royal household to another over the course of his career. He eventually ended up in Cairo, where he became one of the chief judges of the Islamic court as an expert on North African Islamic law. He was considered to be an honest judge, and consequently he was fired and rehired five times. He had experienced many such periods of unemployment, which were typically caused by enemies in a royal court or the loss of patronage when a new dynasty replaced by an old one. It was during one such long spell of unemployment beginning in 1375 that Ibn Khaldun retired to a village on the edge of the desert and spent four years writing a multi-volume history of the world. It is the "Introduction," or *Muqaddimah*, to this work where Ibn Khaldun laid out his model of history and society, a new "science of culture" (*'ilm al-'umran*).[2] This introduction was designed to provide the background to his larger history of events, to explain his methodology, and lay out a number of models that explained a series of historical cycles that underlay the rise and fall of dynasties and the relationship between the desert and city.

He began his work with a discussion of methodology focusing on the general difficulties facing any historian or social scientist when dealing with information from the past. Here he condemned the general sloppiness of historians, their credulous acceptance of exaggeration, their lack of clear methodology and failure to understand the process by which untruths clouded their work. He argued that these were not necessarily deliberate errors but rather constituted flaws that resulted from 1) partisanship and wishful thinking, 2) failure to understand the significance of a recorded event, and 3) distortion by direct observers and transmitters.

Partisanship and wishful thinking to Ibn Khaldun was the bane of the historical record. Too often the authors wrote about what they wished had happened, not what did, and that they were so excessively partisan in supporting one side that they often distorted the facts or lied outright. Failure to understand the significance of recorded events was a more subtle error. If we do not understand the context, we may not appreciate why some past events were more important than others. To this end the historian must provide the fundamental background for understanding the dynamics of any particular social system so that we can know what the events there mean, why the same type of event can have a tremendous impact in one system and yet create barely a ripple in another. His third difficulty of untruth was the problematic nature of so called "original sources." Ibn Khaldun was particularly annoyed with the distortion of direct observers. Just because somebody saw something didn't necessarily mean that they saw it accurately, particularly when describing things like the number of people taking part in a battle. Worse, most transmitters of direct observations felt free to edit them in unreliable ways.

All of Ibn Khaldun's cautions would make for useful contemporary reading for beginning historians, but these critiques of the source material were only designed to clear the ground for a more ambitious project. This focused on his belief that historians (and social scientists) must provide context about the social, political, and economic organization of the human societies they are writing about. It was this that inspired him to ask questions about the nature of human society, particularly the dynamics of urban civilization and how human beings interacted with one another. For this he created a set of models of how society worked in particular Islamic societies in the Middle East and North Africa. It was not a universal model, but it covered a very large area and worked very well given the material at his disposal. The set was particularly sophisticated in its integration of ethnographic and economic data that was a key part of his model in describing what he considered to be two distinct and opposing types of societies: desert nomadic civilization and sedentary urban civilization.

Desert civilization was characteristic of those people who engaged in subsistence agriculture or pastoralism in marginal ecological zones such as deserts, mountains, or steppeland. Steppe nomads like the Turks raised sheep and horses, though these they were far removed from the desert areas familiar to Ibn Khaldun. More sedentary mountain villagers like the Berbers and the Kurds mixed agriculture and pastoralism. Bedouin nomads in the deep desert raised camels or camels and sheep in better watered areas. It was these deep desert Bedouin camel raisers that Ibn Khaldun used as his archetypal representatives of a "desert civilization" type. All of these societies had relatively undeveloped economies with little economic surplus, tribal political organization, and a strong sense of social solidarity.[3]

Urban civilization was the product of cities and irrigated agricultural land. It was built on the on the surplus extracted from a subservient peasant population that supported densely populated cities, an economic division of labor, and a complex class system. As an evolutionist, Ibn Khaldun argued that desert civilization must have logically preceded urban civilization because the latter was more complex than the former. He also noted that the population flow was always from desert to city. He argued that no one in his right mind ever gave up the luxury of a city to live in a tent in the desert, other than for a short vacation or through the necessity of exile. On the contrary, everybody from the desert was always looking to move to the city (an immoral desire stressed often in the Bible with its anti-city tales of Sodom and Gomorrah!). One reason for this population movement, he speculates, is that desert life is healthier and so produces an insupportable population growth that creates demographic pressure for people to emigrate.

Ibn Khaldun was a keen observer of life among desert Bedouins. One of their distinguishing features was a social and political organization based on kinship ties that created genealogically related tribes. When two people from the desert first met, they exchanged information about their respective lineages because this determined whether they were likely to be allies or enemies. But ally and enemy were loose categories that depended on context. As an old proverb had it: me against my brother, my brother and me against our cousins; me, my brothers, and cousins against the world. First define your enemy and that will determine your friends. The social structure in such tribes was relatively egalitarian. Their leaders, known as *sheikhs*, depended on gaining the cooperation of their followers through persuasion because they could not command them.

Ibn Khaldun thought that the great political strength of the Bedouin was to be found in their group solidarity or *'asabiyah* in Arabic. Unlike people in cities, they felt a powerful connection to one another and would risk their lives for the protection of the group. They were also better fighters because they had to rely upon themselves for protection, having no city walls or professional soldiers to protect them. In battle they would not run away because the shame of deserting the group was more powerful than the fear of death, unlike the mercenaries defending the cities for whom dying was bad for business. (This did not mean that Bedouin never retreated, only that they ran as a group and not as individuals.) Even when facing powerful enemies their independence was assured because such outsiders could not possibly pursue them for very long into the desert without getting lost or dying of thirst.

The Bedouins also had significant weaknesses. The first of these was their relatively small numbers when compared to the number of people in the city. The second was that in spite of their political independence from urban areas, desert nomads were surprisingly dependent on economic ties with cities that provided items like metal, cloth, and foodstuffs, as well as a market to sell their animals. As Ibn Khaldun noted,

> While (the Bedouins) need the cities for their necessities of life, the urban population needs (the Bedouins) for conveniences and luxuries... They must be active on the behalf of their interests and obey them whenever (the cities) ask and demand obedience from them[4]

But perhaps their most significant weakness was their tendency toward political fragmentation. Just as strong kinship bonds created a sense of solidarity, the egalitarian nature of these bonds made the Bedouins resistant to accepting the authority of formal leaders. This, in turn, made organizing large groups difficult. This was, in fact, just the downside of an egalitarian system: because everybody thinks that he can be a better leader than the current one, there is a tendency to refuse to obey orders on the grounds that the leader has no right to give you any orders that you do not like. It is tough being a leader when you have to have to cajole your people into action and when every follower can conceive of himself as a better potential replacement.

Now what about the strengths and weakness of sedentary civilization? Because it was based on surplus wealth, Ibn Khaldun made luxury the defining characteristic of urban life, particularly division of labor that made it possible. In cities people were socially isolated but economically interdependent, just the reverse of the desert. Cities were renowned for their specializations in the production of foods, crafts, and as centers of learning and high art. Its social organization was residence based and kinship bonds were weak. Cities had class structures with wide variations between rich and poor, hierarchical political and religious institutions, centralized governments, and rulers with "royal authority." Such authority consists of knowing that when a leader gives a command it will be obeyed because there is a special set of police or military that will enforce that command.

If the strength of the city lay in its command of material resources and highly productive population, Ibn Khaldun also recognized that it had its own set of significant weaknesses. Its population was not as tough as the desert

Bedouin who were used to living under difficult physical conditions. City and peasant populations were uninvolved with government and dependent on either slave armies (*mameluks*) or mercenaries to protect them. Such troops were inherently unreliable, particularly when their pay was in arrears, and they had no vested interest in the community. The same could be said of the ruling dynasty, which often had few or no connections with population it ruled. It should be noted that this was a specific factor in the Islamic city of Ibn Khaldun's time; the Greek *polis* had drawn its strength from a citizen army and even the Roman Empire had recruited its own citizens for service for many centuries. But perhaps the biggest weakness, in Ibn Khaldun's view, was the tendency toward corruption in all spheres of urban life that weakened its social fabric, its *'asabiyah*.

However, Ibn Khaldun did not assume that the people were fundamentally different in the two systems, only that their material conditions socialized them differently. If the Bedouins were closer to being good in a moral sense than were sedentary people, it was only because desert life offered fewer opportunities for corruption. Indeed, for all his praise of Bedouin virtues and urban vices, Ibn Khaldun had a profound respect for cities as the cradle of high culture. Desert peoples, by contrast, had no significant arts and crafts, their knowledge of religion was deficient, and they were ignorant of the process by which wealth in cities was produced and maintained. This last bit of misunderstanding, Ibn Khaldun claimed, made these people dangerous because they were prone to unthinkingly destroy what they did not understand:

> For instance, they need stones to set them up as support for their cooking pots. So, they take them from buildings which they tear down to get the stones, and use them for that purpose. Wood, too, is needed for props for their tents and for use as tent poles for their dwellings. So, they tear down roofs to get wood for that purpose. The very nature of their existence is the negation of building, which is the basis of civilization. This is the case generally with them.[56]

If Ibn Khaldun had ended his comparison here it would have been a major tour de force in comparative social analysis. Instead, it served as only the basis for a series of models that addressed the rise and fall of ruling lineages and dynasties and the life span of states.

Ibn Khaldun's most famous model of dynastic replacement derived from his observation that in the historical record of the Near East and North Africa most dynasties lasted only four generations and that the founders of new dynasties that replaced them tended to have "desert civilization" origins. This was far from a universal pattern as a quick look at long lived dynasties among the Turks, or in China, or even the Byzantine Empire would demonstrate. But it was a remarkably regular pattern in the Arab Islamic world. Pointing again to social context, Ibn Khaldun noted that a fixed concept of "nobility" that permanently separated leaders from followers was impossible within an egalitarian social structure. Unlike in hierarchical social structures where leadership and authority was vested in particular elite social groups, among the egalitarian Arabs no lineage was believed to have an innate claim on leadership. This meant that there was no ideological barrier to the acceptance of talented new rulers, regardless of their background.

The rise of new rulers and the fall of old ones had a regular cycle of replacement that ran four generations in a single lineage.[7] In the first generation a charismatic leader established a new dynasty in a personal struggle for power. Ibn Khaldun called such a founder "the builder of glory," a leader who, through his personal struggles, had come to understand the difficulties inherent in establishing political dominance and, after obtaining power, retained those personal qualities that had allowed him to succeed in the first place. These men were usually products of desert civilization, raised under rough conditions with tough minds. This was reflected in their personal habits. They remained parsimonious and lived a simple life even when surrounded by available luxuries. Stories about insisting on living in a tent in a palace courtyard because they don't want to feel enclosed, or firing the palace cooking staff and barbers on the grounds that a man needs only simple food and can groom himself, thank you, typically attached themselves to such figures.

The son of the founder represents the second generation. He differs from his father in significant ways. First, he inherited his leadership position and did not have to struggle for it. Having sat at the feet of his father and learned how to rule from him, he is likely to be an adequate ruler but lacking the vitality and originality of founder. In Ibn Khaldun's view, experience is always superior to learning so there is no way that a successor can be as great as the founder. This is a result of socialization, not innate characteristics. The second-generation ruler grew up in the palace, surrounded by wealth and was groomed for leadership as a birthright. If human nature is any gauge he probably chafed at his father's cheapness, lack of manners and culture, and tired of listening to endless stories about how many miles of desert the old man claimed to have walked through in his youth.

The third generation leaders begin a period of decline because they are content with simple imitation and reliance on tradition. They lacked independent judgement and implemented policies by rote, based on slavish adherence to tradition, even when such policies had lost their effectiveness or were destructive. Fourth generation leaders marked the end of the line and met a bad end. They assumed the right to rule was theirs by birth and demanded the automatic respect of their subjects. Their arrogance and misrule not only undercut the lineage's political base, but it also led to disaffection and revolt. This revolt allowed the emergence of a rival leader who installed his own dynastic house in power as a new "founder of glory."

This rise and fall of lineages is connected with the rise and fall of states, which covers a similar three-four generation cycle.[8] In this analysis Ibn Khaldun had the advantage of looking at the financial records of a number of dynasties, which he found in the archives of the courts where he served as a bureaucrat. This dynastic cycle combined the personal qualities of dynastic leaders with the economic health of the state. The first generation of conquerors displays the desert qualities that make them tough leaders. Their cheapness means that the treasury's tax receipts are in surplus because they collected money but did not like to spend it. The second generation is characterized by luxury in the royal court and the establishment of institutionalized royal authority. Internally this means that the destruction of the old elite (i.e., the founder's old buddies or brothers), the wholesale replacement of court officials, and a new dependence on mercenary military force. This period of consolidation also shows a large increase in revenue to support large public works projects, but the budget remains in balance. The third generation is all pomp and glory, but this is a false face that hides cowardly rulers and sycophantic court officials. The treasury begins to run large deficits, in large part because officials begin to siphon off revenue for their own use. The state's outer territories begin to break away. The fourth generation experiences a collapse because they have no revenue to pay their troops, no local support, and as leaders they are incompetent. They are replaced by a new dynasty and the cycle begins again.

This short review does little justice to the complexity of Ibn Khaldun's model, but does provide a basic outline and raises some fascinating questions. In any society with an egalitarian ideology we can see similar processes at work. Think of the history of robber barons like J.D. Rockefeller and his descendants who display a similar four-generation model of economic power. Or more provocatively the changing fortunes of the Kennedy clan in American politics over four generations. Forceful and ruthless founders, sons raised to power, ineffective grandchildren followed by incompetent heirs squandering their legacies: these are familiar themes in our own history and are not confined to Ibn Khaldun's medieval Muslim world.

What I am arguing here is that Ibn Khaldun is, at least for the social sciences, one of the best and clearest expositions of an Arab social science tradition of which we in the west are largely ignorant. But we should not be looking to remedy our ignorance simply so to add a North African to our collection. What we should do is take a look at authors from other traditions like Ibn Khaldun because there may be many more jewels still in the sand that we are overlooking. Therefore we need to go carefully through what is available cross-culturally so that we can present our students with the best possible writing and bring them in contact with the best minds of all civilizations. But this is not something that can be done in one lifetime, or perhaps even ten. It is something that can only take place now when we're looking at the entire world and its history as our own cultural heritage, when people are interested at a fundamental level in what one society thinks as opposed to another. And as instructors in a core text social science enterprise, we need to bring in these types of work to our students to see how other civilizations, or in other historical periods, scholars have attempted to explain the way people are organized, as well as why and how. If we do this, I think we will give our students a foundation that is both incredibly broad and incredibly useful, a gift that can transform our own way of looking at the world and dealing with the people in it.

### Notes

1. For a biography, see Muhsin Madhi, *Ibn Khaldun's philosophy of history: a study in the philosophic foundation of the science of culture.* (Chicago: University of Chicago Press, 1971).

2. For a full translation see Franz Rosenthal, Ibn Khaldun: *The Muqaddimah,* 3 vol. (Princeton: Princeton University Press, 1958). Translations cited here are from the one volume abridged 1967 edition.

3. Franz Rosenthal, Ibn Khaldun: *The Muqaddimah: An Introduction to History* (abridged edition). (Princeton: Princeton University Press, 1967), 91-122.

4. *ibid.,* 122.

5. *ibid.,* 118.

6. *ibid.,* 105-106.

7. *ibid.,* 137-138.

# CHAPTER 14

# Teaching the Confucian Analects

*Brian Jorgensen*

While there is some order, both local and general, to the Confucian *Analects*, they are nothing like a logical treatise; nor, as far as I can tell, do they have any overall organic or thematic form; nor is each one self-explanatory. There are, however, clearly recurrent themes and characters: many of the analects contain insights and advice of the highest and richest order, and, taken together, they offer a lively, often charming, altogether profound approach to life, an approach not free, for some, of the romance of the East. They seem full of energy, usefulness, and things to admire, as well as vibrant with the presence of a modest sage who somehow responds to occasions of mind and heart that arise now as well as then.

Why not teach Confucius as he is presented in the *Analects*? That is, not only acknowledge what the higher criticism has discovered or assumed about the various sources, layers, and modifications, as well as the quest for the real, bare-bones Confucius, but also try to use such information, and whatever classroom interest *it* generates, to point to the greater Confucius transcending his skeleton and dressed as traveler, teacher, and *shih*, knight of the way. This person might be compared in his genesis and presence to Plato's Socrates, except that he is the product of memories enhanced not by a single genius but by more than one mind in more than one time, and in that way is perhaps something like a Biblical character. But he's not just an authoritative name, a Solomonic mouthpiece for various incompatible doctrines, but rather someone who manifests a deep consistency that can embrace paradoxes and apparent contradictions, an unlikely but plausible wise man responding to life, having something essential to say to us right now, this minute. In applying this approach I have not been disappointed, and the same may be said, I think, of at least some other students as well.

Looking back at teaching the *Analects*, which is rather easier and more dreamy than looking forward to the next class in which one is scheduled to teach them, it can seem that their nature may be part of their lesson: that the ethical life, like the *Analects*, can be thought of as coming to us in a series of vivid and varied moments partly ordered and partly not, and that learning what to make of these moments is the ethical task. One puts them together, puts together the various themes, local lessons, recurrent occasions, personalities, and reaches of thought, as one might put the examined life together. In this case, the goal of teaching the *Analects* would be to use the text as much as possible. However, the text relies to a significant degree on context; and the themes, for impatient and, at least by their lights, overworked students, may appear contradictory, repetitious, or obscure. And so one finds oneself approaching the *Analects* in what seems to be three ways. These divisions, less evident in the classroom but clear enough for the purposes of this discussion, are the historical, the thematic, and the textual.

### Historical

With the goal of making students aware of some useful historical context, one may learn a little about a number of things. These could include The Shang and Chou dynasties that preceded Confucius, and that Duke of Chou whose absence from his dreams tells the Master something about his current spiritual state (7.5); the Book of Songs, a collection of poems said to have been edited by Confucius; Chinese ritual; Confucius' home state of Lu and its rulers, namely the Duke of Lu and the oligarchy of the Three Families; the kind of times in which Confucius lived, and something about his life, some rival schools of thought, in particular the Taoists, Mohists, and Legalists; and the Chin and Han Dynasties that followed Confucius. This may seem like a lot but can amount to rather superficial but intrinsically interesting knowledge acquired over a week or two—such things as how the brutal Chin emperor unified China and tried to destroy Confucianism; how the Book of Songs contains aristocratic and folk poetry which Confucius interprets in various senses, somewhat the way Augustine or Dante read the Bible, but always with the feeling that we are hearing the hearts of the people and the fine character of ages past; and so on. One may spend part of a class talking about these things or have them at the ready as needed for discussing certain themes or particular analects.

## Thematic

Some themes are evident and some benefit from being brought to notice. Students may be given a list of analects grouped by various subjects, for use in class and as paper topics. The particular themes I stress are the nature of Goodness, the meaning of ritual, the ethical importance of the study of poetry and history, the nature and training of the gentleman, the behavior and resources of the good man in bad times, the undiscussibles, and discipleship and disciples. One may simply ask about any of these themes, with appropriate analects at the ready, or, proceeding from particular analects, move into particular themes. I am not satisfied unless, by the end of the series of classes on Confucius, we have touched on all of these themes.

One may also try to connect the themes of the *Analects* with other readings. In the Boston University Core Curriculum, some such connections are the Confucian gentleman and the Aristotelian gentleman, Confucius and Plato on the meaning of music, on the uses of poetry, on the Good; Confucius, Plato, and Augustine on the stages of a human life. The last is recommended in hopes that students may find it valuable to think about life as something in which their current set of attitudes are no more or less than a particular and at least partially understandable phase, which may be viewed in light of Confucius' description of his own phases:

> The Master said, At fifteen I set my heart upon learning. At thirty, I had planted my feet firmly on the ground. At forty, I no longer suffered from perplexities. At fifty, I knew what were the biddings of heaven. At sixty, I heard them with a docile ear. At seventy, I could follow the dictates of my own heart; for what I desired no longer overstepped the boundaries of right (11.4).

There seems to be something at once reassuring, inspiring, and eye-opening about the progression and the states of mind described here.

Other thematic connections are the following: Confucius' method of teaching vs. that of Plato and that of Aristotle; Confucius' rectification of names and Plato's ruler in the strict sense; Confucius and the Greeks on class differences—the gentleman vs. the small man; Confucius and the Greeks on the nature of rule—the sage, the philosopher-king, the oligarch (the Three Families of Lu); the Confucian undiscussibles vs. western philosophy, theology, and science; the disciples of Confucius and the disciples of Socrates and Christ; the Confucian Way vs. the Way of Lao-tzu; the Confucian Way and the Kingdom of Heaven; the importance of returning to the past, or linking the past and present, vs. the western philosophical approach; and the idea of learning from ritual as opposed to learning from understanding.

As exempla, here are some things that might be said about three particular themes: Ritual, Goodness, and discipleship. *Ritual.* Ritual, li, is a fundamental Confucian category. It includes what we would call social conventions— shaking hands, making eye contact, clothes appropriate to the season; it includes forms for occasions such as games and contests, occasions of state, dinner parties; it includes proper treatment of the profound turnings of life— that is to say, birth, coming of age, marriage, death; and it includes ways of connecting ourselves with things greater than ourselves—the past, the powers of heaven, ancestors. Ritual is useless or bad if done hypocritically or merely formally. It should discipline and awaken the emotions. It was done better in the past. Yet it must always be responsive to the present. It is perhaps most profoundly a set of occasions for awareness as the following analect suggests: and it suggests something about Confucius' approach to teaching and to life:

> When the Master entered the Grand Temple he asked questions about everything there. Someone said, Do not tell me that this son of a villager from Tsou is expert in matters of ritual. When he went to the Grand Temple he had to ask about everything. The Master hearing of this said, Just so! such is the ritual (3.15).

*Goodness.* Confucius refers to Goodness often but refuses to abstractly define it. He measures people, past and present, against it, and finds even highly admirable ones not worthy of being called Good. Goodness is high and distant and seems to recede like the horizon. Yet Goodness is as near as a motion of the hand. It is both a living force and ideal. It is something which one can, apparently, learn to perceive but not define—or at an I least a gentleman resists the urge to define and abstract it. Goodness ought to be pursued with desires as strong as the sexual. Its enemies are cleverness and pretentiousness, greed, resentment, stupidity. It is at once sufficient unto itself, an end, difficult to acquire, fragile, and an aspect of particular things.

*Discipleship.* Confucius, like Socrates or Christ, is a teacher. The compilers of the Analects consider it important to show how he taught, to evoke the theme of discipleship, and to emphasize the importance of something carried on after the master's death. Some evident points seem to be that Confucius treats each disciple differently, does not try to isolate them from each other, listens, creates occasions of freedom as well as of discipline, and himself learns from each other person. Of the disciples whose names we learn, one might emphasize Tzu-1u, Yen-hul, and Tzu-kung. Mastei- Tseng is important, as is Confucius' treatment of his son, Po Yu. But the three mentioned stand out. Tzu-lu is impetuous, interested in force and power, warm-hearted, wanting life to be simpler than it is but often unable to see the importance of thought, willing to die for Confucius but hoping not to receive too much wisdom in any given week. Tzu-kung is smart, well-spoken, looking for praise and recognition, in some ways invaluable, yet in some ways limited. Confucius, who says "a gentleman is not an implement" (11.12), surprises Tzu-kung, who wants to hear about himself, by calling him a dish. But when Tzu-kung asks "What kind of dish?" Confucius answers, "a sacrificial dish of 'ade" (5.3). We may infer that Tzu-kung's is a character of containment. It is finely shaped to hold fine stuff in a way that both calls attention to itself and points toward connection with the ancestral and heavenly powers. As a thing of receptivity and polish, its particular use is more like an ornamental holding in preparation (the 'ade vessels were not heated) than it is like cooking and sublimation. As a precious container it is to be differentiated from, say, a stream that flows on and on (9.16). Yen-hui is quiet, can understand more than his master says, can live for extended periods of time in the Good, and dies young. The *Analects* include Confucius' grief and disappointment at Yen-hul's death, registered both at the time and many years later, as well as his reaction to the mystery of this quiet person.

*Textual.* With historical and thematic concerns in mind, one may spend some significant part of classroom time on particular analects. I ask each student to come to class with observations or questions about three analects, and I come with some of my own as well, each year a somewhat different list. Almost always the list will include one or two analects from Book 10, which focuses on particular ritual actions, and some analects on poetry, perhaps including the one about the cherry branch and love (9.30). This year, one might seek a place for the following:

> The Master addressed [his son] Po Yu, saying, have you done the *Chou Nan* and the *Shao Nan* [the first two books of the Songs] yet? He who has not even done the *Chou Nan* and the *Shao Nan* is as though he stood with his face pressed against the wall! (17.10)

If it seemed likely that the class might respond, one might emphasize how Confucius repeats the names of the books a second time rather than referring to them as them or these.    This may be taken to indicate respect and more: that these are names one should know as what they are, not merely by the place they occupy in some set.

Class discussion might center on it being Confucius' son who is addressed and on the nature of poetry as revealed by the simile Confucius uses, which implies that a man who lacks certain particular basic sets of utterances shaped in his own language, shaped as if once and for all, is like someone with his face pressed against a wall. To know certain poems is, then, a form of awareness, openness, and orientation', it is a set of perceptions, skills, and habits that offer an escape from a perhaps reassuring ignorance which is ultimately a frustration; it is an ability to walk in one's world on the edge where the past meets the present. It is these rather than the maintaining, actively (the face is pressed), of a consistent posture in relationship to a strong, solid, protective fixture, some object no one in their senses could truthfully deny, here signifying insentience. In short, poetry is an escape from the undeniable but ridiculous.

One might also emphasize the analect that says:

> The Master said, Ritual, ritual! Does *it* mean no more than presents of jade and silk? Music, music! Does it mean no more than bells and drums? (17.11)

If students were disappointed with Bridges to Babylon, the latest Rolling Stones concert, the second part of this is something they might want to think about. And how often one might want to utter the first part about, for instance, Christmas or Easter, however precious the objects exchanged.

And for the teacher himself, Confucius offers the sense of a figure out of the distant past whose words and presence may resonate today, as in the analect that says:

> Tzu-lu was spending the night at the Stone Gates [that is, in some place of frontier or coming and going]. The gate-keeper said, Where are you from? Tzu-lu said, From Master K'ung's [Confucius']. The man said, He's the one who 'knows it's no use but keeps on doing it,' is that not so? (14.41)

The *Analects* ends there-, Tzu-lu s reply is not recorded.

**Works Cited**

Arthur Whaley, trans., 1989. The Analects of Cofucius. New York: Random House.

CHAPTER 15

# Core Texts and
# The Cultivation of Virtue:
# Reading Confucius Reading Plato

*Jane Kelley Rodeheffer*

> The Way of the Great Learning consists in uncovering shining virtue;
> Renewing the people; Coming to dwell in the highest good.[1]

So begins the *Ta-hsüeh* or *Great Learning,* a text of the Confucian school. It is characterized by the tradition as "the gate through which the beginning learner enters into virtue." In what follows, I will begin by reflecting on the teaching of this brief text in light of the Confucian understanding of *jen,* or humanity, which is the central virtue of Confucian thought. The Chinese character *jen* depicts a person standing next to the number two, thus suggesting the sociality inherent in being human. The three most essential characteristics of *jen,* as developed in the *Ta-hsüeh* and the *Analects,* are communal self-awareness, learning, and piety. These virtues are also central to the Platonic dialogues, and especially to the *Euthyphro,* where the relationship between learning and piety is explored in some depth. Indeed, a careful reading of the *Ta-hsüeh* and the *Analects*, pursued within the context of a cross-cultural dialogue, can help to bring the central concerns of Plato's *Euthyphro* into sharper relief. Euthyphro boasts of having superior knowledge of divine things (5a), and he separates himself from others in suggesting that he is wise about things of which the multitude has no knowledge(6b). His piety is called into question by Socrates when he tells of his plan to prosecute his own father for the murder of a hired man. The Confucian texts suggest that the cultivation of virtue begins with the person in relation to others and that communal self-awareness and filial piety can provide important correctives to the potentially dangerous effects of "wisdom," which can cause one like Euthyphro to stray from the path of right action. Such commonalities serve as a very rich beginning point for cross-cultural dialogue.

To read the *Ta-hsüeh*, *Analects,* and *Euthyphro* side by side is not to engage in a kind of facile reductionism in which the Confucian texts are seen as representing classical Eastern cultural views and the *Euthyphro* as representing the foundations of Western culture. Rather, in the Confucian texts, as well as in the early dialogues of Plato, one finds shared problematiques, what the Confucian scholar Tu Wei-Ming calls, following Benjamin Schwartz, a "fruitful ambiguity"[2] with regard to areas of common human concern: learning or self-cultivation, moral virtue, piety, and human relatedness. Across the country, faculty who teach in Core programs are being challenged to broaden their conception of liberal education to include the study of non-western cultures. Such study is necessary if they are to educate citizens for a world in which distant cultures are increasingly interdependent. Cross-cultural teaching that focuses on shared human concerns as confronted by very different traditions can awaken genuine inquiry across cultural boundaries. At the same time, such an approach is the best way to avoid two common but troubling types of distortion. Martha Nussbaum calls these *descriptive chauvinism*, which "consists in recreating the other in the image of oneself," and *descriptive romanticism*, which "consists in viewing another culture as excessively alien and virtually incomparable with one's own, ignoring elements of similarity and highlighting elements that seem mysterious and odd."[3] As core texts, the *Euthyphro, Ta-hsüeh,* and *Analects* need to be presented not as *the* voice of their culture but as one important current of thought within a complex culture. If such presentation is attuned to the social and historical context of each text, a dialogue between the *Euthyphro* and the Confucian texts can provide insight into two cultures' ways of posing questions about the virtuous life.

We will begin our dialogue with the *Ta-hsüeh*, by asking why the Confucian tradition came to understand this text as the gateway to those wishing to enter into virtue. The text of the *Great Learning* reads as follows:

I. The *Tao* (Way ) of the great learning consists in Uncovering Shining Virtue; Renewing the People; Coming to Dwell in the Highest Good.

II. Knowing what to abide in, the fixed direction is then determined, and having established the fixed direction, one is able to achieve insight. This insight is followed by a tranquil equanimity. Being in good order, one is able to deliberate with an unperturbed heart-mind. Tranquil deliberation enables one to achieve the desired end.

III. Things have roots and branches. Events have an end and a beginning. To know what is first and what is last is to draw near to the Tao.

IV. When the old sages desired to make manifest their shining virtue to the people under heaven, they first established order in their own states. Wishing to make perfect their states, they first brought harmony to their own households. Wishing to establish order in their household, they first disciplined their persons. Wishing to discipline themselves, they first made straight their own hearts. Wishing to make straight their hearts, they first made pure their thoughts and intentions.

   Wishing to become one with their thoughts and words, they sought to extend their knowledge to the utmost. This completion of knowledge consists in investigating the nature of beings.

V. Once beings have been examined, knowledge is attained. When knowledge is attained, thoughts and intentions are made pure. When thoughts and words are sincere, the heart-mind is made straight. When the heart-mind is properly positioned, the person is disciplined. When self-discipline is achieved, then the household is in order. When harmony is in the household, then the state will be in good order. When the state is in order, then there will be peace among all the people under heaven.

VI. From the son of heaven down to the common people, each and every person must consider self-discipline to be the root of all.

VII. It cannot be when the root is in disorder that its branches will be in order. To consider the thick as thin (the important as trivial) and the thin as thick (the trivial as important), this is not possible.

In developing his metaphor of the root and branches from chapter IV, Confucius begins by discussing the branches (i.e., the proper ordering of the state and the household), before taking up the discipline of the person. At this point, the branches become a single trunk, and the discussion moves inward to the proper ordering of the heart, the thoughts, and the ability of the person to perfect his or her knowledge of the nature of beings. Chapter V, the *Tao* or Way, branches outward from the interior landscape of the person to again encompass the family and one's kinship relations, the state, and finally, the kingdom (or literally, the people under heaven), at whose head stands the emperor who is referred to as the son of heaven.

In this brief text, the Confucian school conveys a vision of reciprocal harmony between the interior "setting in order" of the person and the outer order of the social, political, and religious spheres. Confucius held that shining virtue is innate in every person, and while it can only be uncovered through self-cultivation, it is implanted in human beings by heaven itself: "Heaven produced the virtue that is in me"(7.22). The full realization of this reciprocal harmony between the inner life of the person and the outer order of social, political, and religious structures is the *Tao*, a Way that incorporates every aspect of human experience.

It is because the teaching of the *Great Learning* articulates the cultural legacy of the *Tao* and its all embracing order that its rhythmic sentences can serve as the gateway for learners who wish to enter into virtue. Before they can take up the more isolated and specific topics of the *Analects*, learners must have a vision of the *Tao* as the ancient Way of their culture, a Way that must be preserved, renewed, and carried forward in the contemporary world.

To bear the *Tao* forward is to be a person of *Te* or moral virtue. The character *Te* is a composite of the characters for a person in action, to make straight, to see, and heart. Virtue involves both vision and action. The virtuous person is one who sees straight into the heart with the eyes of his or her cultural tradition and acts upon such vision, reaching out to foster and integrate all aspects of human life: "Great is the *Tao* of the wise and virtuous one. Abundant, it brings forth and nurtures all things and reaches up to the height of heaven."(Chung Yung 27.1-2) The *Great Learning* thus teaches that the discipline and cultivation of one's own person as well as the renewal of others must always be understood against the background of the *Tao*. These moral activities, like the learned investigation of the nature of beings, cannot be isolated from their place in an all-embracing order.

The Confucian view of order derives from the religious views of early China, where kin members were interconnected in relationships that were governed by an ideal of harmony and strict rules of decorum or *li*. This kinship order was in turn held together by the authority of *Ti'*, the high god. Benjamin Schwartz points out that the order of kinship relations became a model for the social-political order in later dynasties, in which roles and sacred ritual were clearly defined and highly organized.[4]

In contrast to the complex and highly ordered cultural tradition articulated in the *Ta-hsüeh*, the time of Confucius was one of pluralism and internal conflict, wherein he came to believe that the ancient way or all embracing order of the Chou dynasty, the *Tao* whose indwelling laws emanate from heaven, had been lost. With it, the memory of the highest good and the way of life that seeks and embodies it had also been lost. Confucius writes, "I hand down but do not create, standing by and loving the words of the ancient ones." (7.1) He thus saw his role as one of preserving the *Tao,* although like Socrates' profession of ignorance, Confucius' description of himself as a preserver and not a creator is clearly ironic. His communication of the tradition in the *Analects* is that of a moral exemplar. Through analogy and evocation, he creates a model for the renewal of the *Tao* in the contemporary world. Speaking of the virtue of Confucius, one of his disciples says,

> So earnest, he is humanity; As deep as a whirlpool, he is an abyss;
> so all embracing and vast, he is heaven itself. (Chung Yung 32.2)

In searching for the lost *Tao* and asking what makes human beings stray from right action, Confucius evokes a vision of *jen,* or virtuous humanity, in all of its dimensions and capacities.

How is the vision of Confucius instructive for our understanding of the questions posed by the *Euthyphro?* Like Confucius, Plato understands that posing a question about virtue—in this case, 'What is piety?'—Is embedded in a much larger context. Not only does Euthyphro lack knowledge of the ancient way, and an appreciation of its depths, but in coming to view his wisdom as singular and transcendent to that of the many, he has isolated himself from those very relationships in which self-cultivation and right action are nourished. In the *Analects*, Confucius underscores the importance of interpersonal relations, familial as well as social, in one's self-cultivation: "Now the person of humanity (*jen*), wishing to become established in virtue and wisdom, seeks to establish others; wishing to become greater himself, he seeks to make others greater." (6.23) Not only does Euthyphro believe that he knows things -divine things- of which the many do not know (6b), he says that when he speaks about divine things in the Athenian Assembly,—they laugh at me as if I were mad." (3c)[5] He dismisses the laughter of the many as mere jealousy, and he later states that the Athenians also think he is mad for prosecuting his father. (4a) Apparently this does not concern Euthyphro. He thinks that his role as seer has given him insight into pious action and has set him "apart from the many" (5a). If this knowledge should lead him to harm other persons, even his own father, he will not hesitate. Nevertheless, Euthyphro is not eager to test the Athenian view of him (3d), and this would seem to include Socrates, for when Socrates entreats him to continue the search for a definition of piety at the end of the dialogue, he begs off, saying he must go. In a Confucian sense, Euthyphro wishes neither to be established in virtue nor to establish others.

The *Ta-hsüeh* reminds us that "each and every person must consider self-discipline to be the root of all," for "it cannot be that when the root is in disorder that its branches will be in order." (VI-VII) In a discussion laden with irony, Socrates gives the reasons for Meletus' claim that he has corrupted the young:

> He appears to me to be the only one of our public men to begin in the right way, for the right way to begin is to attend to the young, and make them as good as possible—just as a good farmer is likely to give his attention to the young plants first, and the rest later. And so Meletus no doubt begins by clearing away us, the ones who corrupt the young plants, as he says. After this, he obviously will care for the older ones, and will thus bring many precious blessings upon the city. (2c-3a)

Socrates ironic description sheds suspicion on the intentions of Meletus, which are far from pure. As a poet, Meletus is concerned that the ancient Way of piety, which is preserved within traditional poems and stories about the gods, remain stagnant, rather than being carried forward and renewed in the contemporary world, as Socrates seeks to do. Only if wisdom about things divine remains in the hands of the poets can they maintain their influence in Athenian society.

Like the author of the *Ta-hsüeh*, Plato realizes that the proper cultivation and right ordering of the young cannot be achieved unless the state, and those elders who govern it, are also in order. While the irony is completely lost on him, Euthyphro does realize the necessity of such reciprocal harmony between the root and the branches, for he replies to the above description of Meletus' intentions with the following comment:

> I wish it were so, Socrates, but I fear it will go the opposite way. It looks to me like he begins by harming the very heart of the City when he undertakes to wrong you. (3a)

Euthyphro s comments belie some insight into the central role of Socratic questioning in the life of the *polis*. As a *Chun Tzu* or profound person, Socrates actions reflect the most authentic manifestation of *jen* (humanity). In referring to him as the heart of the city, Euthyphro suggests that in its deepest reality Socrates virtuous humanity reaches out to foster the harmony and good order not only of the *polis* but also of the world beyond his time and place. Euthyphro s insight into Socrates internal harmony as a complement of the harmony of the *polis* gives the reader reason to hope that at the dialogue s end the *elenchus* has had a positive affect on him and that when he parts from Socrates, he does so in the realization that he is in need of further cultivation if he is to pursue right action.

Socrates' expresses shock at Euthyphro's plan to prosecute his father for the murder of a hired man, for such action is in clear defiance of the traditional Athenian views of piety in both a religious and a familial sense. His ignorance of and lack of reverence for his own cultural tradition, together with his isolation from people of principle in whose company he might be rectified, has led Euthyphro to a concern with small things and a disregard for greater affairs. In both a Platonic and a Confucian sense, such a concern is characteristic of one who is deficient in an understanding of the *Tao,* as well of the *Te (*virtue), for it is through *Te* that one makes the *Tao* meaningful in one's time and place.

Euthyphro's concern with small things is evident in his desire to avoid what he refers to as "pollution." When asked why he is prosecuting his father for murder, Euthyphro states that regardless of who the murderer was, if the act was not justified, one must prosecute the murderer because "the pollution is the same if, knowingly, you associate with such a man, and do not cleanse yourself, and him as well, by bringing him to justice." (4c) Plato suggests here that what Euthyphro is really concerned with is a small advantage; the effect of his father's crime on his own standing with the gods. Like Plato, Confucius also viewed such small-mindedness as reflecting a lack of virtue:

> The virtuous person sets his heart on moral action; the small person (the one lacking in virtue) sets his heart on the earth. The virtuous person seeks moral sanctions; the small person seeks favors. (4.11)

The similarities do not stop there. In developing his discussion of small mindedness in the *Analects*, Confucius draws on the example of a son who, like Euthyphro, wishes to prosecute his father.

> Do not wish for quick results; do not look for small advantages. Wishing to have things done quickly prevents the goal from being reached. Looking to small advantages prevents great affairs from being completed.
>
> The Duke of She declared to Confucius: "Among my people there was an upright man named Kung. His father stole a sheep, and he, the son, testified to the fact." Confucius said: "In my part of the country, the upright person is different from this. The father hides the son, and the son conceals the father. Uprightness rests in this also." (13.17-18)

The juxtaposition of the Confucian text with Plato s discussion of

Euthyphro s situation thus helps to underscore the fact that Euthyphro s action has larger implications than avoiding pollution. On a Confucian view, to disrupt the order of familial piety for selfish reasons is to disrupt not only one s relations with one s father but the order of government and the relation of human beings to the will of Heaven, which has placed those laws of order within each person. Disruption of the rules of propriety without the proper discrimination is also undermining of the development of one s own virtuous humanity, for *jen* requires for its flourishing a proper ritualistic expression in one s behavior toward both family members and others:

> Boldness without ritual propriety leads to confusion; Straightforwardness without ritual propriety becomes rudeness. When profound persons perform well their duties to their own kin, The common people are inspired to virtuous humanity; when old ties are not neglected, the common people are not mean. (8.2)

The virtuous person must strike a balance between learning and ritual propriety, as Socrates suggests in his admonition to Euthyphro that he will incur the wrath of both gods and men if he breaks with the rules governing filial piety without first providing a coherent *logos* for his action.

There is evidence in the *Euthyphro* to suggest that Plato shares the Confucian caution against disrupting the traditional rules of propriety. When it becomes clear to Socrates that Euthyphro does not know what piety is and that his claim to a divine wisdom that transcends the knowledge of the many is empty, he provokes Euthyphro with the following challenge:

> If you did not have clear knowledge of piety and impiety, you could never have undertaken to prosecute your aged father on a charge of murder for the sake of a servant. Instead, you would have feared to risk the anger of the gods on the chance that your action should be wrong, and would have been ashamed before men. (15d)

While a careful reading of the *dialogue* can uncover Euthyphro's isolation from the community and the cavalier and thoughtless nature of his action, reading the dialogue together with the *Ta- hsüeh* and *Analects,* which share some of the same concerns as the *Euthyphro,* can aid the reader in seeing the implications of the actions of both Euthypro and Socrates for an ever-widening horizon of human reality. As the *Ta-hsüeh* points out, this reality moves outward from the well-disciplined thoughts and intentions of the inner person to interpersonal relations and an ordering of the household based on rules of filial piety, eventually extending to the proper functioning of the state and a reciprocal harmony between the human and the divine. The rules of propriety or *li,* which govern every aspect of the Confucian view of moral, social, and religious order, provide a powerful corrective to a pursuit of learning that isolates one from the human community:

> The person of wisdom and virtue, vast in learning, who submits
> himself to the restraint of *li* (ritual propriety), is not likely to
> Overstep the boundary of what is right. (6.25)

In conclusion, we might ask whether Socrates pursuit of learning really measures up to Confucian standards of piety. In stating to Euthyphro that he finds it difficult to believe the Homeric stories about the gods (6b), Socrates seems to call his own piety into question. Unlike the impiety of Euthyphro, however, that of Socrates is born of a genuine pursuit of wisdom in the context of human relationships. He is both pious and impious at the same time, questioning the gods but doing so at the bidding of a god, Apollo, who has attached him to the city in order to renew the Athenian tradition and thereby bear the Way forward.

I have pursued here a method of placing two classical core texts from very different traditions in dialogue with one another. In focusing on their shared pursuit of abiding human questions, our reading of the *Euthyphro* in light of the *Ta -hsüeh* and the *Analects* has resulted in a sharpened appreciation of the ever-widening domains of human relatedness at work within a Platonic dialogue, in which every thought and action, from the impure intentions of Meletus and the pursuit of small advantages on the part of Euthyphro, to the pious questioning of Socrates, is seen to either foster or undermine the authentic manifestation of humanity throughout the community. If the Confucian sage is the complement of heaven, then Socrates is the complement of Apollo, insofar as his profound humanity reaches out to cultivate the virtue and wisdom not only of Athenians and their descendants but that of the ancestors themselves. In the *Apology,* Socrates tells his supporters that after death he hopes to keep company with the likes of Hesiod and Homer in Hades, "examining and investigating people there, just as I do here, to discover who among them is wise, and who thinks he is, but is not." (41b)

Space does not permit a more exhaustive comparison between these texts, nor does it allow for an account of either the historical situation of the authors or the various ways in which their accounts of the cultivation of virtue differ from one another. While these components are essential to the effective presentation of such texts in the classroom, my aim here has been to focus exclusively on various ways in which a careful reading of the Confucian texts with the dialogues of Plato allows one to engage in inter cultural comparison at its most nourishing and suggestive level: that of fundamental questions about abiding human concerns and the implications of such questions for the continuation of human civilization.

## Notes

1. All translations from the Chinese are my own. In translating the entire *Ta hsüeh*, and passages from the *Analects*, I have followed the Chinese text as it appears in *Confucius*, ed., James Legge (New York: Dover, 1971).

2. See Tu, Wei Ming, *Confucian Thought* (Albany: State University of New York Press, 1985), 16, note 24.

3. Martha C. Nussbaum, *Cultivating Humanity* (Cambridge, MA: Harvard University Press, 1997), 118, 123-24.

4. Benjamin I. Schwartz, *The World of Thought in Ancient China* (Cambridge: Harvard University Press, 1985).

5. All translations from the Greek are my own. I have followed the Greek texts of the *Euthyphro* and *Apology* as they appear in *Plato*, Volume I, (Cambridge, MA: Harvard University Press), 1982.

CHAPTER 16

# Confronting Preconceptions Concerning the Past in *Gilgamesh* and its Biblical Parallels

*James M. Vest*

One of the constants of teaching core texts is the issue of what to make of the past. As we all discover, student attitudes toward the past vary widely, from naive veneration to rabid hostility to rank indifference. In the classroom we can draw attention to passages that address this problem—the nature and importance of "former times"—in even the earliest known texts. We can, for example, encourage students to contrast the tendency in *Gilgamesh* to equate what is past with what is bad to the alternative view presented in Genesis that the past is superior to the present. We can structure discussion around ways these ancient works grapple with issues of anteriority, habituation, and value development in the context of an evolving sense of community. We can posit a Proustian world in which past and present are vitally linked through certain stimuli, including habits of mind. This approach, which involves inviting our students to examine their own judgments concerning the past in light of ways that very issue is treated in core texts, can provide a unique springboard for discussions of the importance of the past, of commemorations of it, and of how it may be understood.

Many core texts seek to situate the narrative present in terms of a presumably connected narrative past. In *Works and Days,* Hesiod outlines the stages of history in terms of a succession of ages leading down to experiences in his own time. For Hesiod these past ages offer a useful perspective on the present, if not a compelling etiology for it. Similarly, in his history of the Peloponnesian War, Thucydides cites examples from the Hellenes' earlier conflicts with the Persians, indicating that there should be some logical, useful, perhaps even necessary connection between the two. Herodotus and Livy take pains to mention past waves of legendary movers and shakers whose activities in some sense set up the "current situation" they are chronicling. The concept of legacy is central to these works, and Polybius will go so far as to make it part of his paradigm for tracing the rise and fall of all societies.

This predilection to view existence in terms of epochs representing successive adaptations in human conduct or in the human condition is something we can help students recognize and critique as they read. I think this is a viable strategy in Humanities sequences and in other courses that treat core texts selected from different periods. And I would like to suggest that such courses can begin to good effect with two of the most ancient of texts, which themselves comment on earlier times in intriguing ways: the opening episodes of *Gilgamesh* and the chapters immediately following the creation stories in Genesis.

Gilgamesh himself is introduced as one familiar with prior times, "of the days before the flood" in Sandars' version (61). In this story the hell-raising young Mesopotamian leader needs someone to curb his wild behavior and bring it in line with the well-defined social order in the city of Uruk: "the king should be a shepherd to his people" (62). His boon companion, "his second self," Enkidu, is described as follows: "His body was rough; he had long hair. . . . His body was covered with matted hair. . . . He knew nothing of the cultivated land" (63). This portrayal of one who ran with the wild animals, sympathized with their plight when hunted, and ate grass with them in the fields (64-65) purposefully distinguishes him from his contemporaries. Enkidu's appearance and demeanor are described as being of a different sort from those around him. He is depicted as a "savage man" (64). To accomplish what he needs to in the narrative present (i.e., the taming of Gilgamesh), Enkidu must abandon his roaming, Neanderthal ways.

We are told that, after being introduced to civilization through the ministrations of a temple prostitute, Enkidu grew "weak, for wisdom was in him" (65). Like his counterparts in Eden who partook of the fruit of a tree "of knowing" that is "desired to make one wise" (3.5-6), Enkidu must start wearing clothes, don the accouterments of civilized life, and begin eating and drinking like a civilized being (67). The text makes it clear that this transition is not easy: "Enkidu could only suck the milk of wild animals. He fumbled and gaped, at a loss what to do or how he should eat the bread and drink the strong wine. Then the woman said, 'Enkidu, eat bread, it is the staff of life; drink the wine, it is the custom of the land' " (67). Her insistence underscores the expectations and imperatives of settled living. "So he ate till he was full and drank strong wine, seven goblets. He became merry . . . and his face shone. He rubbed down the matted hair of his body and anointed himself with oil. Enkidu had become a man" (67). This passage may be read as an account of the epochal transition from migratory to settled lifestyle, and, although innocence and freedom are lost in the process, the emphasis is clearly on the ascendancy of the new over the old, the civilized over the uncivilized.

Passages from Genesis that connect the creation to the flood story address similar concerns but with very different emphases. Here putting on clothes is not a mark of progress, since it is associated with shame, separation from God, and death (Gen. 3.7-19). Similarly, the story of the first fratricide reinforces this notion of decline through time. Students often want to know why Cain's offering is judged displeasing and Abel's pleasing. A possible answer suggested by the text is that whereas Abel's offering was associated with the older, more traditional migratory life of shepherds, Cain's was the result of cultivation. Cain is described as "a tiller of the ground," (i.e., attached to fixed farming practices), a cultivated lifestyle associated with permanent settlements (4.2). Like *Gilgamesh*, the book of Genesis is dealing in large part with tensions between an older migratory, lifestyle and more settled ways. This was a crucial issue for the Hebrews as they became Israelites, an issue that informs the stories of Jacob and Joseph as well as those of the Exodus and reentry into Canaan. (Lest one mistake this issue for one long dead, one need think only of range wars, or of the sometimes violent "no trespassing" disputes still raging in our American backwoods, or of migrant workers globally).

The murder of Abel occurs in "the field" (4.8), whose open spaces may betoken a tension-filled compromise between the brutish state and a state of "cultivation." The curse placed on Cain is instructive in this regard: "When you till the ground it shall no longer yield to you its strength; you will be a fugitive and a wanderer" (4.1). So Cain is sent off, east of Eden, but his wanderings are short lived. He soon settles and, like Gilgamesh, builds a city (4.16-17). In this story, where the word "sin" first appears in Hebrew scripture (4.7), city building is linked with corruption and punishment: the first city is conceived as a refuge for convicted sinners (4.15-17). Cain and his infamous mark reside in a city. Like him the city is branded. Indeed the mark of Cain may be seen as an sign of urban blight. Just around the bend in

Genesis are other blighted cities: Babel, Sodom, Gomorrah. In these Hebrew texts cities are viewed as immoral places, refuges for concentrations of overweening human pride, selfishness, and decay.

Within this context the bizarre accounts of the Nephilim and of naked, drunken Noah may make new sense. When students gravitate, as they will, to these perplexing passages, their curiosity may be turned to instructive purpose in the context of what we have noted concerning views of the past. In the case of the Nephilim—"sons of God . . . [who] took wives for themselves" from among human women (6.1-2.) we see a clear (if cryptic) allusion to a former time, a past epoch when relations between humans and divine forces were substantially different, in which godly beings mated with human females to produce heroic, mortal offspring. A progression of eras is assumed, much as in Hesiod's progression of ages. As in Hesiod, an earlier age is perceived as superior in terms of deeds and mindset, producing "the heroes that were of old, warriors of renown" (6.4), a former age when mortals were closely allied to the divine.

One of the oddest things about this passage is that it forms the immediate backdrop for the story of Noah, which begins in the next verse (6.5) and seems to unfold from it. Our limited time here precludes a thorough comparison of the flood narratives in *Gilgamesh* and Genesis. Yet it is worth noting that, when things settle down after the flood, Noah is pointedly identified, like Cain, as "a tiller of the soil" (9.20) and that his occupation gets him into trouble in a way that may remind us of Enkidu: Noah "planted a vineyard and he drank of the wine and became drunk and lay uncovered in his tent " (9.20b-21). Here the scene of the old man's naked drunkenness is recounted within the context of a settled lifestyle and its luxuries, an ambiance of cultivated living. The implicit connection between drunkenness and the settled lifestyle that accompanies planting and cultivating is highly suggestive here, as it is in *Gilgamesh*. The difference is that in the case of Enkidu, drunkenness is embraced as natural to civilized society and therefore acceptable, whereas in Genesis it is viewed as a deleterious effect of civilization.

The idea of being settled so as to produce bread and wine is held up as beneficial in *Gilgamesh*; however, in these Hebrew texts that stage of human development is problematized. In *Gilgamesh* it is presented as an integral, even desirable part of becoming civilized. There cities are perceived as centers of social life and order, imposing bastions associated with the strength and prestige of a local deity. This story is in essence about the training of a brash young man who is portrayed as, first and foremost, ruler of that city, but nonetheless brutish, in need of taming and civilizing. Cities are viewed favorably in *Gilgamesh*: cities serve not only for protection but also for perpetuating the heroic exploits of champions such as Gilgamesh, as his story is recorded on stone to be preserved in his city of Uruk (61). This distinctive central idea is reinforced by the fact that among the survivors of the flood in *Gilgamesh*, in addition to the family of old Utnapishtim, are craftsmen whose function is presumably to help rebuild flooded cities (109).

Having established these textual reference points we can move with our students toward an examination of sociological and philosophical/theological hypotheses. To what extent is the equation of what is past with what is bad in *Gilgamesh* connected to an ameliorative view that encouraged young Mesopotamians to strive to outdo their forebears? To what extent is the contrasting view in Genesis of the past as superior to the present age linked to the Hebrew concept of society's devolution since creation as a result of human rebelliousness and sin? How does that idea connect to the preeminent Hebrew concepts of covenant and promise? How do these systems of thought compare with our own?

Our goal with our students is comparable to the goals of the authors of these ancient texts: to situate and localize the present in terms of past patterns, to encourage in this generation of students some sense of who they are relative to what has come before. This narrative tendency to regard anteriority judgmentally—as object of veneration or as source of resentment or as insignificant inconvenience—the storyteller's inclination to look to the past in order to discern its connections to the present, the daunting challenge ultimately to attach oneself to the past or to distinguish oneself from it, can be usefully integrated into our teaching. By emphasizing these texts' atten tion to anteriority and their insistence on its pertinence to contemporary living, we can help our students examine more fruitfully their own predisposition—be it hostile, idealizing, or oblivious—toward "those times," and hence toward our common present and future.

## Works Cited

Altar, Robert and Frank Kermode, eds. *The Literary Guide to the Bible* (Cambridge, MA: Harvard University Press), 1987.

Heidel, Alexander ed. and trans. *The Babylonian Genesis* (Chicago: University of Chicago Press, 1963).

Metzger, Bruce M. and Roland E. Murphy eds., *The New Oxford Annotated Bible*. New Revised Standard Version. (New York: Oxford University Press), 1991.

Moyers, Bill. *Genesis: A Living Conversation*. ed. Betty Sue Flowers. (New York: Doubleday, 1996).

Sandars, N. K. ed. and trans. *The Epic of Gilgamesh* (New York: Viking-Penguin, 1972).

# CHAPTER 17

# In the Medieval Gap with Dante's Admiral Beatrice

*James F. Walter*

In the middle of *The Divine Comedy*, the pilgrim Dante faces his own medieval gap when he stands looking across the stream of Lethe, which is all that divides his earthly journey along paths of knowledge of good and evil from a more paradisal, unhampered pursuit of the full truth of the ultimate cause of the universe. Accompanied by his pagan guide Virgil and a Christian companion Statius, Dante sees, in light from Eden on the other side of Lethe, the familiar form of Beatrice Portinari, who has come directing a festal pageant of many vessels to help her beloved Dante cross the water separating him from her. She is, he says, "Just like an admiral who goes to bow and stern, watching his men at work on other ships, encouraging their earnest labors." Admiral Beatrice actually appears as the driver of a two-wheeled cart drawn by a gryphon, representing the compound being of the incarnated Son of God. Her cart, near the middle of a procession of white-robed figures who represent books of the Old and New Testament, is flanked by dancing girls representing the four cardinal and three theological virtues. In the sky overhead, seven trails of light flowing like jet-streams from a marvelous candelabra at the head of the procession are reference points for navigation. This light, according to Genesis first-created before the physical light of the heavenly bodies, empowers the synthetic and penetrative vision of intelligent beings who in the state of innocence receive their powers directly from God. Beatrice, restored since her death to Edenic innocence, meets Dante at this moment to test his freedom to cross the gap of Lethe and enter her region of freer speculation regarding the origin and end of creation. She appears, also, as a possible bridge for his crossing of the gap, if he will do the work it takes to read her, and the panoply of visual aids she brings, as bearers of a promise to gratify his hunger for knowledge.

As many commentators recognize, this moment in the "Purgatorio," with the pilgrim set up to be relieved of his first guide Virgil and challenged with new tasks imposed by Beatrice, is pivotal for the entire *Divine Comedy*: Dantist Peter Hawkins says, "two worlds of discourse [condensed for readers in juxtaposed passages of Virgilian lament and Christian salutation] meet at an impasse to reveal the great gulf fixed between them" (113). All alternatives that are critical to human existence for Dante, for his own age, and for our age are concentrated at this impasse (this gap). That the Christian poet has configured the impasse as not merely a gap impeding progress but rather one yielding passage through high mountain reaches to a promised new region of experience is what fundamentally distinguishes his medieval epic from modern pursuits of knowledge. Dante found a way—of imagination grounded in his restored faith in love incarnated for him in his experience of a woman—to cross Lethe in pursuit of metaphysical truth where later travelers have feared to tread. Most hesitant to follow have been enlightened skeptics, captives of methodologically constrained objective knowledge, and planners of progressive curricula whose anthologies offer modern students all of the "Inferno," but little more, as evidence of imaginative life in the Middle Ages and the genius of that period's greatest poet.

The long-prepared meeting of Dante with Beatrice (in Cantos XXX-XXXI of the "Purgatorio") is not presented as an immediate objective drama; rather, Dante, after completion of his visionary journey, uses his imaginative memory interpretively to reconstruct this reunion to aid his readers' understanding. His narration of this event has five parts: (1) Beatrice's initial appearance to Dante amid theatrics of light and sound, evocative of teleological personal fulfillment, marriage, and corporate benediction; (2) a description of Dante's first reactions, embroidered with an overlay of poetic similes that assist the reader to fathom the pilgrim's experience in a meditative distance; (3) Beatrice's prosecutorial indictment against the criminal, whose stance on the hither side of Lethe figures his residual guilt from past knowledge of sin, although his climb to this place has freed him from sinful desires; (4)

Beatrice's cross-examination of Dante, to elicit his spoken acknowledgment of his sin against her and his remorse; and finally (5) Dante's baptismal passage through Lethe that brings him to a consummate reunion with his beloved. The mediating presence of the seven angelic maidens mark the lovers' meeting as providentially ordained by the Divine Will.

Dante, remembering, says that when Beatrice first appeared in a cloud of flowers, like "the face of the sun shrouded by mist," he was so struck by her "high virtue" that he instinctively turned to Virgil, as a child runs to its mother in fear or affliction. Justifiably, commentators have expounded at length on the honor Dante momentarily paid his "sweetest father" by expressing his emotion in those same words Dido spoke in *The Aeneid* to express the passion resurrected in her by Aeneas: "I recognize the signs of the ancient flame." Less remarked is the dramatic irony in Virgil's dismissal from the action of *The Divine Comedy* before he receives his pupil's tribute, foreshadowed by mounting evidence of the Roman Poet's essential displacement in Purgatory. Especially at junctures when the journey's progress through Purgatory has called for existential personal engagement and a lively sense of social belonging rather than concentrated intellectual mastery, Virgil has seemed out of his element, inclined to cover his interpersonal tactlessness with professorial verbosity. In Canto III, for instance, when Dante asks his master why he casts no shadow on the mount (a query that probes to the root of the interdependence of spiritual and material reality), Virgil advises, "Be content with *quia* unexplained." Regardless of this wise counsel, Virgil is not himself content with *quia* moments later as, "standing there, his head bent low, [he searches] his mind to find some helpful way" to begin the climb up the mountain. While the Poet is turned inward in search for a solution to an immediate practical dilemma, his pupil Dante, by looking up, catches sight of a crowd of people who, after a momentary exchange of information, will point out "the way." Evidently, in this region, progress from one point to the next is propelled less by individual plotting than by social sympathy and dialogue in a containing plot that incorporates many selves.

Of course, any niggling reader can find other evidence of Virgil's increasing uselessness beyond the infernal stage of Dante's journey. After due acknowledgment of the supreme importance of this exemplar of classical moral reason for the historical Dante's poetic and intellectual development, it is worth noticing that in the Florentine's narrative of Purgatory, the surest causes of ascent are not Virgil's homilies but are actions of compassionate souls who descend at crises either to lift Dante literally to the next level or to energize Virgil to perform the office for which he was commissioned. Even Virgil's famous lecture classifying the kinds and motives of love, delivered on the terrace of the slothful with concise Aristotelian correctness that leaves his charge rather sleepy, pales in comparison with Dante's own subsequent narrative of personal love that moves him and Beatrice through the heavens.

In his reconstruction of his reactions to Beatrice's advent, Dante suggests that, as he first felt "enduring love" freshen his trembling soul, his sense of exposure before her penetrating glance provoked him to bond with Virgil for a fig-leaf to gloss his nakedness. Beatrice headed off his evasion, however, by addressing him to the quick: "Dante," she said, "Look at *me*! Yes, I am Beatrice!" Against his resort to poetic crutches, her calling him by the name that was his before he acquired the tile "Poet" recalled him to existential experience and personal dialogue. Once he realized that "father Virgil" was not there to play his mother, and that he could not avoid the self-knowledge Beatrice demanded, he says, "As snow [melts] upon the spine of Italy . . . . the bonds of ice packed tight around my heart dissolved, becoming breath and water." This very Dantesque simile describes the lover's release from Stoical pride such as, in the "Inferno," causes souls like Count Ugolino to hold all their uncertainty and pain inside themselves as frozen tears of anger stockpiled against the world and all its self-affronting evil.

Dante's living tears are not enough, however, for Admiral Beatrice: to command still more of his labor, she spells out his sin, essentially his dereliction of his relationship with her:

> "There was a time my countenance sufficed [she says],
>   as I let him look into my young eyes
>   for guidance on the straight path to his goal;
> but when I passed into my second age
>   and changed my life for Life, that man you see
> [she says to the court of angels]
>   turned his steps to the untrue way,
>   pursuing false images of the good."

Dante scholarship clarifies that in these words Beatrice is accusing her lover-poet, who had dedicated his youthful *Vita Nuova* to her, of turning, after her death, to other inspiration for his later *Convivio*, which he dedicated to a Donna Gentile who represented Philosophy . Beatrice attests that his failure to persevere in his faith in her eternal worth, and the consequent failure of his imagination to follow her to her new existence with God, hardened his heart in a posture of self-sufficiency against besetting fears and desires. Instead of patiently searching his own experience and memory of her for an appropriate theory of life and art, he rushed to theory for a ready refuge from his pain of loss. His wandering from Beatrice in his imagination and poetry made it necessary for her, therefore, to descend to the Dead and recruit Virgil to guide him back to her. If she was calculating on the very root of pagan eloquence that had contributed to Dante s swerving, she followed a good precedent: in an earlier age, Augustine learned to use the misguiding classical education he received from his elders to expose and overcome the very faults that it bred. In brief, Beatrice understood that just as man s work is the cursed inheritance of his fall, so work borne obediently with hope assists release from sin s bondage.

After Beatrice forces Dante to answer a miserable "yes" to her indictment, her beauty is so overwhelming, and his remorse for abandoning her so sharp, that he faints. When he comes to moments later, he is being drawn through Lethe by Beatrice's assistant Matelda. This baptism, by removing all Dante's memory of the sin to which he confessed, restores him fully to the innocence figured by his finally landing on Eden's side of the stream.

The drama of Dante's "re-cognition" of Beatrice unfolds in two parts, the first assisted by the four dancing maidens, the second by the other three. Through it all, Beatrice continues standing in the chariot, where Dante sees her first looking at the gryphon and then directly at him. The four leading Dante to the gryphon's breast instruct him,

"Look deeply, look with all your sight . . . .
for now you stand before those emeralds
from which Love once shot loving darts at you."

What he sees when he looks at Beatrice s eyes are alternating reflections of the two aspects of the gryphon. In other words, he sees her doing theology : meditating the mysterious incarnation of the Divine Nature in the human person of Christ. In a pure and simple objective vision, Dante sees also in the depth of her wonderful emeralds the incarnation of *her* spiritual beauty that is, her intelligent being as she performs the act of knowing God s love mysteriously shining in the harmonies of creation.

Next the other three maidens implore Beatrice, "turn your sacred eyes . . . and look upon your faithful one who came so very far to look at you! . . . unveil your mouth for him." In her compliant smile Beatrice discloses the full power of her eternal love for Dante, who feels it as a consummate satisfaction of his human desire. The meaning of this intimate communion will expand tremendously in the "Paradiso," where Dante tells how a Divine Poet has created the universe such that every thing in it, including the planets and fixed stars, has been created to serve as signs in a vast semeiotic of personal converse among humans and between God and humankind.

I have attempted to explicate Dante's portrayal of Beatrice in *The Divine Comedy* as an Admiral, who, at an impasse in her beloved's life, commands the timely arrival of a fleet of cohorts, encourages transformative labor, and accomplishes a higher will. I have suggested that, especially for modern readers, Dante's narration brings this impasse to focus as a medieval gap, or perhaps a threshold, where we are asked to weigh the value of faith in revealed truth, the uses of metaphysical speculation on eternal causes of the universe, and evidence that the experience of love between historical persons incarnates the "Love that moves the sun and the other stars."

One interpretation of the Middle Ages, argued eloquently by Marina Warner in a 1989 essay "Personification and the Idealization of the Feminine," is that, for readers who are enlightened regarding the real sources of power in the world, these thoughts may be a sinkhole in which idealist dreamers lose their force to change the world's history for the better. In the art of the Middle Ages, Warner says, male artists simply gave new spins to a traditionally conventional image of the idealized feminine that had nothing to do with real women in the middles ages, who remained powerless and exploited. However inspiring women may appear in allegorical poems such as *The Divine Comedy*, she says, they "rarely closed the rift between fantasy and reality; and in [this] connection lies the power of images, written or visual, to structure our world for the better" (91). This idealizing of the feminine, Warner believes, caused "the vulgar fact" of the condition of real women to be "forgotten, or perhaps [not quite to] be faced, and the historical splendors and possibilities of women's participation in the Middles Ages were neglected in favor of contemporary romancing" (109).

Warner's fundamental thesis is that real power to improve the world begins with a scientific history (cultural studies) that exposes the rhetorical sleights that in past ages have drawn a veil of illusion over reality. Unblinking historical eyes, she maintains, by seeing how and by whom the veil was drawn teach us how to rip it off for a vista of a new world freer of rhetorical and political exploitation. Nevertheless, Warner indulges in a little "contemporary romancing" herself as she neglects to say anything about powerful pressures in the thought of the Middle Ages for close knowledge of the existential realities of life, just as she hurries past the fact that for Dante Beatrice was no mere allegory. When Beatrice was alive (and even after she died), she was a real woman for Dante, a person Dante saw many times in Florence, who had a voice he heard and a history deeply imprinted in his imagination. By her noble character and demeanor, her intelligence, and her outspoken modesty (as well as her beauty), she moved Dante as nothing else moved him in his life. She was much more down-to-earth, certainly much closer to the "vulgar fact" than Warner admits. In describing the reunion he imagines with Beatrice in the "Purgatorio," Dante remarks the power of her "piercing virtue" to move him to act in faith and trust, to see himself in the most naked honesty, and to dedicate his poetry to expression of truths at once the most intimately personal and the most distantly metaphysical. Thus, he saw in her an incarnation of the Divine Love in human form, an image of Christ revealing Divine purpose to her pilgrim-poet-lover. Because of his faith in the revelation that came to him through his experience with Beatrice, Dante would not have hesitated to say that she empowered him to write a poetry that truthfully reveals the ultimate cause and goal of the universe.

A chief value of Dante for contemporary readers is that he helps us consider whether we are ever free of what mystifies, blinds, and lures us to further knowledge, and whether truthful owning up to our submission to such otherness is not the beginning of a human wisdom conducive to human happiness. For his ability to unsettle us in the theoretical resorts to which, perhaps, we all too hastily run these days, and for his disclosure of an actual past that continues to provide material for our interpretation of ourselves in the present, his *Divine Comedy* (all of it!) should be on the reading list of every undergraduate needing to know where we are and what we're doing there.

## Works Cited

Hawkins, Peter. 1991. "Dido, Beatrice, and the Signs of Ancient Love." *The Poetry of Allusion: Virgil and Ovid in Dante's "Commedia,"* ed. Rachel Jacoff and Jeffrey T. Schnapp. Stanford: Stanford University Press, 113-130.

Warner, Marina. 1989. "Personification and the Idealization of the Feminine." *Medievalism in American Culture*, eds., Bernard Rosenthal and Paul E. Szarmach. Binghamton, NY: Medieval and Renaissance Texts and Studies, 85-111.

CHAPTER 18

# Machiavelli's Debt to Medieval Thought

*By Margaret Heller*

If you read a history of political thought in the Middle Ages, you will typically find in it a judgement such as this one by Joseph Canning: "the Middle Ages were the seed-time of European civilization: without a knowledge of them, it is not possible fully to understand political thought in the later centuries."[1] If this is true, then the medieval period might to be expected to figure prominently in general accounts of the development of western culture. Yet so often the medieval contribution is barely acknowledged in writings which mean to treat the tradition of the West as a whole. Great Books reading lists also may follow a common pattern of neglect. I recently came across a web site called "The Master Works of Western Civilization" which has put together various lists of "the quintessential works of Western Civilization."[2] The compilation features thirty-seven Greek plays and twenty-eight nineteenth century European and American novels, but only six works written from the sixth to the fourteenth centuries. The balance in the curricula of many core text courses is not dissimilar.[3]

It would be interesting to try to understand what it is about medieval texts which prevents them from being perceived as "great," or even as important, but that is beyond the scope of this paper. All I really want to establish is that they *are* important for understanding the western tradition, and that their neglect distorts how we interpret modernity, beginning with the Renaissance. Ideas of the early modern period which were claimed to be either original or recovered from ancient thought often really had medieval antecedents. The debt of modern thinkers to the Middle Ages was generally unacknowledged by them, however, for they wanted to create their own foundations by choosing their parents (the ancient Greeks and Romans), or by giving birth to themselves. Do we want to accept this? My answer is no: if we read core texts in order to know ourselves by becoming acquainted with the intellectual foundations of the West, it is odd that we believe that this could be possible without close attention to the Middle Ages, the period of Europe's formation. To make my case through a particular text I have chosen what I trust is a counter-intuitive example, Machiavelli's *Prince*.

There are certainly obvious grounds for thinking that in this treatise Machiavelli intends to break completely with everything medieval. His double project of the recovery of ancient models of excellence and the discovery of what he calls "an original set of rules" pointedly ignores the Middle Ages. Machiavelli seems, in fact, to go out of his way to defy medieval conceptions of the political good, such as those articulated in Dante's *Divine Comedy*. Asserting that the true standard of justice is to be found in the obtaining and retaining of power, he *re*commends that a ruler seek success through any means necessary, including hypocrisy, treachery, and cruelty. *The Prince* appears to reverse the equation of the *Divine Comedy* by which if you want earthly paradise you end up in hell, but if you want heaven you can reach earthly paradise. Now it is: if you act in the light of heaven you cause hell, but if you accept hell it is possible to achieve earthly paradise. Nevertheless I hope to show that even this unmedieval position is strongly conditioned by a medieval background and cannot be interpreted apart from it.

Let me begin by quoting two passages from *The Prince*:

> But since it is my intention to say something that will prove of practical use to the inquirer, I have thought it proper to represent things as they are in real truth, rather than as they are imagined. Many have dreamed up republics and principalities which have never in truth been known to exist; the gulf between how one should live and how one does live is so wide that a man who neglects what is actually done for what should be done learns the way to self-destruction rather than self-preservation.[4]

The rest is up to you. God does not want to do everything Himself, and take away from us our free will and our share of the glory which belongs to us.[5]

The first manifests what can be termed a radical secularity. Here justice is not a transcendent reality to be grasped by contemplation, but rather something to be discovered in the material world itself and possessed concretely. As the temporal realm is one of shifting circumstance and human desire, the good of the city can only be realized if justice is adapted to the realities of change and ambition and not derived from otherworldly principles.

The second reveals, though, that this secular outlook is fundamentally Christian; it belongs neither to paganism nor atheism. Machiavelli does not doubt that the individual ruler's self-assertion and desire for glory are acceptable and even pleasing to God. As with many other Renaissance figures, be they artists, natural philosophers, or discoverers of new worlds, Machiavelli is confident in the righteousness of what Pico della Mirandola calls "holy ambition."[6] The Prince is not informed by that ancient tragic sense of contradiction between what the individual desires and what Destiny decrees or between the soul's true happiness and its imprisonment in the body. Nor does it assert human freedom against the divine. Could there be such self-assurance on the part of a ruler who has abandoned, or feels abandoned by, God? Machiavelli's Renaissance prince is no Dr. Faustus; he basks in God's recognition of his excellence.

But how can this radical secularity, this worldliness which does not refuse evil, co-exist with a Christian's confidence in divine notice? The conception that an individual's concerns in the world can be independent from his concerns for his ultimate end is surely not a medieval one. Yet it is the logical conclusion of a certain understanding of the relation between sacred and secular which developed in the late Middle Ages. The distinction between the two realms was not new. Early on in western Christendom, Papacy and Empire considered themselves to be divinely ordered authorities with different but complementary roles. Discerning the just relation between their mutual autonomy and unity proved, of course, to be difficult and it was the source of continual conflict and numerous proposed solutions in the medieval period. Thomas Aquinas' work in the thirteenth century was perhaps the greatest attempt to formulate the proper balance between the secular and sacred within a single order, whereby "grace does not abolish nature, but perfects it."[7] The assertion and eventual defeat of papal power, the Babylonian captivity, and the Great Schism, all in the fourteenth century, brought into question the very possibility of a balance; increasingly the temporal and the eternal, reason and revelation, were thought to be unconnected. We can see this tendency in Dante's *De Monarchia* (c. 1312), which argued that man has two quite separate goals, both equally derived from God: "the bliss of this life" and "the bliss of eternal life."[8] As a consequence humankind needs two modes of government, each with autonomy in its own sphere. Yet for Dante there is still an ultimate connection between the two insofar as secular authority is subject to the Church in matters which concern salvation.

A more radical separation between the secular and sacred was made by the nominalist William of Ockham in his *Short Discourse on Tyrannical Government,* written about 1340. After the Fall temporal power and the power to appropriate temporal things were given to all mankind, believers and non-believers alike, "by a special grant from God."[9] As temporal power is both divinely ordered and ordered without any reference to salvation, it is essentially independent of religious direction.

The theological ground of this political principle was not, as might be expected, a new assertion of the independence of humanity but rather a new assertion of the freedom of God. The nominalists held that the mediating systems of realists such as Thomas Aquinas obscured the clear distinction between the Creator and His creation, thereby diminishing His majesty. The material world does not and can not function as a bridge to the divine; on the other hand, it does bear the stamp of God's handiwork in its own right. What creation is, is what God has willed. For the nominalists, a deep sense of awe before the majesty of God *and* an assertion of the independence of the material world are two sides of the same coin. These sides continue to co-exist through the Enlightenment in the thought of Hobbes, Locke, Voltaire, and even Hume.

It is not such a large step from William of Ockham to Machiavelli. If the reconceptualization of the temporal or secular realm is taken into account, the references to God in *The Prince* no longer seem insincere or contradictory. It is not surprising that, as medieval theologians came to emphasize God's will rather than His reason, a subsequent political thinker might come to emphasize a ruler's ambition and prowess rather than his vision of the Good. Machiavelli turns away from "what ought to be" according to reason toward "what is" as discovered by observation: he looks for justice in the recorded actions of those great men who have been most effective. Effectiveness or success is achieved by acting in accordance with God's will, that is, by discerning what is to be done:

> But to come to those who became princes by their own abilities and not by
> good fortune, I say that the most outstanding are Moses, Cyrus, Romulus,

Theseus, and others like them. Although one should not reason about Moses, since he merely executed what God commanded, yet he must be praised for the grace which made him worthy of speaking with God. But let us consider Cyrus and the others who acquired and founded kingdoms: they were all praiseworthy, and their actions and institutions, when examined, do not seem to differ from those of Moses, who had such a mighty teacher.[10]

According to his famous formulation, prowess in the created world results in justice: "you cannot have good laws without good arms, and where there are good arms, good laws inevitably follow."[11]

My general point is in not in the end about Machiavelli; it is about how the meaning of modern secularity can be misunderstood if not given its fuller content and true context in the Middle Ages. The existence of "the medieval gap" in a typical Great Books curriculum is to a large extent the result of its own historical origins. Liberal arts education as we know it began primarily with the educational program of the Renaissance humanists, who were in competition with the Church-dominated universities. The humanists deliberately passed over medieval intellectual traditions and discovered alternative models of justice in ancient texts studied directly. But for us to continue to follow them in giving the Romans and especially the Greeks so much attention, and in giving medieval thinkers so little, only serves to distort our understanding of the real historical origins of many aspects of contemporary western culture, including its assertion of the dignity of the individual, its accomplishments in modern science, and its development of representative institutions. If we who teach in core text courses really intend students to know themselves, we must "please, mind the gap."

## Notes

1. Joseph Canning, *A History of Medieval Thought 300-1450* (London; New York: Routledge, 1996), 187. See also Antony Black, *Political Thought in Europe, 1250-1450* (Cambridge: Cambridge University Press, 1992), 191.

2. "The Master Works of Western Civilization. A hypertext-annotated compilation of lists of major works recommended by Drs. Adler and Eliot, Charles Van Doren, Anthony Burgess, Clifton Fadiman, the Easton Press, and many others," http://www.eskimo.com/-masonw/mwwc.html.

3. E.g. "St. John's College List of Program Readings," http://www.sjca.edu/college/readlist.html.

4. Niccolo Machiavelli, *The Prince*, trans. George Bull (London: Penguin, 1961), 90-91 (in XV).

5. Machiavelli, 135 (in XXVI).

6. Pico della Mirandola, *Oration on the Dignity of Man*, trans. Charles Glenn

Wallis (Englewood Cliffs, N.J.: Prentice Hall, 1985),7.

7. Thomas Aquinas, *Summa Theologica*, I, 1, 8, ad 2, in *The Basic Writings of St. Thomas Aquinas*, trans. Anton C. Pegis (New York: Random House, 1948).

8. Dante, *On World-Government*, trans. Herbert W. Schneider (Indianapolis: Library of Liberal Arts, 1957), 78.

9. William of Ockham, *A short discourse on the tyrannical government over things divine and human, but especially over the Empire and those subject to the Empire, usurped by some who are called highest pontiffs*, trans. Arthur Stephen McGrade (Cambridge: Cambridge University Press, 1992), 89.

10. Machiavelli, 50 (in VI).

11. Machiavelli, 77 (in XII).

# IV. New Perspectives on Shakespeare as Core Text

CHAPTER 19

# Shakespeare in the Core Curriculum

*David Bevington*

I address my subject as chair of one of the core humanities courses at the University of Chicago. It is a freshman humanities course, spread over three quarters, called "Greek Thought and Literature." We study ancient texts from Homer down through Plato and Aristotle. The third quarter deals largely with philosophical texts. In general we proceed historically: Homer and Herodotus in the first quarter, which perhaps some pre-Socratic philosophers; Thucydides, Aeschylus, Sophocles, and perhaps one play by Aristophanes in the second quarter; some more Aristophanes, Euripides, and the philosophers in the third quarter. We give our instructors some leeway, but this is the basic plan.

This course is one of a number of Core humanities courses at the University of Chicago. There used to be only one course for all students, back in the 1940s and 50s. Since the late 60s we have moved toward a more pluralistic scheme. Students can take "Human Being and Citizen," "Readings in World Literature," "Readings in Cultures," and still others. "Human Being and Citizen" is a Great Books course, not organized historically as is "Greek Thought and Literature." I am comfortable with the plan, for while it lacks the college-wide cohesiveness of a single humanities course for all students, it does still provide a genuine core experience.

One aspect of this that I want to stress, is that a course like this one does wonderful things not only for the students but for the University community. It's a remarkable opportunity to teach a faculty whose members have taught not simply the standard English and American literature courses but also Kant, Thucydides, Sophocles, Tolstoy, Lucretius, Virgil, and many others. There is a shared richness that we all profit from. I sense much the same richness at gatherings of the Association for Core Texts and Courses. At a session on Shakespeare during the 1998 conference in Asheville, a group of colleagues interested in Shakespeare and his role in the core humanities experience turned out to have, in its membership, a number of teachers who were prepared to talk about Shakespeare in the context of Plato's *Republic,* Machiavelli, and Montaigne. The Great Books background provided a kind of enrichment of perspective that is too often lacking even at gatherings of Shakespeare experts, as for example at the meetings of the Shakespeare Association of America. I profit greatly from those annual gatherings, but I don't expect to hear much talk of the Platonic dialogues.

One especially rewarding insight for me at the 1998 meeting of the Association for Core Texts and Courses has been that of seeing how the idea of core texts can operate in other broad areas, like the Social Sciences, and how it can incorporate new texts without giving up the emphasis on the Great Books of Western Civilization. I was impressed by the talk given by Thomas Barfield, from Boston, on the writings of Ibn Khaldun. I certainly had not heard of him. This fine address had an added impact on me because I attended, the previous evening, a colloquium on the question: what can the idea of core education offer to a central Asian country like Tadzhikistan? What would the core experience be like in such a country, and what texts would be appropriate in that setting? The questions raised an issue that I confess I hadn't thought much about previously: what is the role of the core in the Third World? And how can such a question help us to think through ways in which our own notions of the core can be updated and expanded?

As a society, we in the Association for Core Texts and Courses need to worry about taking on the appearance of a rearguard movement the chief function of which is to hold out against post-modernism and try to turn the clock back. It is important that we not be pigeon-holed into what appears to be a conservative stance opposed to multiculturalism. Can there be room in a core program, as at the University of Chicago, for a course like "Reading in Cultures" that deals largely in post-modern issues and methods of reading? Such a course attracts many of the younger faculty coming to the University. We must be careful not to give the whole field of multiculturalism to post-modern criticism and thus accentuate a polarization between it and a more traditional core curriculum.

What excited me about Tom Barfield's presentation was its success in proposing for us a text from outside Western Civilization which beautifully fufills the idea of a core text and is at the same time genuinely friendly to our multicultural world. This is a text I am anxious to teach in my own courses. The text offers an arresting theory of the rise, growth, and cyclical decay of tribal organization. It does so from the point of view of a medieval author in the Middle East, theorizing about his subject in a successful attempt to see a cyclical pattern. It is sufficiently broad in its implications that one can see ways of applying the theory to the rise and fall of civilizations elsewhere. It is a new, Third World, text with universal implications.

As an author, Khaldun offers an arresting contrast with Shakespeare. I choose Shakespeare because I teach and edit him professionally. Khaldun represents a text not heard from on most campuses. Shakespeare runs to the opposite extreme. He is universally familiar, and, as a Dead White European Male, would seem to represent just the kind of authority figure in literature that postmodernism wishes to challenge. Shakespeare is a major presence, along with Plato and Socrates, at this conference. Shakespeare has become essential to the core experience. What better author could we choose from English Literature and poetry? He is so widely the choice in colleges today that he survives and thrives while many of his contemporaries like Marlowe and Spenser and Ben Johnson are in danger of disappearing from the curriculum. Often he is the one author whom our students—even our English majors—still study in the era before 1800.

There has been a good deal of worry lately in conservative quarters that Shakespeare too is on the decline, because according to the statistics, there are many fewer required courses in Shakespeare than was the case earlier in the century. I don't worry about this. Shakespeare seems to be able to sell himself. Our English Department does not have a requirement that students take Shakespeare, and I support that position. Enrollments are holding up well, because students find Shakespeare genuinely exciting. What a pleasure to have students who have chosen Shakespeare because they want the course, not because it is a requirement!

Paradoxically, Shakespeare is not only on the decline in our classrooms; he turns out to be the darling of postmodern criticism. He is remarkable for his ability to respond to any current critical question with a pertinent and critically sophisticated answer. He serves well the demands of feminist theory, or destruction, or New Historicism. A good number of the most visible of modern theorists are Shakespeareans like Stephen Greenblatt.

But are we happy with what postmodern criticism does to Shakespeare?

At a Shakespeare session at this conference, the participants in a discussion of *The Tempest* seemed at first reluctant to allow the use of New Historicist questions dealing with colonialism and neocolonialism. Is Prospero a colonialist? The group preferred to talk about ethical responsibility and choices, and to see Prospero in more traditional terms as a artistic figure standing very much at the center of the play. There was a disinclination to allow that he bullies his daughter in patriarchal fashion or that he is a kind of a slave owner. My own response is that one need not choose between ethical readings of the play and postmodern ones. These last twenty-five years of critical exploration have been exhilarating—not without their excesses, of course, but genuinely stimulating and insightful. It's a mistake, in my view, to think that one can discuss *The Tempest* today without reflecting on what the post-colonialist world can ask in the way of new questions.

*The Tempest* is such a vital core text, in other words, because it offers itself to such a range of contrasting interpretations. This is not to say that one's teaching need turn to the kind of relativism of allowing that anything goes. There are values in *The Tempest* that are visible and significant. But we do need to open up the play to a wide cross-section of perspectives.

Even if Shakespeare is doing well in the core classroom, his texts are on the defensive in our culture more generally, and for reasons that are worrisome. He opens up issues of social conflict that some people would prefer not to hear about, or expose their children to. We learn how some libraries are removing *The Taming of The Shrew* from their shelves because of worries about feminist sensibilities, or getting rid of their copies of *The Merchant Of Venice* because of worries about antisemitism. *Othello* is similarly under attack. The complaints come from the left and right. A headmistress of a private girls' school in England recently decided not to arrange a trip for students to see *Romeo and Juliet* because, she observed, it is so relentlessly and onesidedly heterosexual.

I thought about the *Merchant of Venice* a lot when I was invited to a meeting of the German Shakespeare Gesellschaft in Weimar, Germany a couple of years ago. Weimar is close to the World War II concentration camp in Buchenwald. The Shakespeare meeting happened to coincide with the commemoration of the fiftieth anniversary of that camp. There, in Weimar, the home of the Weimar Republic after World War I, the national acting company of the city chose to mount a production of *The Merchant Of Venice*. It was an arresting performance.

As one came into the theatre, one immediately saw over the stage a huge banner reading *"Jedem das Eines,"* "To each his own" —the legend that notoriously appeared over the entrance to Buchenwald during World War

II. The concept of this production was that a group of bored German officers acting as the authorities at Buchenwald during the war had decided to entertain themselves by mounting a production of *The Merchant of Venice*. They dragooned three inmates of the camp, three Jewish inmates, to impersonate Shylock, Jessica, and Tubal in their show. First they ordered these inmates up on stage, forced them to strip naked, and insisted that they sing the camp song. The effect was unimaginably degrading. Then they got on with the play. The commandant of the camp played Antonio, the merchant. Two younger officers shaved their legs, rolled up their trousers, and did drag versions of Portia and Jessica. As the play proceeded, things turned nastily against Shylock, of course, with the result that in the climatic trial scene the camp commandant appeared for a time to be at the mercy of a knife-wielding Jewish inmate. Order was restored, if order is what I mean. The antisemitic gloating of Gratiano — "A second Daniel, a Daniel, Jew! / Now, infidel I have you on the hip" (4.1.331-2) was unbearable painful. I was struck with the chilling authenticity that the young German actors brought to their roles as Nazi officers, insulting and humiliating their inmates. I was no less struck with the remarkable courage and self-examination that were required to mount such a production a few miles away from Buchenwald as part of the commemoration of that terrible event. This German acting company, and their German audience, were not turning away from what was so awful about the play and its implied comment on their own twentieth-century history. The play was offered as a vehicle for remembering and reflecting on one's own crimes of intolerance and hate.

Contrast this astonishing production with another that I saw only a few weeks later. This was in Lincoln, Nebraska, at Nebraska Wesleyan University. I had been asked to attend and critique a production of *The Merchant of Venice* by students of that school, located as it is in an essentially all-white, Protestant, Middle Western part of our country. The students played it as a straight comedy. Shylock was the heavy, the blocking figure whose overthrow was necessary for the comic completion of the love plot and the final joyful reunion of all the Christian friends, together with the newly converted Jessica, now the Christian wife of Lorenzo and hence no longer a Jew.

During a discussion afterwards, which I was asked to chair, and which included all the cast and many members of the audience, I asked the young women playing Portia if she had experienced any uneasiness with her role in the discomfiture and overthrow of Shylock. "Oh, no," she replied. "He got what he deserved." The cast were generally of this opinion. In the audience, on the other hand, a Jewish Rabbi spoke up. He hated the play, and wished never to see it performed again; if he could destroy all copies of the play he would gladly do so. He was there, he explained, solely because an adopted non-Jewish member of his family had a role in the production. He went on to explain, with my encouragement, what it was like to be a rabbi of a somewhat beleaguered flock in a place like Lincoln, Nebraska. It was an electrifying evening, no less so than that I had spent in Weimar, Germany, even if the nature of the emotional conflict was strikingly different.

Out of this pair of experiences I came to a renewed sense of the value of the play as a catalyst for critical thought about issues of ethnicity, belief, and tolerance. Whether or not there is a residue of antisemitism in Shakespeare's text) and it certainly can be argued that there is such a residue (the play is thoughtfully complex and sensitive that it cannot help but encourage necessary reflection in all of us. It is a core text in the best sense of the concept.

*Othello* is certainly another. I have been struck by a recent book by Ania Loomba, called *Gender, Race, Renaissance Drama* (Manchester: Manchester University Press, 1989). Ania Loomba grew up in New Delhi. She teaches at the University of that city in an English faculty that includes 700 to 800 members; *Othello* is probably read by more students in that University system than any where else on the globe. The author takes the opportunity to write about *Anthony and Cleopatra* from an Eastern perspective. To her, the play is basically about an Eastern woman, Cleopatra, confronting, and in an important sense triumphing over, the West symbolized by Rome and Octavious Ceasar. Proceeding from such an analysis, the author then asks of herself: here I am a woman brought up in India as colonized by the British, in a world where I was taught that *Othello* is not about race but is an object lesson in the necessity of wives being obedient to their husbands. How am I, in the India of the late twentieth century, after the departure of the British, supposed to teach this text? Do I want to teach it at all? Is it not a symbol of British domination of my country? Should I, like my colleagues, go on teaching Shakespeare, or should we throw all of this over and turn to texts by Indian writers and modern authors in other countries that have been routinely excluded from curriculum until now? Here was a configuration of Shakespeare as the Dead White European Male author that seemed to urge the adoption of a new course. And yet Ania Loomba did not make that choice; she still teaches, and writes about, not only Shakespeare but his contemporary dramatists. What she and her colleagues found, of course, was that Shakespeare as a text was open for the kind of skeptical investigation of race and ethnicity and colonialization that she and her colleagues wished to pursue. Shakespeare is alive and well in New Delhi today, but perhaps in a guise that might be almost unrecognizable by the traditionally British-taught Indian women of an earlier generation who had taught Ania Loomba at Miranda House.

A similar transformation can be seen to have taken place in the producing and teaching of Shakespeare in South Africa in the days following the official end of Apartheid. One part of the story is of Janet Suzman's decision to mount a production of Othello in Johannesburg just shortly before that official end of Apartheid, when one could sense that change was imminent but that is might take years and might be a bloody affair. Janet Suzman is a White South African woman who had become prominent on the English stage; in fact, she had starred as Cleopatra in a very successful production of that play in Stratford-upon-Avon in 1972.

On this occasion, Suzman chose to cast, in the role of Othello, John Cadi, perhaps South Africa's best known black actor. He had not done Shakespeare before this. Opposite him, Suzman cast a very blonde South African actress, and, in the role of Iago, an actor with a frightening capability for playing the part of a brutal police officer. The stage was thus set for a production that was stirringly timely. The audience was racially mixed. The production, available in videotape, breathes with the excited tension of the surroundings of *Othello* on film.

As an intriguing aftermath, I had occasion to hear Janet Suzman speak at a gathering of the International Shakespeare association in Los Angeles in April of 1996. I didn't want to miss that, since I had admired her production so greatly. I was made uneasy by the speech, however, and my uneasiness was confirmed by the response to the speech of my South African colleagues, all of whom hated it. As much as they admire Suzman, they sensed a kind of white person's condescension in the story that Suzman must have been unaware of; I'm sure she would have been saddened to learn how poorly the speech went over in these last quarters. The problem was that she had cast herself in the role of the enlightened liberal white woman, taking on the white man's burden of teaching Cadi how it was possible for him to act Shakespeare. Not being familiar with Renaissance theatre, Cadi, in her account, had floundered with the language, had felt defeated, and had wanted to quit. She helped him through it all. Here, for me, was one more indication of how troublesome the play is, and how necessary it is that we reflect on our own feelings of racial prejudice as we watch such a play.

*Othello* certainly dramatizes a problem of racism that seems deeply ingrained in Venetian society, so much so that it is expressed not only by riff-raff like Roderigo and cynical villains like Iago but also by upstanding senators like Desdemona's father, Brabantio. Sadly, Brabantio needs little encouragement from Roderigo and Iago to come to the conclusion that something unnatural has happened in the elopement of his daughter. It must be magic, he concludes, because his own blood daughter would not "natu-rally" do something so against her "nature" as to fall in love with a black. Even more painfully, this is the racist idea that Iago manages to persuade Othello to believe in, to internalize in his own sense of self. "Haply, for I am black / and have not those soft parts of conversation / That chamberers have, or for I am declined / Into the vale of years (yet that's not much) she's gone," Othello concludes (3.3.279-83). Once he accepts that premise, his decision to kill Desdemona follows as a foregone conclusion. This internalization of racist attitudes in Othello's own consciousness is deeply painful, once again, but is vitally important to talk about with students.

*Hamlet* presents a different kind of situation as a core text. We do not encounter here issues of racial difference or slavery or ethnic and religious hatred. The issues are more those of murder and revenge and Christian for-bearance. *Hamlet* is nonetheless an unavoidably central icon of our culture, and one that must be taken hugely into account. It's a tribute to Shakespeare, I think, that the play has managed to survive its own oppressive mythology as being the most essential of tragedies. How does one stage, yet again, "To be or not to be?" Actors and directors alike wrestle with this difficulty. (One of my favorite solutions was that of Robert Falls, at Wisdom Bridge Theatre in North Chicago around 1970, who, in a modern dress production, chose to have his Hamlet spray- paint the words "To be or not to be" on a bulkhead, and then, as the smell of the spray-paint drifted through the audience, stand back admiring his own work and say, "That is the question!")

One approach to the timeless attractiveness of *Hamlet* is to discuss the play in terms of love and friendship. The play is full of misogyny; that is indeed a problem like racism or ethnic hatred not easily eradicated from today's culture. "Frailty, thy name is woman!" Hamlet exclaims(1.2.146), in response to what he sees as the deplorable and disgusting carnality of his mother. The painfulness of this perception colors Hamlet's relationship with Ophelia. His own behavior is coarsened and made more violent as the play proceeds. Under these circum-stances, love does not fare well.

*Hamlet* was written around the time of *Trolius* and *Cressida* and some of the other darker sonnets, shortly after *Much Ado About Nothing*, a time in Shakespeare's life in which, as Richard Wheeler argues (*Shakespeare's Development and the Problem Comedies: Turn and Counter-Turn* (Berke-ley: University of California Press, 1981), the playwright turns from his ear-lier and happier romantic comedies, with their charismatic and loyal young heroines, to situations in which the specter of female willfulness and incon-stancy is perceived as a major problem. Earlier, as in *Much Ado*, female profligacy is readily imagined by the anxious male psyche but is entirely chimerical; Hero did not sleep with other men before her marriage, and the illusion of infidelity is finally dispelled. With the Dark Lady sonnets and *Trolius* and *Cressida*, on the other hand, Pandora's box has been opened; the prospect of actual infidelity is at hand.

In the great tragedies, accordingly, love and marriage are put to a new and severe test. Lady Macbeth is a frightening manifestation of woman as monster, only briefly adumbrated in earlier plays. King Lear's ravings about women as centaurs "Down from the waist" (4.6.124) elaborates a similarly disturbing image. *Hamlet* inhabits a similar world of frightening prospects of female monstrosity.

Under these misogynstic pressures, other relationships take on a new value. In place of unsatisfactory love relationships or marriages we are invited to admire loyal servants, true friends, and some kind children. In *Hamlet*, some of these issues come to the fore in the closet scene, Act 3 Scene 4, when Hamlet confronts his mother with her presumed guilt. Having been instructed by his father to "Leave her to heaven/ And to those thorns that in her bosom lodge" (1.5.87-88), Hamlet resolves to "speak daggers to her," though he will "use none" (3.2.395). He is still highly affronted with her behavior, but is also determined to try to bring her to her senses rather than simply humiliate her. She is very resistant at first (as portrayed, for example, by Julie Christie in Kenneth Branagh's recent movie version). She refuses to let her son speak to her like this. After the death of Polonius, however, and in response to Hamlet's insistence that she confront her own complicity in her husband's murder (whatever that degree of complicity may be), Gertrude seemingly begins to listen to what Hamlet has to say about habit—about how easy it is to get into bad habits and so hard to get oneself out again, but not impossible if one works on it a step at a time. "Go not to my uncle's bed," Hamlet urges. "Assume a virtue, if you have it not" (3.4.166-7). Gertrude wonders if Hamlet is simply mad, but seemingly does not listen, and subsequently acts in such a way as to show that she is newly obedient to Hamlet's instruction. He has told her not to give away his secret of being only seemingly mad; she honors that command by lying to her husband when he enters. "Mad as the sea and wind with both contend / Which is the mightier," she tells Claudius in response to his request to know "How does Hamlet?" (4.1.6-8). Later, she disobeys her husband as well, in a significant gesture of loyalty to her son. Claudius orders her, "Gertrude, do not drink", but she drinks the poison anyway: "I will, my lord, I pray you pardon me" (5.2.293-4). She lies and disobeys because her son has begged this loyalty to her, and she has chosen her son over the husband that, as she now begins to understand, is a murderer. Her disobedience is much like that of Emilia in *Othello*, who, having finally comprehended what her husband Iago has done, answers his order that she remain silent by saying, "Tis proper I obey him, but not now" (5.2.203).

Thus, erotic or romantic love in these great tragedies yields pride of place to friendship and to loyalties of parent and child. Hamlet and his mother both die tragically, but they die reconciled; Hamlet has succeeded in winning his mother back from the detested uncle. And with Horatio, Hamlet finds a wonderful consolation in friendship. They love to argue with each other; they respect differences; they refuse to allow worldly consideration to interfere with the disinterestedness of their love for each other.

Here, perhaps, is one more way in which Shakespeare's plays can be brought into the context of current critical discourse, with its New Historicist and feminist concerns, and still honor the play as a central part of the core curriculum. Shakespeare can usefully be seen as a central to the entire matrix of what post-modern criticism is all about. Students, readers, and critics need to keep coming back to these texts in order to explore the kind of rich literary layering of meaning that we all cherish as central to the core experience. Shakespeare does not merely survive; he flourishes today, and not because he offers a respite from contemporary criticism but because he is so able to endow it with critical purpose and insight.

CHAPTER 20

# Prophecy Eclipsed: *Hamlet* as a Tragedy of Knowledge

*William Franke*

To define what is distinctive about knowledge in the humanities, by contrast with what has tended to be the dominant paradigm for knowledge in modern culture, namely, science, it is instructive to consider *Hamlet* as a tragedy of knowledge. The play was written probably in 1600 and at any rate at the opening of the 17th Century, the golden age of the rise of modern science. Its language and imagery are tinged with the new vocabulary and embody the new sensibility and outlook together, and in tension with, the old. Thematically, moreover, *Hamlet* wrestles with the incalculably far-reaching meaning of this transition from an older, traditional *epistème* or general framework for knowledge based on revelation, particularly the biblical revelation of the ultimate ends and context of human life as resting upon a metaphysical order of being, to a scientific world-view in which knowledge, now sought preeminently through the physical senses and their direct perceptions, lacks all transcendent foundation. The tragic loss involved in this transition is made palpable and poignant both in the overarching conception and in the imaginative and expressive textures of the play.

Shakespeare inherited and indeed provided some of the most compelling representations of what has been dubbed "the Elizabethan world-picture," featuring a three-tiered universe reaching both above and below the world accessible to mortal sight into the realms of heaven and hell. This outlook is represented in *Hamlet* as having fallen into crisis and as tragically unable to endure the strain under which it is placed by new perspectives that the emerging culture of the Renaissance is opening, propelled to a considerable degree by the impulses imparted by scientific method and discovery. At issue in *Hamlet,* among other things, is a transition from what we may call the age of prophecy-in which a whole world-order and a future destiny, including an afterlife, were accepted as revealed-to an age of science, where what is true is equated with what can be proved by empirical evidence—'the sensible and true avouch of mine own eyes," as Horatio so vividly puts it.

In the age of prophecy, the most authoritative knowledge was supposed to come from sources higher than the senses. A vision or a spirit could reveal truths that were incapable of being proved by empirical methods. The impetus to the action of revenge, which is the central business of *Hamlet* at the level of plot, comes from just such a prophetic revelation, an apparition from the other world. Hamlet's murdered father comes back from the dead, from the world of eternity, to tell him the truth about how he died and demand from his son that justice be done upon the usurper for his crime. When Hamlet first hears this disclosure he exclaims, "O my prophetic soul!" (1. 5.40). He is evidently saying that he had already inwardly divined the true course of events and their concealed guilt, as if by revelation from a higher source. And in any case, whether as divined or as revealed by the ghost, the kind of knowledge he acquires in connection with his father can aptly be said to be "prophetic' in nature.

And yet this prophetic revelation—his own father come back from the dead to inform him directly of its cause—becomes enmeshed in a web of doubts and eventually even play-acting generated by attempts to test and prove its authenticity. Hamlet is later heard saying, "I'll have grounds more relative than this" (11. 2. 570), which means, of course, even more pertinent circumstantial evidence than he has already. But this statement also ironically says that all the grounds Hamlet is seeking to ascertain can at best be only "relative." By failing to embrace the certainty offered him by the actual presence of the father speaking directly to him as a voice of essentially divine revelation, he condemns himself to having no sufficient but only "relative" grounds no matter how far he carries his investigation. Of course, the uncertainty is deeply rooted in Hamlet's character and even more deeply in the emerging character of the new, Renaissance individual as grounded in an objective, material world and as losing its bearings in a transcendent, spiritual reality. In this way, *Hamlet is* dramatizing far-reaching shifts in the whole nature and foundation of knowledge that are being experienced in Shakespeare's time.

The eclipse of prophetic vision ushers in an age of skepticism represented from the play's outset especially by Horatio, who is unbelieving with regard to "this thing," the "apparition" of the dead king Hamlet reported by Bernardo and Marcellus, holding it for nothing more than their "fantasy" (1. 1.23ff). Horatio's rational suspicion of superstition is but one expression of a crisis of traditional belief in all sectors, not only religious but also political. The general cultural predicament is one of a defunct moral and spiritual order. On a political plain, it translates into the crisis of state noted at the outset as following upon the death of the king, indeed in Denmark and in Norway alike. The deceased kings Hamlet and Fortinbras are chivalric figures who had engaged in a noble duel "by a sealed compact / Well ratified by law and heraldry" (1.1). They are succeeded respectively by the usurper scorned by Hamlet as "[a] king of shreds and patches" (111.4.104) and by the "young Fortinbras" who has "Sharked up a list of lawless resolutes" (1. 1.98). Against the former generation of kings' lawful and valiant warring, the present marshal maneuvers are described rather as an unruly mob's marauding. These are the earliest signals of the general moral degeneration that upsets Hamlet and provokes his scathing eloquence.

Hierarchies of value in the traditional medieval world-view depended upon a supreme and divine good, namely, God, and an animate universe of angelically guided spheres, and without this the whole structure of the moral order and of the social world, no less than of the physical cosmos, collapses. 'The world is out of joint." "It is the times." "The times now give it proof." *Hamlet* shows extreme sensitivity to its own time as a time of crisis. Formerly this world, both natural and social, fit into and was supported by a cosmic order. Hamlet evokes this old world-picture, become, however, stale and tacky like discarded theatre scenery, in describing his sense of the rottenness and corruption of life as he experiences it in the present:

> this goodly frame the earth seems to me a sterile promontory, this most excellent canopy the air, look you, this brave oerhanging firmament, this majestical roof fretted with golden fire, why it appeareth nothing to me but a foul and pestilent congregation of vapors. What a piece of work is a man, how noble in reason, how infinite in faculties, in form and moving, how express and admirable in action, how like an angel in apprehension, how like a god: the beauty of the world, the paragon of animals. And yet to me, what is this quintessence of dust?  Man delights not me ... (49.2.287-97).

Man here is no longer 'crowned with glory and honor," as in Psalm 8. Although conceived as an endlessly wondrous creation, precisely as in the biblical vision, yet he is reducible to his material substance, and that itself to mere ashes. The 'goodly frame of earth" and 'excellent canopy" of the air are likewise reducible to mere inert elements. The majesty of the creation has fled. Its material reduction has undermined the spiritual vision of transcendent values as inscribed everywhere in the visible universe. The excellence of God's name is no longer manifest in all the earth. Hamlet frames his discourse within the old order of earth and sky and man, with his place of special prominence in the hierarchy, but all the magic of it is gone. It depended upon a transcendental order that conferred a radiance from above. When taken in and for themselves rather than as a manifestation of divinity, the physical phenomena of the heavens are just a foul and pestilent congregation of vapors, just as man without any relation to immortal being, no longer in God's image, is but "this quintessence of dust."

Of course, Hamlet still has one foot in the former, nobler world of theological and chivalric tradition as his very insufferance of the present evil age indicates. He is possessed by the vision of the prophetic past which haunts him in the shape of his father's ghost. That this sensibility is no longer commensurate to the corrupt and wider world in which he lives determines his demise. Such a nature as his cannot survive, neither psychically nor physically, in the Denmark Hamlet himself describes, and bitterly denounces. Thus, although Hamlet has a spiritual revelation (a direct disclosure from a spirit), and to this extent remains in touch with the older epistemological order, he is not able to sustain belief in it. He too is complicit in the degenerate new order, as his unsparing self-deprecation acknowledges, for example, in the soliloquy beginning "O, what a rogue and peasant slave am I!" (11.2.516). The immediate presence of his father's spirit fades to a spectrous appearance of a ghost, for Hamlet, eminently representing the skeptical consciousness of the new age, almost ceases to believe in all but material reality. Correspondingly, all his nobler values are shaken. He falls tragically into a world of sheer materiality, brute fact, rough manners, and political Machiavellianism. He does still express an ideal vision of love, for example, in his statement that his father was "so loving to my mother, / That he might not beteem the winds of heaven / Visit her face too roughly" (1.2.140-42). But even this very tender tone of filial reverence eventually sinks, in the course of the crisis that he is represented as undergoing, to the level of raw sexual innuendo concerning "c(o)untry matters" (3.2.105).

In the harsh, disenchanted new perspective, everything that was able once to give clear purpose to life turns obscure. Even the overwhelming presence of the father, at first observed by all together on the watch, and giving Hamlet irresistible resolve and purpose, becomes dubious and apocryphal. Hamlet lives essentially in a region of doubt, where clear, unambiguous revelations are a thing that can only be imagined as having existed in the past or that are staged precisely in their process of disappearance. The presence of the father internally in Hamlet's spirit is fundamentally troubled and vulnerable to being declared illusion. He has to *write down* the command enunciated by the ghost of his father, thus giving it the form of an external, material entity ("My tables—meet it is I set it down"—1.4.107). This substitutes for the immediate spiritual presence of the father a concrete empirical object, a positive existence he can be sure of but one which is no longer the bearer of unequivocal testimony, no longer the immediate presence of the father's spirit but truly only a 'sheeted" ghost, a blatant artifice. The problems of doubt and delay are in this way shown to derive from epistemological conditions enacted in the opening scenes giving the impulse to the action and setting up the plot of the play.

Hamlet's world as a whole is turned to irreality by its being out of joint with the metaphysical order that alone was able to guarantee and found moral ideals. Hamlet's heart is disposed to believe in these noble values, but his intellect has become skeptical, like that of his fellow-student, Horatio. This disunity within him and the disintegration of the moral universe to which he ideally belongs engender a split that becomes virtually, whether literally or not, madness. Given the constraints of a corrupt social world, only in madness can the dictates of the heart and the truth perceived by the soul be expressed. It is the "prophetic soul" within him and its incompatibility with the world around him that at least incipiently drive Hamlet mad (though at least sometimes he is in control of it, as when he says that he is mad but "north northwest" and again "mad but in craft").

Despite his innate idealism, Hamlet is deeply submerged in a material vision of the world, as is the modern age that is here seen in its birth. Among the many casual, apparently innocuous indications of his falling under the influence of the new, mechanistic, scientific outlook replacing the spiritual vision of the Middle Ages is the closing formula of his letter to Ophelia: 'Thine ever-more, most dear lady, whilst this machine is to him" (49.2.22-23). The machine metaphor shows itself here as coming into vogue to describe what formerly were sacrosanct mysteries of divine creation. Another telling sign, this time specifically of Hamlet's infection by the moral relativism that follows the collapse of the metaphysical world-order, is his remark, 'there is nothing either good or bad, but thinking makes it so" (49.2.243-44). The emphasis on the times, on the changing fashions of London theatre, for example, also indirectly indexes the demise of stable, hallowed values as a newer, crasser logic of commerce and expediency, devoid of morality, usurps their place.

*Hamlet* still embodies the values of the medieval world, but now in a new age of skepticism these values are in crisis. Young Hamlet has studied in Wittenberg, learned certainly about the latest scientific discoveries and been exposed to new cultural currents. He is a youth and as such represents the future. But the play concerns his relation to the past, embodied in the form of his father-or rather, not quite embodied, since his father has become a ghost. Hamlet, however, is not sure he believes in his father. He loses touch with the transcendental ground of his existence and with the noble past communicated through tradition.

These remarks are meant to indicate the lines of interpretation that would guide a comprehensive interpretation of *Hamlet* as a humanities text so as to illustrate the distinctive kind of knowledge that can be aquired through this type of study. They suggest that *Hamlet* itself begins recording the story of how in the modern age, beginning with the Renaissance, humanistic knowledge is endangered in ways relating to the rise of science as the dominant paradigm of knowledge. This is true today especially in the university where humanities and science share the liberal arts curriculum and are studied together, despite their, in some respects, radically different methods and goals. A text like *Hamlet* demands to be taught in such a way as to emphasize the relational, contextual nature of knowledge—which is traditionally projected as relation to an other world and which literature is perhaps best equipped to exemplify and render intelligible to students in a culture increasingly geared to the processing of knowledge as information. Hamlet demonstrates in an eminent manner the risk of loss of traditional, unscientific forms of knowledge and the tragedy that this entails. Core courses have a responsibility to resist this result by historically circumscribing scientific knowledge and rendering evident its limits and by proposing traditional alternative models for human awareness and inquiry.

## Note

1. E. M. W. Tillyard, *The Elizabethan World Picture* (New York: MacMillan, 1944). See also Arthur O. Lovejoy, *7he Great Chain of Being: A Study of the History of an Idea* (New York,: Harper & Row, 1960); William James lecture at Harvard, 1936). Quotations of *Hamlet* are from the Norton Critical Edition, ed. Cyrus Hoy (New York, 1963), with consultation of the text in the *Riverside Shakespeare,* text ed. G. Blackmore Evans (Boston: Houghton Mifflin Co., 1974).

CHAPTER 21

# Speech in Dumbness: Female Eloquence and Male Authority in *The Winter's Tale*

*Ellen Belton*

The notion of women's verbal incontinence is proverbial in English Renaissance drama (Jardine 1983, 103-140; Woodbridge 1984, 189-207). In Shakespeare, however, it is often deployed ironically, as in the scene in which Hotspur uses women's reputed inability to keep a secret as his excuse for not telling his wife where he is going *(Henry the Fourth,* 1.2.3.). (It is Hotspur who cannot control his tongue, not Lady Percy.) But though injunctions to women to be silent are common in Shakespeare, so are exhortations to speak. Such exhortations encourage women to use language but in a manner clearly circumscribed by masculine restrictions and inscribed with the signs of masculine hegemony (Belsey 1985, 149-191; Callaghan 1989, 74-89). One of the most notable and absolute silences in Shakespeare, however, is the silence of Hermione that begins in Act 3 of The *Winter's Tale* and extends almost to the end of Act 5. Harvey Rovine says that this silence at first represents Hermione's "tragic separation from Leontes," later her desire to "entice" him, and finally her joy at "being reconciled with Leontes and ending her sixteen years of silent humiliation" (Rovine 1985, 50-51). Valerie Traub, on the other hand, reads Hermione's stillness as part of a strategy by which "women who are perceived by men as erotically threatening are monumentalized, their erotic warmth transformed into the cold, static form of jewels, statues, and corpses" (Traub, 18). In my view, Hermione's "speech in dumbness" is eloquent not merely of her own emotions and desires on the one hand and not merely of an authorial strategy of containment on the other but of the failure of language itself in a patriarchal society. To appreciate the full significance of this mute eloquence we must look back to the way language works, and doesn't work, in this play.

*The Winter's* Tale opens with a pair of seemingly playful contests that both question and reaffirm the authority of language, the first between Archidamus and Camillo (1.1), the second between Polixenes and Leontes (1.2). In each, while claiming that words themselves or their own mastery of words is inadequate, the participants struggle to outdo one another in verbal compliment and courtesy, while attributing to one another the proficiency they themselves lack. "There is no tongue that moves, none, in the world, / So soon as yours could win me," says Polixenes (1.2.20-21), as he denies Leontes' request that he extend his visit; these words simultaneously acknowledge his friend's mastery of language and demonstrate its insufficiency. This formulation of discourse as a game or a conflict whose object is to "win" is a key to the inadequacy of language in a patriarchal society, suggesting as it does that the goal of using language is to monopolize or preempt meaning rather than to share and disseminate it.

Leontes' failure to change Polixenes' mind prompts his appeal to Hermione in the terms suggested by Polixenes' refusal: "Tongue-tied our queen? Speak you" (27). These words, the first he has addressed to her, contain an important contradiction, one that Leontes himself fails to recognize. On the one hand, strictures against feminine eloquence in Renaissance texts honor women precisely for being "tongue-tied" (Maclean 1980, 61-64). On the other hand, Leontes uses this term pejoratively here, implying that *by not* speaking Hermione has failed in her obligation as a wife, hostess, and queen. His words are not just an invitation to speak then; they are a command. But *by* obeying her husband, Hermione is evoking the tradition that equates verbal freedom in women with sexual promiscuity. Leontes applauds and encourages Hermione's speech, but his words of seeming approval are tainted *by* his culturally determined ambivalence. "Is he won yet?" he asks, but when Hermione replies, "He'll stay, my lord," his comment is: "At my request he would not" (86-87).

Although Hermione has done exactly what Leontes asked of her, we notice an incipient resentfulness and disapproval in Leontes' response.

Perhaps he is jealous of Hermione's eloquence and of the superior power indicated *by* her having "won" Polixenes' acquiescence. Even more ominous is Leontes' answer when Hermione forces him to confess that she has "twice said well" (90):

> Why, that was when
> Three crabbed months had sour'd themselves to death
> Ere I could make thee open thy white hand
> And clap thyself my love.
> (101-104)

Although the onset of Leontes jealous madness has not yet been revealed to the audience, we notice the harshness of the phrases Three crabbed months and sour'd themselves to death, the contemptuousness of Clap thyself my love, the lurking sexual innuendo in Ere I could make thee open thy white hand. Leontes apparent approval of Hermione s speaking well is infected *by* an underlying disapproval of her mastery of language and a suspiciousness of the sexual promiscuity such mastery implies.

Leontes' anxiety about his own authority over language *leads* him defensively to claim for himself a privileged position in interpreting and evaluating the signifying practices of others. In the ensuing sequence where Hermione and Polixenes talk apart while Leontes observes and comments on their behavior, Leontes obstinately and irrationally misreads courtesy as courtship and becomes convinced of Hermione and Polixenes' guilt. But Leontes' jealousy, though it masks itself as sexual in nature, is as much about generativity as it is about adultery. The remainder of the first half of the play (Acts 1-3) may be read as a contest, whose site, like the playful courtesy contests of the play's opening moments, is social discourse but whose goal is the appropriation of language as a sign of generative power.

The debate in Acts 1-3 centers on Hermione's right and the right of her supporters to speak and on Leontes' attempts to thwart or suppress all speech on her behalf. At a deeper level the passionate speech of Paulina and Hermione, like the long silence that follows it, lays claim to a woman's right to construct and legitimize through language her own version of reality. "He must be told on't, and he shall," says Paulina upon learning of the birth of Hermione's child.

> The office
> Becomes a woman best; I'll take't upon me.
> If I prove honey-mouth'd, let my tongue blister,

And never to my red-look'd anger be
The trumpet any more.
(2.2.31-35)

As Hermione and her supporters outdo Leontes in words, Leontes is
driven in self-defense to challenge the authority of language itself, including
even the sacred speech acts of Apollo. His refusal to accept the word of
Camillo, of Antigonus, of Paulina, of Hermione herself, and finally of
Apollo, all of whom attest to his wife's innocence, enacts an almost ritualized
rejection of language and indeed of meaning. In response, Hermione takes
refuge in silence, a form of discourse that must be read, like Cordelials
negations in *Kina Lear*, as protest. In a world where language, even the
sacred speech of the oracle, is branded as untrustworthy, the most eloquent
speech is silence.

In the sheepshearing scene in Act 4, we find a woman's speech once again
firmly enclosed within patriarchal boundaries, as Perdita's welcomes her
guests at the bidding of her adoptive father. Perditals submissiveness would
appear to lend support to Peter Erickson's argument that in The *Winter's Tale*
women are "a powerful force for transforming the men, yet their power as
facilitators is used to reform rather than to transcend the patriarchal framework" (Erickson 1985, 167). Viviana Comensoli takes this view as well
when she argues that the function of most female characters who, like
Hermione, "unequivocally challenge the dictum of silence . . . is to expose
the transgressions of a male who is usually central to the action" (Comensoli
1989, 255). Traub also makes this point, arguing that "assertions of [female]
agency" in Shakespeare are "still circumscribed by a patriarchal discourse
that terms Ophelia's tuneful accusations of sexual infidelity 'mad,' and places
Emilia's and Paulina's resistance to oppression within the iconography of
'shrew'" (Traub, 49).

Still, it is important not to undervalue the power of female agency in this
play. Paulina (and, through her, Hermione) maintains and consolidates her
power in the second half of the play, a power that includes dictating when
and how Leontes uses language. "I like your silence," she says, when
Leontes and the others first behold the supposed statue of Hermione. "It the
more shows off / Your wonder. But yet speak" (5.3.21-22). One aspect of
Paulina's role as facilitator that deserves special attention is her complicity
with the play's author in withholding not only from Leontes but from the
audience the knowledge that the report of Hermione's death is false. This
omission of crucial information, which is virtually without precedent in
Shakespeare, further destabilizes the spectator's as well as Leontes' assump-

tions about language and meaning. By forcing Leontes to depend on her as his interpreter, Paulina assumes a role that closely parallels that of the presenter in a masque, whose task is to mediate between the non-speaking performers and the aristocratic (often kingly) spectators. This role, which in Elizabethan and Jacobean entertainments is performed by a man, sometimes even by the author himself, vividly illustrates Paulina's claim to the generative power of authorship and to the possibility of rewriting the notion of authorship as belonging to both sexes.

The answer to the apparent contradiction between the representations of feminine discourse in the sheepshearing scene and the statue scene lies in the relationship among the three principal women, who are seen together for the first time at the end of the play. A remarkable phenomenon in the reconciliation scene is that Hermione never speaks directly to her husband. Though we are told by the observers that she embraces Leontes and "hangs about his neck" (112), she addresses no words to him, speaking instead only to Perdita. Perdita too, we notice, never once speaks directly to her father, in spite of the fact that they are in two important scenes together (5.1 and 5.3). With Paulina's leave, however, she does kneel and ask the statue of Hermione for her blessing (5.3.42-46). Bruce W. Young underscores the significance of the fact that in this play, as in *Richard III* and All's *Well That Ends* Well, the parental blessing, a ritual commonly associated with the father, is conferred by the mother (Young, 187-188). Young sees the mother's blessing of her daughter as "a reciprocal act: Hermione calls for heavenly grace to descend upon her daughter, yet Perdita conveys grace—love, regenerative power—in return. It is as if Perdita, especially now that Hermione can see and touch her, brings the resurrection of her mother to completion, giving birth to the woman who bore her" (Young, 187). In effect, Hermione's recovery of her voice is precipitated, with Paulina's help, by the recovery of her daughter.

The power of women speaking to and for one another is a vitalizing principle throughout this play. The miraculous reunions in Act 5 can be read not only as a reconstitution of the family, a restoration of male friendship and trust, and a reestablishment of political order and stability, but as an affirmation of the instrumentality of feminine discourse in bringing about social and personal renewal. It is not surprising, then, that Perdita's hesitancy with words, Hermione's silence, and Paulina's tongue-lashings and lies fail to conform to traditional male-centered ways of signifying. Seeking alternatives to Leontes' destructive, destabilizing use of language, these women are compelled to experiment with new discursive practices. Naming their world with wonder, with trepidation, and with pleasure, Perdita, Hermione, and Paulina are also reclaiming that world by forging new connections between speech acts and meaning.

In the last act of the play men submit to and even imitate feminine discursive practice. "I make a broken delivery of the business," says the First Gentleman, describing the reunion of Leontes and Camillo. "... There was speech in their dumbness, language in their very gesture. They look'd as they had heard of a world ransom'd, or one destroyed. A notable passion of wonder appeared in them" (5.2.10-18). This involuntary adoption by men of signifying practices traditionally associated with women, such as "broken" speech or silence, demonstrates the instrumentality of feminine speech acts in recreating the world that had been lost.

Such confirmation of the importance of female generativity counters Erickson's argument for patriarchal repossession. What I think Erickson's analysis misses is that the signifying practice shaped by Hermione, Paulina, and Perdita is inclusive, rather than exclusive. Hermione has never denied the right of men to authorship, as her appeal to the ultimate patriarchal authority, the oracle of Apollo, attests. She pleads only for the opportunity to share that right. Even acknowledging the fact that in the closing speech of the play Leontes reasserts a measure of patriarchal authority, we are unable to ignore the centrality of feminine speech acts to the play's denouement. The difference between Leontes' view of verbal generativity and the view espoused by Hermione, Paulina, and Perdita is that to the women language does not have to be a contested site, and eloquence need not be appropriated by one sex for the purpose of maintaining its power over the other. "I'll use that tongue I have," declares Paulina:

> If wit flow from It
> As boldness from my bosom, let
> It not be doubted I shall do good.
> (2.3.52-54)

## Works Cited

Bamber, Linda. 1982. *Comic Women, Tragic Men: A Study of Gender and Genre in Shakespeare*. Stanford: Stanford University Press.

Belsey, Catherine. 1985. *The Subject of Tragedy: Identity and Difference in Renaissance* Drama. London: Methuen.

Berggren, Paula. 1980. The woman's part: Female sexuality as power in Shakespeare's plays. In *The Woman's Part: Feminist Criticism of Shakespeare*, eds. Carolyn Ruth Swift Lenz, Gayle Greene, and Carol Thomas Neely, 18-31. Urbana: University of Illinois Press.

Callaghan, Dympna. 1989. *Woman and Gender in Renaissance Tragedy: A Study of "King Lear," "Othello," "The Duchess of Malfill and "The White Devil."* Atlantic Highlands, N.J.: Humanities Press International.

Comensoli, Viviana. 1989. Gender and eloquence in Dekker's Honest *Whore, Part II. English Studies in Canada*, 15, 3 (September): 249-62.

Dash, Irene G. 1981. *Woodina, Wedding, and Power: Women in Shakespeare's Plays*. New York: Columbia University Press.

Erickson, Peter. 1985. *Patriarchal Structures in Shakespeare's Drama*. Berkeley: University of California Press.

Gohlke, Madelon. 1980. "I wooed thee with my sword": Shakespeare's tragic paradigms. In *The Woman's Part: Feminist Criticism of Shakespeare*, ed. Carolyn Ruth Swift

Lenz, Gayle Greene, and Carol Thomas Neely, 150-70. Urbana: University of Illinois Press.

Jardine, Lisa. 1983. *Still Hariping on Daughters: Women and Drama in the Age of Shakespeare*. Totowa, N.J.: Barnes & Noble.

Maclean, Ian. 1980. The *Renaissance Notion of Woman*. Cambridge: Cambridge University Press.

Montrose, Louis Adrian. 1986. A *Midsummer Night's Dream* and the shaping fantasies of Elizabethan culture: Gender, power, form. In *Rewriting the Renaissance: The Discourses of Sexual Difference in Early Modern Europe*, eds. Margaret W. Ferguson, Maureen Quilligan, and Nancy J. Vickers, 65-87. Chicago: University of Chicago Press.

Rovine, Harvey. 1985. *Silence in Shakespeare: Drama, Power, and Gender*. Ann Arbor: UMI Research Press.

Shakespeare, William. 1936. The *Complete Works of Shakeakespeare* ed. George Lyman Kittredge. Boston: Ginn & Co.

Traub, Valerie. 1992. *Desire and Anxiety: Circulations of Sexuality in Shakespearean Drama*. New York: Routledge.

Woodbridge, Linda. 1984. *Women and the Enalish Renaissance: Literature and the Nature of Womankind, 1540-1620*. Urbana: University of Illinois Press.

Young, Bruce W. 1992. Ritual as an instrument of grace: parental blessings in Richard *III, All's Well That Ends Well*, and *The Winter's Tale*. In *True Rites and Maimed Rites: Ritual and Anti-Ritual in Shakespeare and His Aae*, ed. Linda Woodbridge and Edward Berry, *169-200*. Urbana: University of Illinois Press.

CHAPTER 22

# Forgiving Prospero: The Audience's "Rarer Action" in The Tempest

*Barrett Fisher*

Why does Shakespeare's *Tempest* end with Prospero's direct address to the audience?

> Now my charms are all o'erthrown
> And what strength I have's mine own,
> Which is most faint. Now 'tis true
> I must be here confined by you,
> Or sent to Naples. Let me not,
> Since I have my dukedom got,
> And pardoned the deceiver, dwell
> In this bare island by your spell;
> But release me from these bands
> With the help of your good hands.
> Gentle breath of yours my sails
> Must fill, or else my project fails,
> Which was to please. Now I want
> Spirits to enforce, art to enchant;

And my ending is despair
Unless I be reliev'd by prayer,
Which pierces so, that it asaults
Mercy itself and frees all faults.
As you from crimes would pardoned be,
Let your indulgence set me free.[1]

It is a commonplace observation that the physical conditions of performance in the Elizabethan theater a tight, enclosing auditorium with a thrust stage, resulting in the close proximity of its audience to actors performing in full daylight led to such dramatic conventions as asides and soliloquies, thus blurring the distinction between the fictive characters playing on stage and the real people watching in the audience. Unlike playwrights in the realist tradition, for whom the proscenium arch stage creates an invisible fourth wall between the play and its spectators, Shakespeare was not particularly concerned with maintaining the illusion of a self-contained world of imaginary men and women who strut and fret their hour upon the stage, entirely unaware of their contingent existence as both characters and actors. Rather, in direct appeals to the audience, his players acknowledge that the action in which they participate is (in Hamlet s words) a fiction or a dream which could not exist without the audience s cooperation and indulgence. In *Henry V*, for example, Shakespeare modifies the classical technique of choric commentary by creating a character named Chorus who narrates the action and invites the audience in his Prologue to Piece out our imperfections with your thoughts : O, pardon! since a crooked figure may / Attest in it little place a million; / And let us, ciphers to this great accompt, / On your imaginary forces work. / Suppose within the girdles of these walls / Are now confin d two mighty monarchies, . . . Chorus returns in an epilogue which recognizes that the story is not concluded (history has been recounted only Thus far ) and concedes the playwright s lack of skill ( with rough and all-unable pen,/ O u r bending author hath pursu d the story ) in order to crave the audience s indulgence: In your fair minds let this acceptance take. In the epilogue which concludes *As You Like It*, the speaker Rosalind concedes that she is departing from the theatrical custom of the day ( It is not the fashion to see the lady in the epilogue ), acknowledges that the female part has been played by a boy ( If I were a woman I would kiss as many of you as had beards that pleas d me ), and ur ges the audience to approve the play: I am not furnish d like a beggar [a self-conscious reference to the character s costume], therefore, to beg will not become me: my way is to conjure you; . . . I charge you, O women, for the love you bear to men, to like as much of this play as please

you: and I charge you, O men, for the love you bear to women , . . . that
between you and the women the play may please. At the end of *A Midsummer Night s Dream*, in a speech which closely parallels Prospero s, Puck
suggests that the play is a Chinese-box of sorts the dream of the lovers
in the woods is contained within the waking world of Athens which is contained within the play called *A Midsummer Night s Dream* which is contained
within the waking world of the Globe Theater[2] and that its success depends
on the kindness of the audience: If we shadows have offended, / Think but
this, and all is mended, / That you have but slumber d here / While these visions did appear. He asks the audience s pardon and twice promises to
 amend, concluding with a gesture which eliminates the physical as well
as the conventional barrier between play and audience: Give me your hands,
if we be friends, / And Robin shall restore amends. [3]

These examples provide three answers to my initial question. First,
Prospero addresses the audience because Shakespeare is a metatheatrical
poet who frequently makes the conditions and conventions of performance
a theme of his plays. In this respect, Shakespeare is more postmodern than
realist in his aesthetic; his art often thematizes its artifice, and is not afraid
to call attention to itself as an imaginative construct. Second, the direct
address to the audience often provides the formal closure required by the
structure of the play; *Henry V*, for example, is a frame-narrative, beginning
and ending with Chorus. Strictly speaking, however, neither the comedies
nor *The Tempest* appears to require such closure; in fact, one could argue that
the epilogues in each of these cases are intended not to close the play formally as an artistic whole but to indicate its incompleteness without the
audience's gracious contribution. (Actually, this is the case in *Henry V* as
well; we are asked not only to pardon the playwright's efforts, but to fill in
the rest of the historical events between the period depicted by the play and
the time of its performance.) And this leads to my third answer, and the main
point I want to argue in the rest of this paper: the epilogue of *The Tempest*
creates an "open" aesthetic structure in order to invite thematic closure or
resolution. As in the other plays cited, but to an even greater degree, *The
Tempest* creates a role which the audience must play in order for the play to
conclude. Because Shakespeare leaves everyone on the island, including
Prospero, the final action of the story (Prospero's return to Naples, the actual
nuptials of Miranda and Ferdinand, which in the comedies would be performed on stage), is left to our imaginations. But, Prospero argues, if we do
not exercise our imaginations in transporting the characters back to Italy, then
they remain stranded on the island, and all of his efforts are in vain. He has
surrendered his magic powers; he has released Ariel from his control and

the only magic which remains is the only magic which has existed all along: the magic of imagination. If we do not exercise that imagination, then Prospero has failed to please us and we have failed to learn the lesson of the play: magic is to be used to bring about moral regeneration, both of those who use it (as Prospero has done in confronting the "three men of sin") and those who are subject to it (as is every other human being on the island, though not all are morally changed by it). Prospero's epilogue reveals that magic is a metaphor for both imagination and grace; the audience is urged to discover and use its own magic in order to provide a good end for the characters and to forgive the players for any shortcomings. Paradoxically, however, the audience's use of this god-like function depends on its recognition of its own human frailty: "As you from crimes would pardon'd be / Let your indulgence set me free."

My argument, then, is that the action of *The Tempest* has a double purpose: while Prospero pursues a scheme to rescue himself from the island through a series of magic tricks in which the action (the tempest in 1.1, the banquet in 3.3, and the masque in 4.1) is revealed as a contrivance by a playwright (Prospero) intended to teach a lesson (Miranda witnessing the tempest, "the three men of sin" tempted by the banquet, and Miranda and Ferdinand entertained by the masque), Shakespeare is teaching his audience how they should respond to his theater. His conclusion, embodied in Prospero's epilogue, suggests a conjunction of imaginative and ethical action: to use one's imagination to "set [Prospero] free" is also to take one's own moral measure and recognize the need for pardon in our own lives. As Hamlet tells Polonius after the latter promises to "use" the visiting players at Elsinore "according to their desert": "God's bodkin, man, much better: use every man after his desert, and who shall scape whipping? Use them after your own honor and dignity—the less they deserve, the more merit is in your bounty" (2.2.527-32). Duke Theseus in *A Midsummer Night's Dream* counsels a similar graciousness to the rude mechanicals who perform their play so ineptly: "If we imagine no worse of them than they of themselves, they may pass for excellent men" (5.1.215-216). Earlier in this scene, Theseus tells Hippolyta that "The lunatic, the lover, and the poet / Are of imagination all compact" (5.1.7-8), but in *The Tempest* Shakespeare extends the power of the imagination by implying that his audience must recognize that their imagination has both an aesthetic and an ethical dimension. To help Prospero back to Milan, to imagine the action of the play as completed, is also to be gracious; it is to be most god-like in recognizing our own need for mercy.[4]

The play's dual purpose thus creates a dual experience for the audience. As we watch the three scenes just mentioned—tempest, banquet, and masque—we see them the first time through our own eyes and a second time through the eyes of the character or characters for whom these spectacles are primarily intended. The reaction of the characters and the instructions or rebukes they receive are intended for us as well; we discover at the end that the entire play has been an object lesson in how to respond to the play itself. Just as the characters then rejoin the "real world" of Italy after learning these lessons, so too do we then rejoin the real world outside the theater; just as Prospero has used his magic arts to teach and acquire wisdom, so too do we use our imaginations to receive pleasure and bestow (and receive) mercy. But it is Prospero who speaks at the end because ultimately his is the greatest lesson: during the course of the play he does not simply use his magic, but he also faces (and overcomes) the opportunity to abuse it as well as the temptation to retain it. By "abjuring" this "rough magic," breaking his staff and drowning his books, he reveals that he has embraced the greater magic of grace, and becomes our example to do the same. In speaking of his enemies, he says, "Though with their high wrongs I am strook to th' quick, / Yet, with my nobler reason, Against my fury / Do I take part. The rarer action is / In virtue than in vengeance" (5.1.25-28). With Prospero as an example of how to treat enemies, how can we deny him if he appeals to us as a friend?

The play begins with a tempest; in a scene of confusion and chaos, a ship founders in a dreadful storm, conflicts between different social classes arise, and everyone prepares to sink—and possibly die. As in a film, however, Shakespeare shifts from this "close-up" on board to a long view from the shore, where Prospero and his daughter, Miranda, watch "the wild waters in this roar," as Miranda describes it, adding: "The sky it seems would pour down stinking pitch, / But that the sea, mounting to th' welkin's cheek, / Dashes the fire out" (1.2.2-5). Even in Miranda's description the audience's imaginative participation is already required; the limited technical resources of the Elizabethan stage would certainly not provide the special effects necessary to create awe and fear in its spectators. Important though Miranda's words are in helping to create the scene, her speech serves the greater purpose of telling us how to react to what we have just seen. In fact, this reaction depends upon an imagination which can supply the images suggested by Miranda's words and place the observer in the position of those suffering on the ship:

O! I have suffered
With those that I saw suffer! A brave vessel
(Who had, no doubt, some noble creature in her)
Dashed all to pieces! O, the cry did knock

Against my very heart. Poor souls, they perished.
Had I been any God of power, I would
Have sunk the sea within the earth or ere
It should the good ship so have swallowed, and
The fraughting souls within her. (1.2.5-13)

Prospero s art (which Miranda ironically wishes she possessed in order to prevent the spectacle in fact created by that art) also provides the first óccasion for instruction of the audience in the commendable use of the imagination. Miranda imagines herself with those in danger, leading to compassion; she imagines what she would do if she had the power of a god, leading to consternation or amazement because she lacks that power . Prospero tells her that he has done nothing, but in care of thee (1.2.16), but Shakespeare s care toward the audience is equally great; as the scene unfolds and Prospero launches into an extended plot exposition, it beomes clear that Miranda is serving in part as the audience s representative on stage. Granted that she is both ignorant and naive at times, yet her initial reaction to the tempest and her active listening to her father s tale encourage us to participate in the drama as it develops. Several times during Prospero s speech she interrupts him with exclamations which reveal how fully she imagines the events he relates and how greatly she sympathizes with his suffering: O the heavens! ; Alack, for pity! ; Alack! what trouble /    Was I then to you! (1.2.1 16, 132, 151-52). Throughout this scene Miranda shows us that exercising the imagination can lead to feelings of compassion.

In act I we also learn of Prospero's opportunity: due to a combination of luck and fate his enemies (his brother Antonio, who usurped his dukedom, Alonso, the king of Naples, with whom Antonio allied himself, and Sebastian, Alonso's treacherous brother) have come within the range of his power. In act III he commands Ariel to present a banquet intended to test their imaginations and reveal their guilt. When the banquet appears, each man is amazed but credulous; in this metatheatrical moment, Shakespeare draws attention to his own artifice, for the pantomime on which the characters comment is also being played for us. Again, the stage effects are technically inadequate to the actual representation, so we take our cues from the characters' comments. Sebastian says: "Now I will believe / That there are unicorns; that in Arabia / There is one tree, the phoenix' throne, one phoenix / At this hour reigning there" and Antonio adds: "I'll believe both; /And what does else want credit, come to me, / And I'll be sworn 'tis true" (3.3.21-25). Sebastian and Antonio assent to the reality of the illusion, but that reaction is not in itself virtuous.[5] Beguilement is not Prospero's only goal; as the

responses of Gonzalo and Alonso indicate, this spectacle is also intended to
sharpen moral judgment. Gonzalo characterizes the "people of this island"
(so he interprets the spirits) as "of monstrous shape, yet note / Their manners are more gentle, kind, than of / Our human generation you shall find
/ Many, nay, almost any" (3.3.30-34). Alonso agrees that the banquet expresses "a kind / Of excellent dumb discourse" (3.3.38-39). In the latter two
responses, Gonzalo and Alonso indicate a willingness to inquire into new
experiences to discover their deeper implications; while Antonio and
Sebastian are concerned with the rather practical question of veracity (what
they see appears to confirm the strange tales of travelers), their companions
are concerned with meaning and even moral implication. Because Ariel does
not confront them with their sin until they approach the banquet, Prospero's
goal must in some way require this banquet. Obviously, the men are arrested
(in both senses of the word) by what they see, but it is the stimulation of the
imagination which is intended to lead them to a confrontation with their
moral failure.

As they approach the table to eat, the banquet disappears and Ariel addresses them "like a harpy"[6]:

> You are three men of sin, whom Destiny,
> That hath to instrument this lower world
> And what is in't, the never-surfeited sea
> Has caus'd to belch up you; and on this island
> Where man doth not inhabit—you amongst men
> Being most unfit to live. . ..
>     But remember
> (For that's my business to you) that you three
> From Milan did supplant good Prospero,
> Exposed unto the sea (which hath requit it)
> Him and his innocent child; for which foul deed
> The powers, delaying (not forgetting), have
> Incensed the seas and shores—yea, all the creatures,
> Against your peace. (3.3.53-58, 68-75)

It is not insignificant that of the three men of sin (among whom Gonzalo
is not included), only Alonso understands Ariel s speech: O, it is monstrous!
monstrous! / Methought the billows spoke, and told me of it; / The wind did
sing it to me, and the thunder, / That deep and dreadul organ-pipe,
pronounc d / The name of Prosper; it did base my trespass (3.3.95-99).
While Sebastian and Antonio resolve to fight the legions of fiends,

Alonso makes the connection between this wonder they have seen, and his connivance at the usurpation of Prospero and cruel banishment of him and his infant daughter. If Miranda shows us imagination turned outward in compassion for the suffering of others, Alonso shows its potential to turn our eyes inward to confront our own guilt.[7]

In act IV Prospero once again makes use of Ariel to prepare a third spectacle, but unlike the first two this does not play a direct part in his larger plan. Whereas the tempest became an occasion for imaginative compassion and the banquet a stimulus to imaginative self-examination, the masque, which is presented largely as pleasurable entertainment, becomes an occasion for a brief philosophical lesson on the imaginary nature of reality itself. Actually, it is not entirely accurate to say that the masque conceals no ulterior motive on Prospero's part: like any responsible father, he is quite concerned that Ferdinand not take any pre-marital liberties with Miranda, so he offers the masque as a wholesome pastime; in addition, the spirits (in the guise of Juno, Iris, and Ceres) present a celebration of marriage and fertility, pronouncing their blessing on the impending marriage. Ferdinand's response to the performance includes a recognition that the actors are spirits, an appreciation for Prospero's wisdom and power, and a desire to live for ever on the island. However, the masque is interrupted by Prospero's sudden recollection of Caliban and the conspiracy against his life. After the general confusion that ensues, and his own brief distraction, he tells Ferdinand that

> These our actors
> (As I foretold you) were all spirits, and
> Are melted into air, into thin air,
> And like the baseless fabric of this vision,
> The cloud-capp'd tow'rs, the gorgeous palaces,
> The solemn temples, the great globe itself,
> Yea, all which it inherit, shall dissolve,
> And, like this insubstantial pageant faded,
> Leave not a rack behind. We are such stuff
> As dreams are made on, and our little life
> Is rounded with a sleep. (4.1.148-58)

Ferdinand s role in this scene combines the function of Miranda in Act 1 with the functions of the men in Act 3. Like Miranda, he is a surrogate for the audience; the reflection on reality is intended for our ears as much as his, because the structure of this scene anticipates the end of the play. After the revels (as Prospero describes the masque) of The Tempest are ended,

Shakespeare wants us to understand that this particular play represents all
drama, and all drama ultimately represents reality. How we respond to drama
will influence how we respond to reality. Like his father, Ferdinand reveals
an aptitude to learn from Prospero s magical displays; he draws the right
conclusions about the spiritual nature of the masque, and he demonstrates
that he has learned to trust Prospero. In their first encounter, when Prospero
had feigned anger, Ferdinand drew his sword and Miranda expressed her
wonder at her father s choler; in this scene, both Ferdinand and Miranda share
the mood of confusion over Prospero s state of mind, but both join in wishing
him well. Clearly, Ferdinand has learned the lessons of humility and obedi-
ence which his labors for Prospero were intended to teach him. As an audience, watching Ferdinand s behavior may also increase our sympathy toward
Prospero and incline us to attend to his well-being at the end of the play.

In light of these three scenes, then, Prospero's epilogue is a necessary
structural means to prevent the audience from (literally) leaving the action of
the play in the theater. By combining the natural images in each of the scenes
I have looked at—tempest, food, and flora—with the themes of those
scenes—compassion, repentance, and wonder—Shakespeare implies that
responding with imaginative sympathy to Prospero's appeal at the end of the
play is a way of carrying the play into life. I must admit to some discomfort
with this conclusion; it sounds old-fashioned and even reactionary in the face
of postcolonial and New Historicist readings of the play which may censor
a Eurocentric attitude toward Caliban as a representative of Native Americans
or the illegitimate exercise of oppressive power by Prospero. However, we
must remind ourselves that while Prospero is not a real person, the action he
is asking us to perform is a real action. Within the world of the play, none of
the spectacles to which the characters respond is "real": the tempest is manu-
factured, the banquet is illustory, the masque is a charade. Nonetheless, in the
world of the play the characters' reactions are presented as genuine; indeed,
they are crucial to their moral and psychological development: a Miranda who
cannot feel sorrow for the "fraughting souls" in the "brave vessel" is unlikely
to befriend Ferdinand; an Alonso who is not struck to the heart by Ariel's
performance as a harpy will not express his penitence and receive back his
dead son; a Ferdinand who cannot be amazed by Prospero's art is not a fit
husband for Miranda or heir of Alonso. We should also remember that
Ferdinand's wish to remain on this paradisal island in not granted, that these
characters, like us, cannot live in the world of artifice; the island is a testing
ground for each of them, just as the experience of theater is a testing ground
for each of us. Gonzalo provides his own epilogue when he exclaims

O, rejoice

Beyond a common joy, and set it down

With gold on lasting pillars: in one voyage

Did Claribel her husband find at Tunis,

And Ferdinand, her brother, found a wife

Where he himself was lost; Prospero, his dukedom

In a poor isle; and all of us, ourselves,

When no man was his own. (5.1.206-13)

To find ourselves we must let Prospero go: this is the imaginative appeal of
The Tempest and the moral potential of all art.

## Notes

1. All quotations from *The Riverside Shakespeare*, ed. G. Blakemore Evans,
2nd ed. (Boston & New York: Houghton Mifflin, 1997).

2. In *The Tempest*, of course, Prospero carries this "nesting" one step further in
his speech to Ferdinand and Miranda after the spirits' masque is broken up. As in
A Midsummer Night's Dream, the world of the imagination or theater is equated
with the dream world, but for Prospero, life itself is a dream.

3. While this is usally glossed as a request for applause, it is not implausibly
an actual offer of physical contact; for example, in a 1997 production directed by
Joe Dowling at the Guthrie Theater in Minneapolis, Puck did in fact come off the
stage to shake hands.

4. This is also the lesson of *The Merchant of Venice*, as expressed by Portia in
a much different context: "We do pray for mercy, / And that same prayer doth
teach us all to render / The deeds of mercy" (4.1.200-202). Interestingly enough,
her argument fails with a man who seems to have no aesthetic pleasures; in particular, Shylock objects to music, and it music which defines the magical world
of Belmont in this play. I realize, of course, that for Shylock music is identified
with the unseemly revelries of the immoral Christians, so this rejection of music
is not necessarily an anti-aesthetic stance. Still, one could argue that Shylock's
refusal to foresee the consequences of his insistence on law is, in part, a failure
of imagination.

5. In Act 2, for example, Shakespeare creates a clear ethical distinction between Gonzalo, who is usually wise and always good-hearted, and the diabolical
pair of Antonio and Sebastian, on the basis of their imaginations. In surveying
the island, Gonzalo imagines it as an ideal commonwealth, as a ruler of which he
would "excel the golden age" (2.1.169); he is mocked by Antonio and Sebastian
for his foolishness, but after Ariel causes the rest of the party to fall asleep, Antonio tempts Sebastian to murder and usurp Alonso by imagining that the latter's
sleep resembles death, and arguing that "My strong imagination sees a crown /
Dropping upon thy head" (2.1.208-209).

6. The invitation to a meal which Alonso refers to as his "last" (3.3.50) is not in-
consequential. On the one hand, it may indicate Alonso's despair; he knows that if

the meal is in fact enchanted he may be risking his life and soul by partaking of it; on the other hand, the suggestion of a "last supper" which the men are then prevented from eating has obvious religious overtones.

7. Despite Prospero's words to the contrary—"They being penitent, / The sole drift of my purpose doth extend / Not a frown further" (5.1.28-30)—neither Sebastian nor Antonio ever indicate genuine repentance, unlike Alonso. In fact, when Prospero threatens the two villians with exposure to Alonso, Sebastian says "The devil speaks in him" (5.1.129) and Antonio maintains an obdurate silence. Alonso enters joyfully into the spirit of celebration and, like Miranda at the beginning, is a willing and eager auditor of Prospero's tale. I would argue for a connection between Alonso's imaginative receptivity to Ariel's speech and his subsequent "regeneration"; of course, he is in mourning for the "death" of his son, so that grief may also contribute to his receptivity, but Antonio also had ample opportunity for grief had he mourned for the "death" of his brother.

CHAPTER 23

# Instructions to Ariel: A Way to Understand Prospero's Political Plan

*Darcy Wudel*

Paul Cantor has suggested, rightly I think, that the Prospero of Shakespeare's *Tempest* must be understood as a kind of heroic figure capable of great action.[1] To put it another way, Prospero, a philosopher, can be a man of action, or, to go a little further, can be a king. *The Tempest*, with its emphasis on the problematic relationship of wisdom and action, is, accordingly, an appropriate foil to books like Plato's *Republic* and Machiavelli's *Prince*. But if we agree that *The Tempest* is worth teaching for these reasons, we need to ask this: how do we get our students to see Prospero as a heroic figure?

What I propose here is a "method" to push students to think seriously about Prospero and what he does. Students, I want to suggest, need to be prompted to think about Prospero's instructions to his servant Ariel. The action of the play implies that there are instructions given, but most often they are not heard. Shakespeare thus makes it clear that Prospero has plans and that he uses Ariel to carry out those plans. Shakespeare does not, however, reveal the nature of Prospero's instructions. So readers of the play (along with their students) are left to think what they might be and think about why Prospero gives them.

In order to show how this method works, it is necessary, first, to look closely at what the text suggests about what has happened before *The Tempest* begins, and, second, to interpret some of Prospero's instructions to Ariel and show what understanding of the play results from those interpretations.

In order to prepare students to think about Prospero's instructions to Ariel it is necessary for them, at the outset, to determine what happened before the play. With a little prodding, they can easily discover this much after reading Acts 1 and 2. Prospero was the Duke of Milan (1.2.57-58). He was married (1.2.56-57). He had a daughter named Miranda (1.2.1, 56-57). He spent an inordinate time studying liberal arts and other secret studies, his library being "dukedom large enough" (1.2.72-77, 109-110). His brother, Antonio, in league with Alonso, the King of Naples, took the opportunity presented by Prospero's love of study to usurp Prospero's throne (1.2.66ff). Prospero and Miranda were put into a boat and left to drown (1.2.144-151). But they were supplied with provisions and books by Gonzalo, a counselor to the King of Naples (1.2.160-168). Subsequently, they came to an island with magical powers that Prospero was able to turn to his own use: in particular, Prospero was able to free the spirit Ariel from a tree and make him a powerful servant (1.2.248-299). Alonso, his son Ferdinand, his brother, Sebastian, Gonzalo, and Antonio, have sailed to Tunis for the wedding of Claribel, the King's daughter, to the King of Tunis, and they are now returning to Italy (1.2.67-69). At Prospero's bidding, Ariel has created a tempest that brings them and others to Prospero's island, and he has dispersed groups of survivors around the island (1.2.193-238).

Now this is not an exhaustive list of what students might find, but it is the necessary beginning for understanding Prospero's plans. With this much found, it is appropriate to ask students to look at Prospero's circumstances and set a goal for him. With one voice students tend to say that his goal should be to win back his dukedom. Having said that, they are in a position to see more clearly what Prospero attempts to do.

Now consider some of those instances of Prospero's instructions to Ariel and what students can learn from them.

In Act 1, Scene 2, Prospero gives these orders to Ariel: first, "Go make thyself like a nymph o' the sea. . . (1.2.301306)," and then, when Ariel has done so, tells him, "Fine apparition! My quaint Ariel, / Hark in this ear." Ariel's reply is "My lord it shall be done" (1.2.317-319).

Clearly we are meant to understand that instructions were given; but just as clearly we are meant not to hear what they are. We are thus left to wonder about Prospero's instructions. At this point, one may suggest to students that it is possible to ask what Prospero instructed Ariel to do, and, more importantly, that it is possible to speculate why Prospero instructed Ariel to do so. I ask students to fill in these blanks in an imagined speech from Prospero. "Ariel, go and do _____ because _____ .

What, in this case, do they find? They find that Ariel, having already separated Ferdinand from his father, leads him to an encounter with Miranda which results in their falling in love and being married (1.2.375ff; 3.1.59-91; 4.1.1-142). So the implied instructions are "Go get Ferdinand, and make it possible for him to meet Miranda." Why? "Because I want him and my daughter to fall in love and be married." It is all very pretty when performed, but this way of looking at things reveals Prospero to be engaged in manipulation.

This interpretation is born out if students follow out the further consequences of the love and subsequent marriage of Ferdinand and Miranda. Later in the play, when Prospero confronts Alonso with his treachery, Alonso wishes that his "lost" son and Prospero's "lost" daughter had been united as the King and Queen of Naples (5.1.130-152). He soon learns that he has already been given what he asked for (5.1.166-204). The political consequence of the marriage—which students pretty easily grasp—is to bring Prospero's Milan into a friendly relationship with Alonso's Naples. This marriage will thus build a peace between the dukedom and kingdom (and may also bring about a kind of union of northern and southern Italy[2]). Students may note, as well, that because Ferdinand's sister is Queen of Tunis, the marriage of Ferdinand and Miranda may also give Prospero an influence on the other side of the Mediterranean (5.1.5 13).

Why, in sum, does Prospero want Ferdinand and Miranda to meet? "Because I want him and my daughter to fall in love and be married, so that I can create a safe working relation with Naples and have influence all the way to Tunis." Viewed this way, Prospero has plans at least equal to, if not greater than, a Machiavellian prince.

In Act I, Scene ii, Prospero gives further orders to Ariel. He says, "Hark what thou else shalt do me" (1.2.496). What students find when they look for instructions and reasons is this: Ariel goes to the group that includes Alonso, Sebastian, Antonio, and Gonzalo. He puts all but Sebastian and Antonio to sleep. Their wakeful contemplation of the sleeping King of Naples leads Antonio to suggest another usurpation—that Sebastian should kill Alonso and rule Naples (2.1.290ff).

Acting on Prospero's command Ariel wakes the others just as Sebastian and Antonio are about to execute their plot. By this means Prospero is able to "get the goods" on Sebastian and Antonio, and make them fear on account of what they might have done. In his confrontation with Alonso, he warns them in this fashion:

But you my brace of lords, were I so minded,
I here could pluck his Highness' frown upon you,
And justify you traitors. At this time
I will tell no tales (5.1.126-129).

They are chastened, and Prospero is in control.

What was Ariel instructed to do? "Put all in Alonso's group to sleep except Antonio and Sebastian;" and then later, "Wake the others because Antonio and Sebastian are about to put their plot into action." Why was Ariel instructed to do this? "Because I want to make sure that my brother, Antonio, and Alonso's brother, Sebastian, are in no position to do us harm once we all return to Italy." Prospero clearly wishes to return to a safer Milan and Italy than he formerly faced, and he makes his plans accordingly.

What has been said here does not do justice to all that might be said regarding to Prospero's instructions to Ariel. But with this much done, students can begin to see what Prospero is capable of accomplishing. In short, they are able to see the heroic action of a philosopher. As a result, they will be prepared to see beyond the play to Prospero's return to his dukedom—a dukedom he will, doubtless, rule more wisely and from which he will have a powerful influence. And they will be prepared to see a Duke who spends part of his day, with some security, in the dukedom he first loved—his library.

### Notes

1. Paul Cantor, "Shakespeare's *The Tempest*: The Wise Man as Hero," *Shakespeare Quarterly* 31 (1980): 64-75.

2. See David Lowenthal, review of *Shakespeare as Political Thinker*, eds. John Alvis and Thomas G. West, in *Claremont Review of Books* (May 1984): 12-13. Lowenthal attributes this idea regarding northern and southern Italy to Dick Cox. Cf. Niccolo Machiavelli, *Prince*, Ch.1.

# V. Core Texts and Writing

CHAPTER 24

# *Antigone*, Writing, and Linked Classes

*Terese Balistreri Hartman*

Research on student learning has demonstrated that it is enhanced when students are exposed to material which they can transfer and apply to previous knowledge and to new contexts and that "information organized in personally meaningful ways is more likely to be retained, learned, and used."[1] It is also a known fact that the classics provide layers of meaning as individual texts and this meaning is further augmented when paired with other texts. Therefore, when a history colleague and I were searching for a way to link his World Civilization class and my Freshman Composition course, we turned to the core texts, which are a part of the ten-volume set of classical readings which define the Lynchburg College Symposium Readings Program. We built our link around four shared classical texts which we taught in tandem in our classes so that students could make connections between the two courses almost simultaneously.

When it came to choosing the texts, we first thought of texts which would contain knowledge that we felt was fundamental to a liberal arts education. Also, we needed to choose writings that would mesh well with our respective texts. One of the texts that we chose was the play *Antigone*. We felt that because our country looked ultimately to the Greek ideal of a republic and because so much of our political thought could be traced to the Greek world, Sophocles' play would function well as a core text. We found that *Antigone* not only provided the forum for discussion of Greek theater and an appreciation of the language, but it more importantly presented a myriad of issues for discussion and writing opportunities. Some of these issues dealt with the individual rights versus State's rights. Others focused on the issue of religious freedom versus State law. The fragility and strength of human relationships is yet another issue which is explored in the play. Finally, there were issues which considered the role of men and women in society. This last concern was ultimately the primary aspect of *Antigone* which we chose to explore.

While my colleague and I saw using *Antigone* as a significant text in our courses, the students were bewildered to find that they would be writing papers using classical texts in a Freshman Composition class, especially since we were using a contemporary rhetoric, *Reading and Writing in the Academic Community*, as the primary textbook. In my class, I first dealt with the history of Greek tragedy and the role of women in Greek society. The students were given discussion questions and worked in groups to gain an understanding of the elements of the play. We then read three essays in our rhetoric which dealt with gender bias in language and stereotypes: "Gender and Language," by Laurel Richardson; "Real Men Don't, or Anti-Male Bias in English," by Eugene R. August, and Deborah Tannen's, "Put Down That Paper and Talk to Me." The background material that I had given the students reinforced my history colleague's unit on ancient Greek society. There would have been no way to ascertain if our goal to enhance student learning by making connections between the two courses had been achieved if it were not for our writing assignments.

My writing assignments were designed to give the students an opportunity to compare and contrast one of the three contemporary essays which treated gender bias in language or stereotypes with *Antigone*. The students were to list at least three elements which both texts shared and discuss how these elements affected the characters' perception of themselves, others, or their world.

At first students were skeptical that connections could be made. Then they were amazed to find that common stereotypes for men as well as women existed in *Antigone*. One stereotype that August discusses in his essay is the fact that men are subject to negative stereotyping. One such stereotype is that "crime and evil are usually attributed to the male."[2] For example, Creon pronounces his anathema on the "man" who has tried to bury Polynices. He fumes: "What? What man alive would dare?" Later he swears to Zeus: "If you don't find the man who buried that corpse, / the very man, and produce him before my eyes, / simple death won't be enough for you, / not till we string you up alive / and wring the immorality out of you."[3]

Likewise the students came to realize that women also suffered from stereotyping in Greek society. The idea of stereotyping women is considered in Laurel Richardson's "Gender and Language." Richardson shows how language undermines women's equality with men. Linguistic practices define females as "immature, incompetent, and incapable," in order to show how women are defined in terms of their relationships to men, whereas men are defined in terms of their relationship to the world.[4] Certainly these ideas are clearly articulated in several places throughout the play. One particularly poignant reference occurs during the conversation between Ismene and Antigone. Ismene is horrified at the fact that Antigone is disobeying the law of the king. She tells her:

> Remember we are women,
> we're not born to contend with men. Then too,
> we're underlings, ruled by much stronger hands,
> so we must submit in this, and things still worse. [5]

It is likewise interesting for the students to see how Antigone breaks this stereotypical perception of women with her assertive, articulate, and public renunciation of Creon's decree. In her essay, "Put Down That Paper and Talk to Me," Deborah Tannen discusses the ways in which men and women communicate. She postulates that women tend to engage in "rapport-talk," which tends to be private and is used to maintain relationships; whereas men tend to engage in "report-talk" which tends to be public and is used to preserve independence and "maintain status in a hierarchical social order."[6] One way which women use "rapport-talk" is telling secrets. Ismene reflects this aspect of communication when she says to Antigone: "Keep it a secret. I'll join you in that, I promise." [7] Here Ismene is trying to protect Antigone from punishment from the law as well as confirming her love for her, even though she will not join Antigone in her mission. Likewise, when Antigone is able to break the stereotype of the woman, Creon understands her strength. After Antigone publicly proclaims that her loyalty to her brother is governed by "the great unwritten, unshakable traditions"[8] of the gods, Creon responds:

> This girl was an old hand at insolence
> when she overrode the edicts we made public.

> But once she had done it-the insolence,
> twice over-to glory in it, laughing,
> mocking us to our face with what she'd done.
> I am not the man, not now: She is the man
> if this victory goes to her and she goes free.[9]

Needless to say, Creon will not be swayed from his goal of seeing Antigone punished for her crime.

In my colleague's history course, these same students were asked to write another comparison and contrast essay. Before they had read *Antigone* and studied Greek culture, the students had studied the cultures in India, Mesopotamia, China, and Egypt. After they had studied Greek culture, they were asked to compare gender roles in *Antigone* with the gender roles with one of these cultures. The students could make the connections between the openness for women in Egyptian society and Antigone's lowly role in Greek society, when Ismene reminds her that "Now look at the two of us, left so alone . . . think what a death we'll die, the worst of all / if we violate the laws and override/the fixed decree of the throne, its power- / we must be sensible . . . . I'm forced, I have no choice-I must obey / the ones who stand in power."[10] Or the students could compare gender roles in the Greek society itself. They could choose to look at the way the men and women interacted in the play which depicts Greek society in the Bronze Age to see the similarities and differences which exist with that of Greek society in the fifth century Athens, when the play was written. The students could explore fifth century Greek society to see if it echoes Creon's words: "From now on they'll act like women. / Tie them up, no more running loose; . . ."[11]

Using *Antigone* with these writing opportunities enabled our students to become familiar with a significant classical text from the ancient Western world and to make connections with our contemporary world. The writing helped them to enhance their knowledge by seeing the play through diverse historical lenses and in different dimensions. Through this knowledge, the students were able to create essays which deepened in their critical understanding of the text and to come to a realization that the classics not only teach us how things have changed, but how they have remained the same. One hopes that the study of core texts will fulfill the final words that are articulated by the chorus of *Antigone:* "The mighty words of the proud are paid in full / with mighty blows of fate, and at long last / those blows will teach us wisdom."[12]

## Notes

1. Thomas Angelo, from his article from Session 56: "A Teacher's Dozen: Fourteen (General) Findings From Research That Can Inform Classroom Teaching and Assessment and Improve Learning" (AAHE's 1993 National Conference on Higher Education).

2. Eugene R. August, "Real Men Don't, Or Anti-Male Bias in English," *University of Dayton Review* 18 (Winter/Spring 1986-87), 115-24. Rpt. in *Reading and Writing in the Academic Community*, eds. Mary Lynch Kennedy and Hadley M. Smith (New Jersey: Prentice Hall, 1994), 222.

3. Sophocles, *The Three Theban Plays:Antigone, Oedipus the King, Oedipus at Colonus*. trans. Robert Fagles (New York: Penguin Classics, 1984), 71.280-281; 74.356-350.

4. Laurel Richardson, "Gender and Language." Rpt. in *Reading and Writing in the Academic Community*, eds. Mary Lynch Kennedy and Hadley M. Smith (New Jersey: Prentice Hall, 1994), 209, 211.

5. Sophocles, 62.74-77.

6. Deborah Tannen, "Put Down That Paper and Talk to Me." Rpt. in *Reading and Writing in the Academic Community*, eds. Mary Lynch Kennedy and Hadley M. Smith (New Jersey: Prentice Hall, 1994), 229.

7. Sophocles, 85.99.

8. Ibid., 82.505.

9. Ibid., 83.536-542.

10. Ibid., 62.70-74.

11. Ibid., 90.653-654.

12. Ibid., 128.1468-1470.

CHAPTER 25

# Memories, Stories, Histories: Student Journal Writing and the Construction of Meaning

*By Katherine Platt*

This essay focuses on a journal writing assignment that is part of a first year foundation course in the History and Society Division at Babson College in Wellesley, Massachusetts. The course is called "Memories, Stories, Histories: Constructing Self in the 20th Century." The journal writing assignment is structured around the reading and rereading of a collection of poems by Ursula Duba entitled, *Tales from a Child of the Enemy* in parallel with the assigned texts of the course. Before discussing the book and the writing assignment, let me provide some context about the college, the curriculum, and the course in which they are situated.

## The College

Babson College offers undergraduate and masters degrees in business administration with a special focus on entrepreneurship. Undergraduates take approximately 50% of their credits in the Liberal Arts at the foundation, intermediate, and advanced levels of the curriculum. Significantly, although the students graduate with a degree in business, they all take increasingly demanding and intensive courses in the Liberal Arts as they proceed through their four-year program. Consequently, our Liberal Arts foundation courses in the first year are not a once in a lifetime taste of the Liberal Arts for non-majors. They are, in fact, foundational to further study. This kind of an integrated curriculum allows us to create courses with the developmental trajectory of the students in mind.

**The Curriculum**

Our first-year foundation courses are predisciplinary (just as the students are) in the sense that they are issue-and theme-focused with the objective of establishing a foundation of abilities and intellectual standards. Among these are the ability to read texts of the highest literary and cultural quality deeply and inquiringly, the ability to interrogate the text and to interrogate one's own thinking in conversation with that text, the ability to identify themes and patterns of themes across a body of literature, the ability and willingness to revisit a text with an enriched perspective, the ability to mobilize a text-supported argument, and the ability to tolerate and explore ambiguity.

Intermediate courses in the Liberal Arts are introductions to disciplinary and interdisciplinary study, including the theories, methodologies, and bodies of data specific to particular scholarly domains. The developmental objectives of this level of the Liberal Arts curriculum include the ability to identify, understand, and apply disciplinary and interdisciplinary concepts; the ability to frame and articulate penetrating problems and questions; the ability to analyze such problems and questions in terms of particular ways of knowing; the ability to hypothesize defensible solutions or explanations to such problems and questions; and the ability to understand the usefulness and the limitations of different ways of knowing.

The advanced level of the curriculum allows for a focused and in-depth applied program of study based on a self-designed learning plan. The focus on student abilities and competencies rather than mere transmission of knowledge in the earlier levels of the curriculum prepares the students to construct and pursue a coherent set of courses and projects tailored to their own educational objectives. The long-range goal of this process is to graduate people who have taken responsibility for envisioning and owning their education and who will be life-long learners.

**The Course**

"Memories, Stories and Histories: Constructing Self in the 20th Century" is one of a number of semester-long History and Society foundation courses which is either preceded or followed by a companion Arts and Humanities foundation course. Two such companion courses are "Myth, Law and the Moral Imagination" and "The Individual in Communities."

"Memories, Stories and Histories" features the social and psychological construction, destruction, and reconstruction of identity set in the context of major 20th Century international, national, and social conflicts. These include imperialism, WWI, and the Holocaust, the Vietnam War and the lingering conflicts of race, class, and gender inequality in America. The course is designed to introduce students to a range of issues, concepts, and ways of knowing that resonate with each other and recur in various manifestations over the arch of the course. Among the most important of these are the concept of the self as a complex social construct, the concept of personal agency in the face of institutional and structural oppression, and the relationship of memory and stories to history.

An important decision in the design of this course was to assign only primary texts. In addition to being of the richest literary and cultural value, all of the primary texts we chose also provided a "road in" or entry point into the psyche of an eighteen-year-old. This might be a point of empathy or identification, a provocation, or a conflict or question: some "hook" that would engage the student emotionally as well as intellectually.

We excluded the secondary interpretive texts one would expect to find in a History and Society course and that we had used before in earlier versions of this course. (William Pfaff's *The Wrath of Nations*, Richard Rubenstein's *The Cunning of History*, Jonathan Shay's *Achilles in Vietnam*, and Michael Walzer's *On Toleration* are among the secondary texts that we have used.) Without the mediating voices of interpretive texts, the students were left to find authority in their own reading and develop individually and collectively an original narrative out of the themes and primary texts of the course. Thus, as they studied the social construction of meaning as one of the core themes of the course, they also constructed meaning out of their experience of the course. Recognizing processes within the texts and then experiencing them within themselves is one part of the dynamic that makes this course distinctly foundational and integrative. The journal assignment described below particularly facilitated this dynamic.

### The Book

Tales from a Child of the Enemy is written by Ursula Duba (b. 1938) who spent the war years of her early childhood in Cologne, Germany. The defining experience of this collection and perhaps the poet's life was in 1958 on holiday in Antwerp, when nineteen-year-old Duba went on a blind date with a Jewish boy. In "Blind Date," Duba writes:

> her handsome date
> and she were dancing
> cheek to cheek
> to a slow blues melody
> when he asks her
> what do you think of Auschwitz
>
> she thought he meant Austerlitz
> and replied
> that she wasn't much of a history buff
> and didn't care about Napoleon and his battles. (43)

The ensuing all-night conversation is her first exposure to the Fact and facts of the Holocaust. This revelation shatters the German "victim identity" prescribed at home and school and initiates a life-long struggle to situate herself in relation to the historical realities of World War Two:

> till the end of her life
> she would have to prove
> that she wasn't one of them
> like the ones who had kept silent
> like the ones who had colluded
> like the ones who had participated. (44)

The chief value of this collection is the way Duba problematizes all such explicit identities and explores the underlying debates and denials. The survivor's fear that some moment of ignorance had made her a perpetrator ("As You Wish, Madam" and "If Only I Had Known"), the colluder's defense that he was really a victim ("The Victims"), and the bystander's shrug of innocent ignorance ("Family Secrets") are examples of how she disturbs the surface of historical identity.

Each poem has its own internal punch, often resulting from a shift in focus from the "micro" experience of the individual to the "macro" forces of history in which the individual is caught. For example, the lens in "A Slice of Bread" zooms in on the six-year-old who is beaten for asking for a second piece of bread and zooms out to the disenfranchisement of the silent socialists and to the carpet-bombing of Cologne. The "micro" and "macro" views are held together by the common thread of powerless rage.

The whole collection has a terrific cumulative punch derived largely from the range of perspectives the poet is able to represent convincingly. These include the perspectives of different historical moments: 1943, 1958, 1985; the perspectives of different ages of the poems' narrators: child, adolescent, adult; the perspectives of different nationalities and ethnicities; but, most important, the perspectives of different relationships to the Holocaust: victim, survivor, resister, bystander, sympathizer, perpetrator.

This book of poetry is an excellent "freestanding" companion to the texts assigned for classroom discussion. This is partly because the direct and accessible narrative style makes it easy to read without classroom exegesis. More important is the resonance of the collection with the themes of the course. *Tales from a Child of the Enemy* is a record of the struggle to understand the relationship of memory to stories to history. It also highlights and problematizes concepts such as the reflexivity of identity, meaning that one's identity is socially constructed and, at the same time, one's action, agency, reaction, and reflection are constitutive of social forces and patterns. These themes are at the core of the course and make all of the assigned texts "speak to each other."

### The Journal Writing Assignment

After reading the first two texts of the course, Things Fall Apart by Chinua Achebe and *All Quiet on the Western Front* by Erich Remarque, the students were asked to read the entire collection of poems *Tales from a Child of the Enemy* and to write a one page reflection on one or two poems or the whole experience, as they wished. They were asked to be ready to read their journals aloud in class. As they finished each of the next three books—*Fragments* by Binjamin Wilkomirski, *Survival in Auschwitz* by Primo Levi, and *War: A Memoir* by Marguerite Duras—they were asked to choose two poems and write a one-page reflection on them informed by their reading of that book. Again, they brought their journals to class and randomly were asked to read them aloud. As they finished each of the last three books in the course—*The Bluest Eye* by Toni Morrison, *The Things They Carried* by Tim O'Brien, and *Two or Three Things I Know for Sure* by Dorothy Allison—they were asked to take any two of the six poems they had already written about in their journals and write a one page reflection about them informed by their reading of the current book. The last journal entry was based on a rereading of the whole collection informed by reading their first journal entry. By the end of the semester, all of the students had read aloud from their journals at least once.

There were a number of reasons why this assignment worked very well.

It was a refreshing change of pace and format from other course activities in that we did not discuss the collection in the classroom as an assigned text. The journal readings in class were not graded or critiqued in class, but there was a significant social reward for high quality effort and presentation. The openness of the assignment made room for exploration, reflection, and a greater degree of creative risk-taking.

The assignment also gave the students the experience of reading, rereading and revisiting texts as a normal part of a literate life. By the end of the assignment, they had read the whole collection at least two times and some poems they had read and written about three or four or more times from different and increasingly rich perspectives. They were amazed that each visit rendered more material for reflection. As Patrick Brown, a student, put it:

> Duba's *Tales from a Child of the Enemy* continues to amaze me every time I reread it. When I first read the collection of poems, I only saw the superficial stories and meanings behind them. However, as I continued to read the different poems after reading the different books as the course progressed I began to see the way that they related themes across to those other books, whose subjects were about people from different times and places, but still the story lines related. This book has been like a house that every time I go into and look around has more rooms, with complex halls leading you through.

Equally important was their realization that this richness of material came from the new questions they were able to ask of the texts, not simply from the texts. Such an inquiring imagination is evident in Tim Yantz's journal entry:

> In Ursula Duba's poem, "As You Wish, Madam," a young girl sends her mother off to the gas chambers unknowingly. In stark contrast, though, Dorothy Allison's sister sends her off to her father knowing of the abuse that will follow. It makes me wonder about the young girl and if she would have taken the place of the mother given the chance and knowing the consequences. On one hand she would die at the hands of the Germans. But on the other, she would have to live with the guilt that she had made the choice to save herself. This is the problem that faced Dorothy Allison's sister, whether to be the victim or to allow another to be the victim. I don't know which would be worse.

In their journals, the students had seven separate experiences of making one text converse with another, another habit of a literate life. In the seventh such experience, one of the texts held in conversation with another was their own earliest journal entry. Most of the students were astonished by how

much their interpretation of *Tales from a Child of the Enemy* had changed
and deepened as a result of rereading it through the lenses of other resonant
texts. Their development as readers, thinkers and writers was very visible
to them. Adam Bomberger states:

> My first journal entry was a brief overview of each poem, and then I described
> my reaction to it. Most of my comments are generalizations; they're too
> vague. Once we started relating the poems to the novels we were reading the
> deeper meanings began to unfold. I never thought I would be able to link a
> poem about the holocaust to a book about a lesbian growing up in the south.

Seeing the distance they had traveled was important because this moment
of self-assessment gave the students some extra clarity and confidence as
they prepared for their final paper assignment.

The final paper of the course was to develop an extended connection
between one of the poems discussed in one of the last three journal entries,
one of the last three books, and one of the central themes of the course. Two
popular themes were the social construction of gender and the relationship
of memory and stories to history. Although the students did not formally
write and revise drafts of this final paper, in essence they had been preparing
to write this paper from the time that they started their journals. Each journal
entry was practice at the skills they needed for the final paper. The students
were aware that the journals had more than one purpose and that the greater
thought they put into their journals early on, the farther along they would
be when it came to writing their final papers. Having one assignment dove-
tail into another in this way helped students see their own development and
added to the coherence and momentum of the course.

In summary, the assignment worked because it kept all of the course texts
alive and in conversation throughout the course, it allowed for extensive
practice of skills essential to ultimate success in the course, and it provided
opportunities for self-assessment along the way. However, I think the most
important reason this assignment took off was that over and over again the
students were doing the thing they were studying. As they studied an eighteen-year-old coming into historical and ethical awareness, they also became
aware of historical atrocities and related ethical dilemmas in a new way.
Chris Patrinos reflects,

> Before this class unfortunately if a friend did make a rude comment about a
> Jew, black, lesbian or whatever it was, I would probably keep it inside of
> myself that what he is doing is wrong. But now that I realize what people went

through, for example in "The Sundial" (by Duba) and Dorothy Allison, I now am going to try to express my feelings more to my friends and hopefully it will change their mind just a bit.

As they studied memory and history as personal and social narrative, they narrated their own encounters of the personal with the social. As they studied the implicit search for a listener embedded in all storytelling, they became more compassionate listeners. As they studied the problematic categories of perpetrator, victim, bystander, they understood the need to become witnesses.

I will close this essay with Jonathan Zissi's especially poignant expression of willingness to become a compassionate witness:

> The one main thing I think about differently after studying all the themes and reading all the books with tremendous atrocity and oppression is the current situation in Kosovo. As an Albanian (-American), you would think I was so worried and interested in the crisis. Honestly, before reading these books and understanding these themes and how they applied I had no interest and couldn't understand or envision what they were experiencing. Now, I have a great understanding of all these themes and can understand how they relate to my fellow Albanians…. I feel connected to my culture now….. I am thankful I read all these books and learned to see the connection. It's real! As I am unfortunately seeing with my own people.

## Note

1. Many of the ideas in this paper, including the original conception of the journal writing assignment, are attributable to my colleague, Prof. Stephen Collins, with whom I created this course. I wish to thank him heartily. I would also like to gratefully acknowledge the invaluable education I have received from all the History and Society colleagues who have worked on and taugt the foundation courses, including Professors Michael Bruner, Kandice Hauf, Janet Landman, Lynn O'Brien Hallstein, and Blake Pattridge.

## Works Cited

Achebe, Chinua. 1994. *Things Fall Apart.* New York: Bantam Doubleday.

Allison, Dorothy. 1996. *Two or Three Things I Know for Sure.* New York: Penguin Books.

Duba, Ursula. 1995. *Tales from a Child of the Enemy.* New York: Penguin Books.

Duras, Marguerite. 1986. *The War: a Memoir.* Trans. Barbara Blair. New York: New Press.

Levi, Primo. 1996. *Survival in Auschwitz.* Trans. Stuart Woolf. New York: Simon and Schuster.

Morrison, Toni. 1994. *The Bluest Eye.* New York: Penguin Books.

O'Brien, Tim. 1991. *The Things They Carried.* New York: Penguin Books.

Pfaff, William. 1993. *The Wrath of Nations: Civilization and the Furies of Nationalism.* New York: Simon and Schuster.

Remarque, Erich. 1982. *All Quiet on the Western Front.* Trans. A.W. Wheen. New York: Ballantine Books.

Rubenstein, Richard. 1987. *The Cunning of History: The Holocaust and the American Future.* New York: Harper and Row.

Shay, Jonathan. 1994. *Achilles in Vietnam: Combat Trauma and the Undoing of Character.* New York: Simon and Schuster.

Walzer, Michael. 1997. *On Toleration.* New Haven: Yale University Press.

Wilkomirski, Binjamin. 1996. *Fragments: Memories of a Wartime Childhood.* trans. Carol Brown Janeway. New York: Schocken Books.

CHAPTER 26

# Writing About and Through Herman Melville's *Moby Dick*: Reading and Thinking Interdisciplinarily

*David Sokolowski*

What reading and writing and thinking should be is often revealed to us by those who don't or can't attend academic conferences. At one point in "The Library Card," the famous excerpted chapter XIII from Richard Wright's semi-autobiographical *Black Boy*, the young narrator, kept unknowing and invisible in his racist world, describes the effects of reading his first real book, H.L. Mencken's *Book of Prefaces*:

> But what strange world was this? I concluded the book with the conviction
> that I had somehow overlooked something terribly important in life. I had once
> tried to write, had once reveled in feeling, had let my crude imagination roam,
> but the impulse to dream had been slowly beaten out of me by experience.
> Now it surged up again and I hungered for books, new ways of looking and

seeing. It was not a matter of believing or disbelieving what I had read, but of feeling something new, of being affected by something that made the look of the world different. (218)

Later in the piece, Wright will add the following: "The plots and the stories in the novels did not interest me so much as the point of view revealed. ... it was enough for me to see and feel something different" (219). In the following passages, Wright suggests that what matters about his reading is the imaginative vision afforded through being encouraged to see through a variety of different perspectives. The narrator's reading allows him to get up and outside the walls of his narrow world and see and feel differently by viewing it through different eyes. What is implied in these passages is that Wright is not concerned with what the author writes about or, for that matter, the conclusions the author comes to about his or her subject. As he says, he's not interested in believing or disbelieving the argument or subject matter of any work, which is necessarily limited; rather, what captivates Wright is the frame of mind, way of knowing, approach, perspective—call it what you will—revealed to him by his reading. Wright's take on reading is expressed earlier by Ralph Waldo Emerson, who says at the beginning of his essay "Self-Reliance": "I read the other day some verses written by an eminent painter which were original and not conventional. Always the soul hears an admonition in such lines, let the subject be what it may. The sentiment they instil is of more value than any thought they may contain" (492). I tentatively apply the term interdisciplinary to the kind of reading and thinking Wright and Emerson advocate, if we are careful to define interdisciplinarity always in an adverbial sense, as being an action, the nature of which is to focus as much or more on how we read rather than on what we read. Reading and thinking interdisciplinarily encourage not one way of looking at something, which necessarily sets limits as to what we can know about it and in doing so fosters the illusion of determinacy, but multiple ways of knowing that reveal a plenitude of meaning.

If Wright's and Emerson's interdisciplinary approach to reading and thinking has value, and I believe it does, it carries with it implications regarding writing assignments involving core texts. The primary implication is that we should not emphasize writing merely ABOUT these texts; rather, assignments should be designed so that student's write THROUGH these texts. Let me try to explain. Assignments that ask students to write about a text carry with them the assumption that a text represents a world unto itself, not a way of looking at that world or a window on the world, if you will. This manner of writing can have rather debilitating effects on students since what they face is an exercise with a predetermined end. That is, they are going to paraphrase what an author is saying and although this isn't unimportant, it's just that if this becomes the final goal, we've taught them only a slavish adherence to someone else's thought and have robbed the text of its final indeterminate mystery. Writing assignments that are designed to have students write not only about a text but through a text, however, go some way toward avoiding what Walker Percy calls "the loss of the creature" and toward restoring what he calls "the sovereignty of the knower over the known" (59), a stance in which the student's own vision, like Wright's vision, is not obliterated but rather enhanced by the text or texts about which he or she is asked to write. Writing through a text implies establishing connections between it and other things, such as one's own experience or one's experience of other texts.

Yet it is difficult when teaching core texts to enable students to write not only about the work but also through the work. In attempting to impress on our students the relative importance of these works, we sometimes foster in the students an adherence to what the work is about rather than teaching them to use the work as a vehicle for thinking. The texts become not the means of acquiring a new vision, but ends in themselves. Sometimes the trick comes in selecting a work that consciously invites being read, thought, and written about from a variety of different perspectives. But short of this, it means teaching core texts in a way that enables our students to read, think, and write through them and not just about them. Here, I want to turn to Herman Melville's *Moby Dick* because it is a classic text that is consciously interdisciplinary in its approach to reading and thinking. *Moby-Dick* is two things simultaneously: it is a text whose very subject matter—what it is about—concerns reading and thinking about texts interdisciplinarily, and it is also a text that can be used as a window on other texts. In brief, it is a text in which "aboutness" and "throughness" mirror each other, where the very ways of reading and knowing become subject matter itself.

To start with, in what way is *Moby Dick* about reading and thinking about texts interdisciplinarily? The answer would seem to lie in its conscious indeterminacy or its attempt to preserve this indeterminacy. In "The Indeterminate *Moby-Dick*" Millicent Belle writes: "*Moby Dick* is certainly one of those works of the past that embrace a calculated indeterminacy beyond even the indeterminacy that may be present in all texts" (31). In pointing out *Moby Dick's* indeterminacy, Belle does not make the mistake, as others have in the past, of saying that its quest for meaning ends at meaninglessness, although meaninglessness might be one take on the book. As Belle points out: "Melville's masterpiece does not boil down in our trypot, and if it states anything it is that experience is ultimately irreducible to thought—but it is itself reducible neither to this meaning nor to any other" (31). Belle here insists on the concept of a plenitude of meaning in *Moby Dick*, brought about by Ishmael's interdiscipli- nary vision or his habit of seeing the whale or text from a plethora of differ- ent perspectives. It is not as if one approach to the whale Ishmael takes invalidates another approach. Rather, the perspectives taken on the whale form an attempt at understanding or at least as full of an understanding of the whale as it humanly possible to attain. That no full understanding is achieved or can ever be achieved becomes unimportant. Nina Baym makes this point by saying that *Moby Dick* makes it clear that "the quest for truth is significant and mean- ingful even if no truth is attained and that a book embodying such a quest is certainly meaningful and significant" (quoted in McSweeney 110).

Perhaps the crucial chapter in *Moby Dick*, wherein this idea of a plethora of perspectives contributes to a plenitude of meaning that yet falls short of the truth, is Chapter 42: The Whiteness of the Whale. In this chapter Ishmael speculates on why the color of whiteness acts both to comfort and appall, reassure and frighten. Having explored the significance of the whale's whiteness from a dizzying array of perspectives, Ishmael concedes that this characteristic, like others, ends in indeterminacy:

> But not yet have we solved the incantation of this whiteness. . . .
> Is it by its indefiniteness it shadows forth the heartless voids and immensi-
> ties of the universe, and thus stabs us from behind with the thought of anni-
> hilation, when beholding the white depths of the milky way? Or is it, that as
> in essence whiteness is not so much a color as the visible absence of color,
> and at the same time the concrete of all colors; is it for these reasons that there
> is such a dumb blankness, full of meaning, in a wide landscape of snows—
> a colorless all-color of atheism from which we shrink? (263-264)

The cumulative effect of this chapter and other chapters like it wherein Ishmael approaches the whale or text from a variety of different approaches is to give to the reader a sense of the plenitude of meaning surrounding the whale while at the same time asserting its essential mystery. Like the skin of the whale, a sheet of paper on which Ishmael observes an etched hiero- glyphics, the color of whale and all of its other characteristics both reveal and conceal, impelling us onward toward a truth we will never find. This, of course, takes us back to the Wright and Emerson, who read texts, as Ishmael reads the whale, less for what they say than for the expanded vision that their various points of view afford. In fact, you could say that Ishmael is preserved in the end because he does not adopt what any single point of view on the whale would dictate.

The whatness of *Moby Dick*, its status as a book about interdisciplinary reading and writing, leads us finally to how it and other classics can be read, thought about, and written about. Generally, what I do with the writing assignments I give on the novel is have my students use *Moby Dick* as a means of reading others texts we will have read in the course. Therefore, I try to encourage the kind of writing through a text that the text of *Moby Dick* actually enacts. One assignment that I tried last semester was to have students use *Moby Dick* to read Nathaniel Hawthorne's *Scarlet Letter*. In particular, I had student select characters from *Moby Dick*, such as Ahab, Ishmael, and Pip, and explain how each of these characters would "read" or interpret Hester Prynne's scarlet letter. It was a successful assignment, I think, because the students were forced to appropriate viewpoints—from inside the text—to interpret something outside the text. This act of writing through *Moby Dick* helped them appreciate more what point of view provides, new eyes on the world that expand its meaning.

## References

1. Bell, Millicent. 1985. "The Indeterminate *Moby Dick*." *Approaches to Teach ing Melville's Moby-Dick*. Ed. Martin Bickman. New York: Modern Language Association. 23-31.

2. Emerson, Ralph Waldo. 1995. "Self-Reliance." The Norton Anthology of American Literature. Shorter Fourth Edition. Ed. Nina Baym. New York: W W. Norton and Co., 492-508.

3. McSweeney, Kerry. 1986. *Moby-Dick: Ishmael's Mighty Book*. Twayne Masterwork Studies. Boston: Twayne Publishers.

4. Melville, Herman. 1964. *Moby-Dick or, The Whale*. Ed. Charles Feidelson, Jr. Indianapolis: Bobbs-Merrill Educational Publishing.

5. Percy, Walker. 1975. "The Loss of the Creative." *The Message in The Bottle*. New York: Farrar, Straus and Giroux.

6. Wright, Richard. 1937. *Black Boy. A Record of Childhood and Youth*. New York: Harper and Brothers Publishing.